GLOBAL JUSTICE

Global Justice

Defending Cosmopolitanism

CHARLES JONES

OXFORD
UNIVERSITY PRESS

OXFORD

UNIVERSITY PRESS

Great Clarendon Street, Oxford OX2 6DP

Oxford University Press is a department of the University of Oxford.
It furthers the University's objective of excellence in research, scholarship,
and education by publishing worldwide in

Oxford New York

Athens Auckland Bangkok Bogotá Buenos Aires Calcutta
Cape Town Chennai Dar es Salaam Delhi Florence Hong Kong Istanbul
Karachi Kuala Lumpur Madrid Melbourne Mexico City Mumbai
Nairobi Paris São Paulo Singapore Taipei Tokyo Toronto Warsaw

with associated companies in Berlin Ibadan

Published in the United States
by Oxford University Press Inc., New York

British Library Cataloguing in Publication Data

Data available

Library of Congress Cataloging in Publication Data

Jones, Charles, Dr.
Global justice : defending cosmopolitanism / Charles Jones.
Includes bibliographical references and index.
1. Distributive justice. 2. Wealth—Moral and ethical aspects.
3. Utilitarianism. 4. Human rights. 5. Economics—Moral and
ethical aspects. I. Title.
HB835.J66 1999 330.1—dc21 98-54457
ISBN 0-19-829480-8

1 3 5 7 9 10 8 6 4 2

Typeset in Times by Graphicraft Limited, Hong Kong

Printed in Great Britain
on acid-free paper by
Bookcraft Ltd, Midsomer Norton, Somerset

ACKNOWLEDGEMENTS

This book has been five years in the making, and I have incurred a number of debts along the way. My first acknowledgement must be to the supervisors of my doctoral research in the Government Department at the London School of Economics and Political Science, John Charvet and Brian Barry. As co-supervisors, they offered sensible, insightful—and often conflicting—advice at every stage of the writing process. One benefit of co-supervision is that it creates greater scope for individual judgement, since one is often forced to decide for oneself which way to turn when one's two main critics reach different judgements about the quality of an argument. This is especially interesting whenever both critics develop a reasonable case for their positions. John Charvet possesses an enviable openness to critical discussion and argument, along with an ability to isolate strengths and problems in a text and suggest specific strategies for improvement. In addition, I should mention that Brian Barry's published work on justice and impartiality has been an inspiration to me, despite my disagreements with certain aspects of his particular approach.

I owe a special debt of gratitude to the three readers for Oxford University Press, two of whom are now known to me. David Miller, both in his published writings on nationalism and in his comments on my entire manuscript, provided many challenging rebuttals to my claims and led me to change my view somewhat on that important topic. Simon Caney's work is much more in line with my own, but that did not stop him from offering an enormous number of critical suggestions directed at the arguments of the book, suggestions that usually required significant rethinking on my part. The third reviewer also made many helpful comments and suggestions for improvements, for which I am grateful.

I am also indebted to Chris Brown who, in his work on international relations theory, in some correspondence during the early stages of my research, and in his comments on an earlier version of this work, did much to clarify for me the issues at stake in the international justice debates.

The following individuals were kind enough to offer written comments on various chapter drafts, or on earlier versions of the entire manuscript: John Baker, Alan Carter, Daniel Bell, Michael Donelan, Nigel Dower, Gerard Elfstrom, Anthony Ellis, Mervyn Frost, Robert Goodin, Mike Green, Tom Hurka, Will Kymlicka, Susan Mendus, Jan Narveson, and

Stephen Nathanson. Of those referred to here, Gerard Elfstrom deserves special mention, since he was good enough to point out the embarrassingly large number of weaknesses in my arguments, and provided many helpful comments on several chapters at an early stage, some of which I have incorporated into my final draft. It is difficult to overestimate the importance of this sort of feedback, and I am especially grateful to all of these people because I know how time-consuming a job it can be, especially when it is done well.

I am also thankful for the helpful advice I received on various aspects of my work from Joseph Carens, Gerald Dworkin, Iseult Honohan, Attracta Ingram, Jim Levine, David Lloyd Thomas, Richard Noble, Robert Orr, Vasilis Politis, Sam Scheffler, Adam Swift, Alan Weir, and Jo Wolff.

Audiences at the following meetings heard different parts of the book and offered questions and objections that forced me to rework my arguments: the LSE Seminar in International Political Theory, the LSE Ph.D. Workshop in Political Theory, the Tenth International Conference on Social Philosophy (Helsinki, Finland, 1993), and the United Kingdom Political Studies Association Conference (York, England, 1995). I also benefited from reactions of audiences at Trinity College Dublin, University College Dublin, the Queen's University of Belfast, and the University of Ulster, Coleraine.

Earlier versions of Chapters 5 and 6 appeared in Ian Shapiro (ed.), *NOMOS XLI: Global Justice*, Yearbook of the American Society for Political and Legal Philosophy (New York: New York University Press, 1999), and the *Journal of Applied Philosophy*, 13/1 (1996), 73–86.

This book emphasizes the need to focus on institutions in order to protect basic human rights, and it is fitting that I thank the several institutions that supported me during the years this book was written. The facilities provided by the LSE Department of Philosophy and the LSE Centre for the Philosophy of the Natural and Social Sciences were instrumental in the progress of my research, especially in its early stages. The Social Sciences and Humanities Research Council of Canada provided funding over three years without which my work would not have been possible. And the Council of European Studies at Columbia University provided assistance which enabled me to attend an important conference on the ethics of nationalism at the University of Illinois at Urbana-Champaign in April, 1994. My most recent debts have been incurred in Ireland, where the Boole Fellowship in Philosophy at University College Cork enabled me to pursue my research with mercifully little in the way of administrative or teaching duties. The University, and in particular the Department of Philosophy, is a wonderful place to work, due in no small part to Des Clarke's direction of the Department.

Over many years now, my mother, brothers and sisters have supported me—both financial and morally—and for this I am grateful. The book is dedicated to my parents, in gratitude for their care and concern during my formative years. My wife, Beth Donen Jones, has been the most important person in my life for some time, and she has supported me, at no small cost to herself, through all of the ups and downs of the writing process. One other person has recently been competing with her for my attention: our son Jonathan. His birth midway through the first draft of this book slowed my work to some extent, but I am thankful for the opportunity he has given me for a kind of intellectual and moral progress that is different from—though no less important than—the sort urged in these pages.

C.W.B.J.

Cork

CONTENTS

1

Distributive Justice and the International Context

The responsibility for economic and social well-being is general, transnational. Human beings are human beings wherever they live. Concern for their suffering from hunger, other deprivation and disease does not end because those so afflicted are on the other side of an international frontier. This is the case even though no elementary truth is so consistently ignored or, on occasion, so fervently assailed.

(John Kenneth Galbraith, *The Good Society*, 2)

1.1. INTRODUCTION

Serious debates about international distributive justice are a relatively new feature of work in political philosophy. The first significant contribution to the debate, in my view, is Peter Singer's 1972 *Philosophy & Public Affairs* article 'Famine, Affluence and Morality', in which Singer defends far-reaching obligations on the part of the wealthy to feed destitute people regardless of the geographical location of the rich or the poor. What we might call the 'Global Justice Debates' gained a certain momentum in the following years with the publication of work by Brian Barry, Charles Beitz, Henry Shue and Onora O'Neill—to name only the most significant contributors—all of whom (1) defended greater concern for the world's badly off people than had traditionally been the norm, and (2) pointed out the relatively arbitrary moral status of nation-state boundaries (at least when justice is at issue).[1] But, inevitably perhaps, there was an intellectual backlash against the thrust of opinion found in these works.

---

[1] Brian Barry, *The Liberal Theory of Justice* (Oxford: Clarendon Press, 1973), 128–33; Charles Beitz, *Political Theory and International Relations* (Princeton: Princeton University Press, 1979); Henry Shue, *Basic Rights: Subsistence, Affluence, and U.S. Foreign Policy* (Princeton: Princeton University Press, 1980); Onora O'Neill, *Faces of Hunger* (London: Allen & Unwin, 1986).

The most important figures defending the ethical significance of nation-states are David Miller, Michael Walzer, and a host of thinkers, some of whom can be labelled 'patriots' and others I identify as 'neo-Hegelian defenders of state sovereignty'. John Rawls, whose book *A Theory of Justice* revitalized political philosophy when it was published in 1971, himself has defended a *status quo* position on *international* justice, but he remains an important figure in this story mainly because others (notably, Barry, Beitz and Thomas Pogge) have argued that Rawls's own premises lead to radical conclusions about the need for large-scale redistribution of wealth and resources to the world's worst-off people. My aim in this book is to reach certain definite conclusions concerning which side of this dispute has the more reasonable case, and the gist of my view is that distributive justice is best conceived in terms of human rights, from which it follows both that nation-state borders lack any fundamental ethical standing and that the demands of global justice include various positive actions aimed at protecting the vital interests of everyone, regardless of their location, nationality, or citizenship.

According to Joseph Carens, '[c]itizenship in Western liberal democracies is the modern equivalent of feudal privilege—an inherited status that greatly enhances one's life chances'.[2] This claim gets to the heart of the issue. Given the supposed moral arbitrariness of one's ancestry, place of birth, and citizenship, we need to ask why these characteristics should go so far towards determining the likelihood that someone will have either more wealth than they can use or less than they need to live a recognizably human existence.

1.2. DISTRIBUTIVE JUSTICE: THE CONCEPT AND ITS SCOPE

This book is concerned with questions of international morality in general and the problem of international distributive justice in particular. Before outlining and assessing the arguments for and against cross-boundary obligations of justice it will be useful to have before us some general account of social or distributive justice.

In order to clarify the subject-matter of distributive justice, we need to distinguish a number of questions. First, *What is justice?* Here we are

[2] Joseph H. Carens, 'Aliens and Citizens: The Case for Open Borders', in Will Kymlicka (ed.), *The Rights of Minority Cultures* (Oxford: Oxford University Press, 1995), 331–49, at 332.

looking for some broad characterization of the concept of justice—in our case, distributive justice[3]—some common focus of discussion on the basis of which we may engage in disputes about the importance and demands of justice. Good answers to this question will take account of the history of debates on the topic and seek some common ground linking the whole range of them. My answer to the question, then, is that distributive justice has to do with the proper distribution of benefits and burdens among persons. A just distribution is one where each person receives what is his or her due. Notice that we have yet to say what actually is due each person; that is the job of specific, substantive positions on the question of distributive justice. Another, somewhat more controversial claim about the concept of distributive justice is that whatever is a person's due is equivalent to what that person can claim *by right*. In short, a person has a right to that which is his or her due: distributive justice concerns the correct assignment of rights to persons.[4] Will Kymlicka offers a related analysis of the meaning of 'justice' as 'the system of entitlements on the basis of which people can demand social recognition of their legitimate claims (e.g. for resources, freedoms, etc.)'.[5] Hence a system of justice is a system of entitlements that provides the grounds for making claims on others for valued goods. If we think of rights as entitlements, then justice is concerned with what rights we have. The link between rights and justice is evident in common-sense thinking as well. Peter Jones points out that 'when we are denied our rights, we typically respond with indignation or outrage, rather than with mere disappointment; we conceive ourselves as the victims of an injustice rather than as mere unfortunates who have been denied the milk of human kindness'.[6]

David Johnston identifies two important tools of criticism in the liberal tradition: the concept of individual rights and the idea of distributive

---

[3] As distinct from criminal justice, whose concern is the proper assignment of specific sorts of burdens, namely punishments.

[4] See e.g. Alan Gewirth, 'Economic Justice: Concepts and Criteria', in Kenneth Kipnis and Diana T. Meyers (eds.), *Economic Justice: Private Rights and Public Responsibilities* (Totowa, NJ: Rowman and Allenheld, 1985), 10. Readers who deny the existence of rights can ignore this last claim, but only for now. I argue for a particular conceptualization of rights as the proper requirement of justice in Chapter 3.

[5] Will Kymlicka, *Liberalism, Community, and Culture* (Oxford: Clarendon Press, 1989), 234.

[6] Peter Jones, *Rights* (London: Macmillan, 1995), 50. G. A. Cohen makes a stronger claim: 'The language of moral rights is the language of justice, and whoever takes justice seriously must accept that there exist moral rights.' G. A. Cohen, 'Freedom, Justice, and Capitalism', in *History, Labour, and Freedom* (Oxford: Clarendon Press, 1988), 297.

justice. He then makes some historical claims to the effect that rights acquired their normative power by being 'turned against the state', while the importance of distributive justice was exemplified in its use as a restraint on the negative effects of the market.[7] I have no quarrel with these assertions as they describe the development of the central tools of liberal social criticism. But in the present context my claim is that we should not classify matters in this way, since it appears to prejudge the substantive question of the defensibility of positive rights, i.e. rights requiring positive action on the part of duty-bearers. If rights are understood as claims made 'against the state', this suggests that their significance lies only in their guaranteeing a sphere of individual action with which the state must not interfere. But my claim, especially in Chapter 3, will be that rights generate duties of a more complex character than simply ones of non-interference. Moreover, a useful way of stating the requirements of distributive justice is in terms of rights, including rights to assistance when one suffers the consequences of market transactions. In that case, individuals may invoke their rights not only against the *state*, but also, and equally importantly, against the concentrations of *private* power that dominate the global economy. Hence it is misleading to distinguish rights from distributive justice and to link rights only to the defence of individuals against mistreatment by the state.

This distribution of benefits (the basic goods valued by persons) and burdens (the costs they seek to minimize) becomes an object of concern only under certain conditions. These conditions, usefully labelled the 'circumstances of justice', are those features which must be present for there to be a problem of justice in the first place.[8] The circumstances of justice include a certain type of *scarcity* and the consequent *conflict* between persons arising from that scarcity. Moderate self-interest of persons is also a requirement; however, the emphasis should be on the word 'moderate', for the persons who require principles of distributive justice to adjudicate their dispute not only want what is best for themselves; they also aim for a principled arrangement that they can defend to one another.[9] When valued resources are scarce, there is a need for some adjudication between conflicting claims to those resources. Accordingly,

---

[7] David Johnston, *The Idea of a Liberal Theory: A Critique and Reconstruction* (Princeton: Princeton University Press, 1994), 3–4.

[8] For a short and influential recent statement of this notion, see John Rawls, *A Theory of Justice* (Cambridge, Mass.: Harvard University Press, 1971), 126–30.

[9] Cf. Brian Barry, *Theories of Justice* (Hemel Hempstead: Harvester-Wheatsheaf, 1989), 361.

principles of distributive justice serve to generate just distributions of valued resources and disvalued costs, given that desired goods are neither superabundant nor exceedingly rare.

Now that we have some idea of what principles of distributive justice are meant to do, we can ask the second important question: *What does justice require?* This question has been the central preoccupation of some prominent political philosophers in recent years (Rawls, Barry, Dworkin, Cohen, Arneson, Sen, and others). It remains the subject of significant controversies about the proper understanding of *equality* in a theory of distributive justice (e.g. equality of welfare, of resources, of opportunity for welfare, of access to advantage, etc.) and about the proper role in theories of justice of luck and chance on the one hand, and choice and responsibility on the other. Proper examination of these issues would take up an entire volume or more, so despite its importance I will not argue in any detail for one or other answer directly.[10] Strictly speaking, my concern is not with inequality as such but with the specific problem of *poverty*, which is the most pressing problem for theorists evaluating the international sphere. The distinctiveness of this book lies not here but in its investigation of the third main problem of justice, to which we now turn.

Thirdly, and closely related to the second question, we need to ask, *To whom is justice owed?*[11] To answer this question we need to distinguish different possible types of person as potential subjects of justice and then ask whether each is a plausible candidate for inclusion within the scope of distributive justice. A taxonomy of answers to this question should begin by distinguishing what Allen Buchanan calls *justice as self-interested reciprocity* (JSIR, for short) from what he labels *subject-centred justice* (SCJ).[12] Is justice owed only to those who are (actual or

---

[10] For a good account of these issues, including discussions of Rawls, Sen, Dworkin and others, see Richard J. Arneson, 'Equality', in Robert E. Goodin and Philip Pettit (eds.), *A Companion to Contemporary Political Philosophy* (London: Blackwell, 1993), 489–507.

[11] For a clear statement of the importance of this question, see Allen Buchanan, 'The Morality of Inclusion', in Ellen Frankel Paul *et al.* (eds.), *Liberalism and the Economic Order* (Cambridge: Cambridge University Press, 1993), 233–57, especially 235 ff. See also, Stanley Hoffman, *Duties Beyond Borders: On the Limits and Possibilities of Ethical International Politics* (Syracuse: Syracuse University Press, 1981), 150 ff.

[12] Allen Buchanan, 'The Morality of Inclusion', and 'Justice as Reciprocity versus Subject-Centered Justice', *Philosophy and Public Affairs*, 19/3 (1990), 227–53. Buchanan's distinction is related to Brian Barry's earlier distinction between types of contractarian justice, 'justice as mutual advantage' and 'justice as impartiality'. See Brian Barry, *Theories of Justice*, and *Justice as Impartiality* (Oxford: Clarendon Press, 1995).

potential) participants in a mutually beneficial cooperative scheme, as JSIR maintains? Or, as SCJ says, is consideration also due to cooperators and noncooperators alike in virtue of some (set of) characteristics such as capacity for rational agency or capacity to suffer and to experience happiness? Able-bodied contributors to cooperative schemes constitute one kind of subject, handicapped non-contributors another. Who is captured within the scope of justice? We should note that the answers to these questions will not require the acceptance of a duty to recognize only the rights of compatriots (fellow citizens of one's state), since JSIR may include some non-compatriots and exclude some compatriots, for mutually beneficial cooperation is possible with foreigners while some compatriots lack the capacity to contribute to cooperative schemes. Subject-centred justice, on the other hand, certainly will consider it necessary take note of the needs and interests of persons regardless of their state affiliation: at least prima facie, SCJ promises to include all those who qualify as persons according to the criteria in question (e.g. capacity to experience pleasure and pain, or capacity for rational agency). The prominent approaches here are therefore destined to require a rethinking of the problems of international distributive justice. This should be evident in any case, since we should at some stage explicitly consider the moral status of persons of varying geographical and institutional distance from us. Is justice owed only to compatriots, or are foreigners entitled to the same rights as fellow countrymen?

A fourth question represents the flip side of the third question. If we need to know to whom justice is owed, we equally require an idea of *who owes justice* to whomever it is justice is owed. That is, we not only want an account of right-bearers, we also want to know how to assign the duties to which those rights give rise.[13] The two-pronged fourth question, then, is: *To whom should the duties of justice be assigned, and how much of the burdens of justice should each individual or collectivity bear?*[14] The problem of distributive justice is double-sided in the sense that we require the determination of both to whom duties are owed and exactly who should bear those duties (and how much of a burden each duty-bearer should bear).

Answers to these four (or five) questions—about the nature, requirements and scope of distributive justice—are the minimal requirements of

---

[13] See Chapter 3 for more on this theme.
[14] Cf. Henry Shue, *Basic Rights: Subsistence, Affluence, and U.S. Foreign Policy* (Princeton: Princeton University Press, 1980), 112.

an acceptable theory of distributive justice. Moreover, any such theory, as we have seen, requires us to take a position of some sort on the question of *international* distributive justice, for, in answering the third question, the proper response to the needs and desires of members of other states is addressed, while the fourth question implicitly asks after the obligations of persons toward distant others.

But why should an answer to the scope question, the question about who possesses rights, be so urgent or controversial? Isn't it obvious that *every* person is a claimant to the valued resources of his or her society, and that states should recognize the (prima facie) equal claims of all their citizens when making distributive decisions? The short answer to this last question is, simply, No. This is not because all citizens do not have equal rights (they do); it is because this answer fails to consider the claims of *non-citizens*, claims that might turn out to be just as strong as those of citizens. The reason the 'equal claims of citizens' view is not obvious, despite its popularity, is that it makes a questionable assumption about the institutional context in which claims to justice should be considered. To explain what I mean here, I now consider a fifth question: *What are the institutions whose moral character theories of distributive justice should assess?* Answering this question will make it clear that any theory whose focus is limited to the confines of the nation-state is thereby fundamentally misguided. The fact that most theories to date have been only implicitly limited in this way does not excuse them, but it may help to explain why there has not been any widespread questioning of the 'domestic' assumptions at some earlier time.

Like John Rawls, I take justice to apply to the 'basic structure', the main social, legal, political and economic institutions which have such a dominant impact on the life prospects of individuals.[15] Principles of distributive or social justice provide the theoretical underpinning and normative justification for a given set of institutions. This institutional focus is justified, I think, again in agreement with Rawls, by the fact that the way rights are distributed by way of governmental and economic arrangements largely determines persons' chances to secure for themselves the means to pursue a meaningful life. Unlike Rawls, however, I see no reason to restrict our moral focus to the basic structure of any particular nation-state; on the contrary, if one's concern is with the justifiability of the institutions which determine persons' life chances, there

---

[15] Rawls, *Theory of Justice*, 7. The conclusions of Rawls's account of distributive justice are contained in what he calls 'the two principles of justice for institutions', ibid. 302.

are compelling grounds for taking a wider view. The reason should be clear: the institutions and quasi-formal arrangements affecting persons' life prospects throughout the world are increasingly international ones—international financial institutions, transnational corporations, the G8, the World Trade Organization—and the restricted Rawlsian view fails to assess the moral character of those institutions.[16] So the object of our inquiry ought to be what we may call the *international basic structure*, the major institutions in the world as a whole which affect persons and their access to desired goods and resources. The international basic structure includes intra-state, inter-state and non-state institutions.

According to David Miller, conceptual historians 'focus on the way in which the agents in question [i.e. political actors in a given historical period] sought to alter the map [of political concepts] in the light of their argumentative needs. . . . Conceptual history then becomes the study of the (deliberate or accidental) redrawing of conceptual boundaries by actors seeking to articulate novel political standpoints.'[17] We can see the present suggestion in these terms, that is, as part of a recent movement—at least since the publication of Charles Beitz's *Political Theory and International Relations*[18]—to redraw the boundaries of the concept of distributive justice. The aspect of the problem that needs questioning is the assumption, in traditional discussions of that concept (including Rawls's), that distributive justice properly applies only to compatriots.[19] Redrawing conceptual boundaries here means extending the scope of the concept's application, though it seems that much of the rest of what is now meant by 'distributive justice' is left unaltered. It might turn out that the reasons that support redistribution in the domestic case also support an extension of the scope of distributive justice to foreigners. For example, if the requirement to satisfy basic needs goes some way toward justifying redistribution of domestic wealth, then recognizing that distant peoples share those needs will help to ground a case for global redistribution.

---

[16] By referring to the 'Rawlsian view' here I do not mean to exclude from blame most of the other theorists who have written about distributive justice in recent years. On the other side, Beitz, Barry, Richards, O'Neill, Shue, Pogge, Singer, and Elfstrom are some of the philosophers who have had the good sense to go against this particular Rawlsian grain, although none of their views is without its own problems. The arguments of some of these writers are scrutinized in Part I.

[17] David Miller, 'The Resurgence of Political Theory', *Political Studies* (1990), 426.

[18] Princeton: Princeton University Press, 1979.

[19] Cf. Yael Tamir, *Liberal Nationalism* (Princeton: Princeton University Press, 1993), ch. 6, 'The Hidden Agenda: National Values and Liberal Beliefs'.

1.3. HOW TO ARGUE FOR PRINCIPLES
OF INTERNATIONAL DISTRIBUTIVE JUSTICE

I will now outline and defend the main presuppositions of any argument for a set of principles of distributive justice, with specific reference to the international sphere. In short, I maintain that the following must be shown:

(i) the distribution of valued resources is subject to human control,
(ii) those resources are indeed relatively scarce, and
(iii) (at least in the present political context) nation-state boundaries either are or are not relevant for the purpose of determining justice-based obligations.

The first claim to defend, then, is that actions aimed at affecting the distribution of basic goods (or rights to valued resources) are indeed possible. Any reasonable discussion of the grounds for redistribution obviously presupposes that distributional arrangements can be changed if they are found to be unjust. Defence of this claim requires a refutation of what we might call *the incapacity objection*. This objection is especially prominent in the history of attempts to deny the relevance of international justice. It runs as follows: questions about the justice of global resource distribution are beside the point because action to affect such distribution is not possible. We lack the formal and informal global links necessary to control distribution across international borders. Talk of international distributive justice, then, is simply utopian: 'ought' implies 'can' and in current circumstances we cannot, so it is pointless to say that we ought.[20] The condition of the world's poor may be regrettable, but it is a mistake to say that it is an injustice, for that presupposes the efficacy of a global institutional framework for providing a remedy.

There was a time when this objection did have some weight. Throughout most of human history there were neither extensive transport links nor local surpluses of valued resources, and, therefore, it would be pointless to assert that justice demanded the redistribution of resources from one side of the globe to the other. But at this late date the incapacity claim only needs to be stated in order for its falsity to be exposed. We now have the technological capacity to affect the earth's wealth distribution, so

---

[20] For comments on this objection, see Onora O'Neill, 'International Justice: Distribution', in Lawrence C. Becker and Charlotte Becker (eds.), *Encyclopedia of Ethics* (London: Garland, 1992), 624; Onora O'Neill, *Faces of Hunger*, ch. 2; and Barry, *Theories of Justice*, 4–5.

it is perfectly in order to ask about the moral character of that distribution. Arguing for international justice therefore starts from a recognition
of the ability of human actions, individual and institutional, to alter the
distribution of rights to valued resources.

A related objection to the project of questioning the justice of resource
distribution asserts that the inequalities in life prospects, wealth and
resources between persons, and between rich and poor countries, are
natural inequalities. The falsity of this assertion is presupposed in what
follows, and for the following reason. The chronic hunger that hundreds
of millions of human beings now experience is not a fact of nature; high
death rates are not inevitable, even when terrain and climate are harsh.
The key factor in explaining why Africans die in large numbers while
Californians (i.e. desert dwellers) or Minnesotans (i.e. those who have
to live through harsh winters) do not is the robustness of economic and
social structures. Consequently, hunger and famine in distant countries
should be remediable by strengthening the economic and social institutions capable of offsetting the dangers presented by natural processes.[21]
So the world's badly off peoples do not face inevitable comparative
deprivation; on the contrary, the appeal to so-called natural inequalities should be seen for what it is, namely, an attempt to avoid seeking
solutions to a state of affairs whose existence is undeniable. Moreover,
since I consider it to be clear that the present predicament is in part the
product of the workings of social structures *created by* human beings,
and since we and our forebears got us here, we and our descendants
may be able to bring about change for the better if such change is both
feasible and desirable.

I should note at this point, however, that the creation of a state of
affairs by human (individual and institutional) actions is not a necessary
condition for that state of affairs being properly considered the concern
of justice. I disagree with those who claim that a distribution of valued
resources is neither just nor unjust unless it was brought about by deliberate human actions. For if that were true, desperate poverty resulting from
bad luck—for instance, having been born into a poor family in a Third
World country—could not be unjust. It is not that the causal history of
a state of affairs is irrelevant to its susceptibility to justice; rather, it is
that causal background is only one of a number of criteria for determining
when justice applies. Other criteria include the *urgency* of the condition

[21] Onora O'Neill, 'Hunger, Needs and Rights', in Steven Luper-Foy (ed.), *Problems
of International Justice* (London: Westview, 1988), 67–8.

of the individuals involved and the *cost* to others of rendering the required assistance to the deprived.[22] Social causation is obviously relevant to determining duties, since those who were instrumental in bringing about an unjust state of affairs have a special responsibility to ensure that the injustice is eradicated or compensated. But in the absence of action by the primary duty-bearers, others are not simply excused from providing the necessary assistance. Where we can do something about poverty and suffering without excessive cost to ourselves, we should do so, whether or not we directly caused the suffering in the first place. To the extent that much of the world's poverty can be attributed to international arrangements for which we are responsible, however, our obligations to alleviate suffering can only be strengthened.

The second move in an argument about international distributive justice is to show that the valued resources in question are properly thought to be scarce, in the sense that, for whatever reason, there will be a conflict about the preferred distribution of those resources. It may turn out that the most satisfactory resolution of such conflicts will take account of the *reason* for the scarcity's existence. For instance, natural resources such as oil and land are scarce because there is only a finite amount of them on the earth, but a right to a share of income—a different sort of resource or, rather, a claim on resources—is scarce not because some fact about the natural world makes it so, but because every person makes a similar claim to a share of income: in the first case it is a natural fact (combined with the assertion of limited altruism) that leads to a problem of distributive justice, while in the second case interpersonal conflicts, and hence problems of justice, stem from facts about the finitude of rights-distribution (along with the limited altruism claim). It is possible to assign more extensive rights to income, or rights to a larger share of income, to one person or to a minority group of people. But by doing so the rights of everyone else are restricted, since one person's claim to *x* requires not only that others lack that claim but that they have correlative duties to do or forbear in various ways. Rights to a share of income will be contested by persons with an interest in having secure claims to the means to satisfy their needs and wants; in other words, every person will need to reach some agreement with all the others about the distribution of these rights. My tentative claim is that the reason for the existence of interpersonal disputes over valued resources—whether

---

[22] These points about the diverse criteria for judging whether duties of justice exist, and the suggestion of these criteria, are made by Bruce Landesman, 'Justice: Cosmic or Communal?', in Kipnis and Meyers (eds.), *Economic Justice*, 123.

natural (as in the case of land) or otherwise (as in the case of rights to income)—will lead us to alternative grounds for resolving the problems of distributive justice arising in each case.

The next move in an argument for global distributive justice is to assess the arguments for and against assigning special ethical status to nation-state borders. The special nature of this move calls for extended comment, to which we turn in the following section.

1.4. THE INTERNATIONAL CONTEXT

Inequalities within countries are vast and ever-increasing, despite our ability to prevent them. Wealthy individuals separate themselves from the growing mass of domestic poor just as the wealthy nations deny the existence of any obligations beyond the most minimal charity toward the poor countries.[23] The problems of distributive justice within societies such as Great Britain, Canada, and the United States are difficult and controversial, to the extent that one commentator has suggested that 'the task is daunting enough, without the further complexities of international relations'.[24] But an examination of this area of political ethics must focus on the most pressing issues, and *international* inequality is first on this list. The 1992 report of the UN Human Development Program notes that the richest billion people on the earth control 83 per cent of the world's wealth, while the poorest billion are left with 1.4 per cent. Since 1960 this gulf has doubled.[25] Principles of distributive justice ought to tell us the extent to which such inequalities may be justified from an ethical point of view.

Are cross-border inequalities ever properly considered unjust? It is the task of this entire book to answer this question, but here I will address briefly the claim that inequalities can be unjust only when the societies in question form a true social, political, or economic community. Isn't it the case that justice is only possible where there is some communally accepted system by reference to which claims of justice can be adjudicated? Isn't a certain degree of interdependence between

---

[23] For instance, the United Nations recommended level of overseas aid is set at 0.7% of Gross National Product; even so, most of the rich nations do not give even that much.

[24] James S. Fishkin, *The Dialogue of Justice: Toward a Self-Reflective Society* (London: Yale University Press, 1992), 6.

[25] These figures are cited by Noam Chomsky in *Year 501: The Conquest Continues* (London: Verso, 1993), 62. He notes that this doubling is attributed in that report in part to policies of the International Monetary Fund and the World Bank, and to the protectionist policies of OECD governments during the 1980s.

persons a prerequisite of justice? In short, I think we should answer 'No' to both questions. If individuals or groups in a distant country, with whom other countries have little or no contact, suffer violations of what we would call their rights to free speech and assembly and their rights to protection from violent attack, is the lack of cultural and economic cohesion with that country good grounds for others to deny obligations to assist? If we take the aforementioned criteria of urgency and cost to be relevant to determining duties of justice, a case can be made for recognizing the need to respond to violations of rights in distant countries.[26]

Consider the case of the people of East Timor, people who have suffered from brutal violations of their basic rights to life at least since the Indonesian invasion of their country in 1975. What should be the response of the citizens of a foreign country with few or no economic ties to the region and with a significantly different culture? Again, I think the urgency of the claims of the East Timorese makes it plausible to recognize that duties of justice toward foreign and culturally different countries are indeed possible. Much more argument would be needed in order to show precisely what action is required by that recognition, but the unreasonableness of denying the human rights of foreigners is evident. I address the issue of the supposed communal background to justice in Part II, where the arguments of David Miller and Michael Walzer are assessed, but for now I want to maintain simply that the presence of distinct cultures and the absence of extensive contacts between countries does not make it *impossible* for obligations of justice to exist. On the contrary, to say that there is only a duty of charity to provide some aid to the Timorese seems, on the face of it, deeply implausible.

This last point introduces another important issue, namely, the requirements of humanitarianism in international affairs. The main claim I want to make here concerns the relation of humanitarian assistance to demands of distributive justice. What ought to be given in humanitarian aid to others can be determined only *after* an assessment has been made concerning what is owed as a requirement of justice. This is because, without that prior assessment, individuals or states could give 'generously', thinking they were acting charitably, when their giving actually constitutes merely what justice *already* demands.[27] In such cases what is required is taken for what is optional or supererogatory; hence disorganized thinking leads

---

[26] In Part II, I respond to the objection that this ignores the rights of sovereign states.

[27] Cf. Henry Shue, 'Morality, Politics, and Humanitarian Assistance', in Bruce Nichols and Gil Loescher (eds.), *The Moral Nation: Humanitarianism and U.S. Foreign Policy Today* (Notre Dame: University of Notre Dame Press, 1989), 14–16 and 22–3.

to the misidentification of fundamental moral categories and correspond-
ingly skewed assessments of what ought to be done, both individually
and institutionally.

There are a number of central themes in debates about global justice
which get played out in the varying contexts of the different approaches
to the issues. For instance, there is a general problem identified by the
following question: *Can abstract principles apply cross-culturally?* In
discussions of human rights, a specific instance of that general question is
whether human rights are universal.[28] Again, there is *the general problem
of agency*, of which individuals or collectivities should be assigned the
responsibilities to provide which benefits to whom. In the human rights
debate, the questions become, who are rights-holders? and, who are duty-
bearers? In the course of the following chapters, we will examine many
of these general questions while assessing the specific solutions proposed
by alternative moral theories.

The main aim of Part I of this book is to gain an understanding of
the implications for global distributive justice of the dominant contending
theories currently attracting attention in Anglo-American political philosophy. The main contenders are: consequentialism (especially one variant,
utilitarianism), duty-based theories (especially the neo-Kantian approach
developed by Onora O'Neill), and rights-based theories. Each of these
theoretical perspectives can be characterized as cosmopolitan.[29]

The international distributive justice debate is part of the wider discourse of 'normative international relations theory', whose main concern
is to address 'the moral dimension of international relations'.[30] The larger

---

[28] See, for instance, James Nickel's *Making Sense of Human Rights: Philosophical
Reflections on the Universal Declaration of Human Rights* (London: University of California
Press, 1987), ch. 4. Also, Noam Chomsky, 'The US and Human Rights', *Lies of Our Times*
(1993). And see my discussion of relativism and justice in Ch. 7 below.

[29] The reader might wonder why contractarian theories of international justice are not
allocated a chapter, especially since the influential and important work of Beitz, Barry, and
Pogge fit into this tradition. My answer is threefold. (1) The arguments of these theorists are
addressed at various points in the book, so their work is not ignored. (2) The contractarian
approach has much in common with both the basic rights strategy I favour and with the
Kantian view discussed in Ch. 4, therefore some elements of the contractarian approach
are in fact assessed. And finally, I believe there is a problem with any account whose
purported *basis* is what would be agreed by individuals in a hypothetical contractual
situation, since the principles of justice it aims to produce are not in fact adequately defended
by appeal to hypothetical agreement: the correct characterization of the initial choice
situation presupposes a substantive view about justice, hence all contractarian conceptions
of justice are potentially question-begging.

[30] Chris Brown, *International Relations Theory: New Normative Approaches* (Hemel
Hempstead: Harvester-Wheatsheaf, 1992), 3.

picture within which this debate takes place is crucially important to the content of that debate itself, for no answer to the question of the requirements of international justice can be regarded as satisfactory if it fails to address the objections of defenders of state sovereignty, nationality, patriotism, or relativism, to name only the most prominent attempts at restricting the scope of justice. Accordingly, the second half of this work (consisting of Chapters 5 to 8) is devoted to a consideration of these general communitarian challenges to the very idea of international justice —although none of the challengers denies the relevance of justice as it applies to more limited spheres. The question of the ethical status of nation-state borders is the most basic problem facing the theorist of global justice.

I have said that the bast way to approach this question is to look at examples of the main background ethical perspectives. And I have hinted that, following recent tradition, we should distinguish two general approaches to the subject-matter, cosmopolitanism and communitarianism.[31] In Chapters 2 to 4, I assess the merits of three species of cosmopolitanism: utilitarianism, human rights theories, and Onora O'Neill's neo-Kantianism. Then, in Chapters 5 to 8, I evaluate four communitarian accounts of international ethics: patriotism, nationalism, Michael Walzer's communitarianism and, finally, neo-Hegelian constitutive theory. First, I should provide a brief outline of the two general theoretical perspectives.

Cosmopolitanism is a moral perspective with several basic components. The cosmopolitan standpoint is impartial, universal, individualist, and egalitarian.[32] The fundamental idea is that each person affected by an institutional arrangement should be given equal consideration. Individuals are the basic units of moral concern, and the interests of individuals should be taken into account by the adoption of an impartial standpoint for evaluation. Cosmopolitanism as a moral perspective is closely akin to liberalism. John Gray characterizes liberalism as individualist, egalitarian, universalist, and meliorist, where meliorism signifies the 'affirmation of the corrigibility and improvability of all social institutions and political

---

[31] The cosmopolitan/communitarian distinction provides the organizing framework for two recent books on international political theory: Brown, *International Relations Theory*, and Janna Thompson, *Justice and World Order: A Philosophical Inquiry* (London: Routledge, 1992). See also part ii, 'Cosmopolitan and Communitarian Perspectives', in Chris Brown (ed.), *Political Restructuring in Europe: Ethical Perspectives* (London: Routledge, 1994).

[32] See Charles Beitz, 'Cosmopolitan Liberalism and the States System', in Brown (ed.), *Political Restructuring*, 123–36, at 123–7, for related suggestions. I do not address the important point that at least some forms of moral cosmopolitanism would seem to require the inclusion of non-human animals within their purview.

arrangements'.[33] Accordingly, we might understand cosmopolitanism as the ethical standpoint underlying modern liberal political theory, though to some extent even contemporary anti-liberals exemplify some or all of the central aspects of cosmopolitanism, at least when they are considering problems of domestic politics.[34]

The term 'communitarianism' is associated in contemporary political philosophy with certain kinds of criticism of liberalism. Communitarians object to the liberal's supposed commitment to an 'unencumbered self',[35] or to the alleged liberal misunderstanding of the relationship between the individual and the community, or to the liberal lack of attention to the communal origins of principles of justice.[36] As I will use the word, 'communitarianism' refers to the view that a significant source of ethical value is the community (where 'community' itself can be given various interpretations). This distinguishes communitarians from cosmopolitans, since the latter see individuals as the origin of moral worth, quite apart from the community membership of those individuals. The communitarian position, on the other hand, allows that individuals may have intrinsic value—so that individuals may be the legitimate focus of ethical concern —but it assigns ethical priority to *some* individuals (co-nationals or co-citizens) over other individuals (foreigners). Despite certain shared concerns among the thinkers discussed below, this difference between cosmopolitans and communitarians is both important and sufficiently illuminating for my theoretical purposes. Communitarians, in my sense, do not necessarily question the importance of intra-communal justice: they accept that the good society is one whose institutions are consistent with a set of principles of distributive justice. But when considering the issue of international justice, communitarians deny that the arguments

---

[33] John Gray, *Liberalism* (Milton Keynes: Open University Press, 1986), p. x. Roger J. Sullivan, *An Introduction to Kant's Ethics* (Cambridge: Cambridge University Press, 1994), 9, notes that these four features provide a useful organizing framework for understanding the political theory of Immanuel Kant.

[34] A recent attempt to work out the fundamental ideas of the cosmopolitan ethical perspective can be found in Brian Barry, *Theories of Justice* (Hemel Hempstead: Harvester-Wheatsheaf, 1989), and *Justice as Impartiality* (Oxford: Clarendon Press, 1995). Barry's statement of 'justice as impartiality' 'entails that people should not look at things from their own point of view alone but seek to find a basis of agreement that is acceptable from all points of view. The general approach . . . calls on people to detach themselves from their own contingently given positions and take up a more impartial standpoint . . .' *Theories of Justice*, 7–8.

[35] Michael Sandel, *Liberalism and the Limits of Justice* (Cambridge: Cambridge University Press, 1982).

[36] Michael Walzer, *Spheres of Justice: A Defence of Pluralism and Equality* (Oxford: Basil Blackwell, 1983).

for 'justice at home' apply equally to those elsewhere. The communities where justice primarily applies are usually thought to be nation-states, though some thinkers prioritize the nation itself, as distinct from the state. In Part II of this work, we shall look at different versions of these communitarian attempts to limit the scope of arguments about justice.

But why look at these opposing perspectives in the global justice debate? Why not simply focus on what I take to be the correct view and develop that view in more detail? I think there are three good reasons for considering the main competing theories. First, in the interests of achieving a broad scope (though I do not pretend to offer a complete survey), it is desirable to assess the merits and demerits of prominent viewpoints; this will enable us to pick out important claims we might otherwise have overlooked. Secondly, our choice of moral theory has a direct bearing on the features of particular problems that arise. Moral theory does not simply get applied to various pre-existing problems; rather, different theories throw into relief different features of an issue, highlighting those features often at the expense of obscuring others. Concentrating on only one theoretical approach, therefore, may blind us to other morally relevant features of a specific disputed problem. For example, utilitarians can highlight the fact that the present international economic system fails to maximize benefit, but they might have difficulty addressing the problem of agency. (These claims are discussed in Chapter 2.) The third reason for investigating other theories is obvious, but no less important: it is vital that we establish which is the best approach and for what reasons.

The general conclusions reached in these pages about the requirements of distributive justice world-wide can seem both too radical and too conservative, depending on one's favoured approach to these issues. On the one hand, it can appear quite revolutionary to maintain—as I will—that every human being has a right to have her or his vital interests met, regardless of nationality or citizenship, and that the failure on the part of our institutional frameworks to protect those interests constitutes a moral catastrophe. On the other hand, some readers might think that we owe it to one another as human beings to ensure not only that rights to the protection of basic interests are acknowledged, but also that more substantial commitments be made—perhaps, that we recognize human rights to a more extensive list of 'goods' than the one I offer here.

I answer the objection that accepting human rights to the protection of vital interests is too radical a proposal by arguing for the undeniable moral importance of those interests and by showing that it is neither impossible nor too demanding to allocate the duties correlative to those rights. To those who make the second objection, and so see my project as lacking in ambition, I make only two points here. First, I should note that I am sympathetic to an expansion of the commitments of those in the wealthy nations toward those persons who at present suffer from endemic poverty, lack of adequate food and water, complete exclusion from decision-making about questions that directly affect their interests, and the like. But in the interests of practical relevance, I believe that we must start with the least controversial case, namely, the case for human rights to subsistence, liberty, and physical security. Nothing in my argument precludes others from making a case for more extensive obligations. Secondly, the difficulty of offering a convincing argument for cosmopolitanism with respect to distributive justice should not be underestimated. I defend human rights against those who deny their very existence, but that is not all that such a defence requires. It is also necessary to engage in the task undertaken in Part II of this book: to defend the view that persons have similar obligations of justice to all other persons, regardless of national or other community-based duties they might also have, and that the requirements of patriotic loyalty do not rule out the recognition that compatriots and foreigners alike are human beings with equal rights to the protection of their vital interests. The chapters in Part II address what I take to be the most important types of 'limitation arguments', that is, arguments whose purpose is to place limits on the universalist pretensions of the case made in Part I, either by restricting the scope of justice to co-nationals or co-citizens, or by denying that that there can be an account of justice that encompasses anything larger than a more or less rigidly circumscribed community.

As noted earlier, communitarian criticisms of cosmopolitan justice maintain that justice is best reserved for domestic debate, and that nation-states are communities in some sense relevant to distributive justice, while the world itself is not a community in this sense. I introduce the most interesting versions of communitarian justice in Part II, but I should note here my sympathy for the idea that nation-states are not homogeneous entities, nor are they arenas for cosy cooperation between large groups of people committed to some ideal of 'national advancement'. The reality is different. When considering the question of international distributive justice, we do well to keep in mind the fact that nation-states are themselves the focus of conflicts between rich and poor, and that fellow members of the wealthy classes in the world—as well as fellow members of the world's hungry population—might have common interests of greater importance than the interests that bind compatriots or co-nationals to one another. Sentiments of loyalty can run along lines that separate compatriots from one another and underpin bonds toward others with whom some set of important interests are shared.

Everyone would agree that the present international political and economic system is not perfect. Starting from this agreement, I will ask specifically how the international order stands up to justice-based criticism. In other words, my aim is to determine both what is wrong and what can be done to improve matters, at least with respect to the justice of current arrangements. We need to ask the following questions: What reasons are there for the extremes of wealth and poverty that exist in the world? Are such inequalities unavoidable? If not, why might they be considered desirable? The book itself is an examination of arguments for and against the radical inequalities of the international political and economic system by way of an assessment of arguments for and against the assignment of duties of justice toward compatriots and foreigners.

Chris Brown has said that 'in the last resort the extent to which communitarian as opposed to cosmopolitan thought is convincing seems to depend more on the "gut" feelings of individual authors than on the processes of reasoned argument'.[37] While there might be no way to disprove this claim conclusively, this work aims to limit the extent to which gut feelings will decide the large questions of international ethics. My hope is that the following discussions will go some way towards demonstrating that close attention to specific arguments is a fruitful way of achieving progress in international political theory.

[37] Brown, *International Relations Theory*, 75.

I

Cosmopolitanism

2

Utilitarianism and Global Justice

2.1. WHAT IS UTILITARIANISM?

Cosmopolitan justice can take a number of forms, the most important and promising of which are utilitarian, rights-based and obligation-based conceptions. My plan is to outline each of these views in turn, with the goal of showing how an approach centred on basic human rights overcomes the shortcomings of its main contenders. I begin with utilitarianism because its simplicity and direct approach to global justice has a significant initial appeal, and because some of the most notable contributions to the global ethics debates have been utilitarian.[1] It is worthwhile, therefore, to determine the character and plausibility of this approach. However, the difficulties with utilitarian accounts of justice will lead us naturally to my favoured 'basic rights' view, since this view has some sympathies with utilitarianism but differs in precisely the ways needed to overcome the main problems with that theory. Having laid out the gist of the basic rights account in Chapter 3, I then consider the challenge presented by another close cosmopolitan relative, namely, Onora O'Neill's Kantian focus on obligations. I conclude that O'Neill's position is no improvement upon (my preferred version of) rights-theory; and so, by the end of Part I, we will have evaluated the central cosmopolitan theories of global justice, and we will have come to the tentative conclusion that we do best to accept a theory centred on basic rights. Let us begin, then, with utilitarianism.

According to Russell Hardin, utilitarianism 'is the moral theory that judges the goodness of outcomes—and therefore the rightness of actions insofar as they affect outcomes—by the degree to which they secure the greatest benefit to all concerned'.[2] From this definition of utilitarianism, we can distinguish its three central features. First, it is consequentialist. This means that it judges the rightness of actions (or policies) *solely* in

---

[1] For instance, the work of Peter Singer, Robert Goodin, and Gerard Elfstrom, among others, is important, sophisticated, and explicitly utilitarian.

[2] Russell Hardin, *Morality within the Limits of Reason* (Chicago: The University of Chicago Press, 1988), p. xv.

terms of their consequences. Secondly, consequences are understood in terms of the *benefit* embodied in them. Specifically, utilitarians say we should aim to bring about benefit to all of the individuals affected by our actions. And finally, the amount of benefit to individuals should be *maximized*: a policy is to be preferred if it produces more benefit than would any other policy.

Utilitarianism is a clear case of a cosmopolitan theory (as we defined cosmopolitanism in Chapter 1). It will be remembered that cosmopolitans favour an approach that is impartial, non-perspectival, individualist, and egalitarian. Referring again to Hardin's characterization, in answer to the question, 'What is the core of utilitarianism?', he says: 'The fundamentally moral impulse of utilitarianism is the concern with consequences for people in general. Hence, the core of utilitarianism is its consequentialism, its universality, and some kind of value that is value to individuals. The element here that is not fixed is the value theory, which can take diverse contents.'[3] When assessing outcomes, concern should be shown for 'people in general', where no one is to count for more than anyone else, since no one person has more inherent worth than any other. The latter claims embody the utilitarian commitment to egalitarianism, while the former claim recommends an impartial standpoint for evaluation. And it follows that no one perspective or group of perspectives should be privileged when making moral assessments: this is the requirement of non-perspectivality. No one's perspective or interests should be excluded or weighed more heavily than that of anyone else. The individualism of utilitarianism is explicit: whatever constitutes the value which the theory aims to maximize, that value is always and only a property of individual persons. As another interpreter says,

[a]ccording to the utilitarian tradition, the ultimate locus of value is the individual, and the reason for this is that it is individuals, not communities, that can be happy or unhappy, have desires satisfied or unsatisfied, and so on. We may speak of a community as wanting something, but this, utilitarians believe, can always be translated into some set of statements about the interests of individuals that compose the community.[4]

---

[3] Hardin, *Morality within the Limits of Reason*, 19.

[4] Anthony Ellis, 'Utilitarianism and International Ethics', in Terry Nardin and David R. Mapel (eds.), *Traditions of International Ethics* (Cambridge: Cambridge University Press, 1992), 172–3. While this is true of the *tradition* of utilitarianism, utilitarian individualism is by no means as inevitable as this passage makes it seem. A prominent utilitarian, Derek Parfit, in *Reasons and Persons* (Oxford: Clarendon Press, 1984), argues that the ultimate unit of morality is the discrete experience; given that view, the individualism might be hard to retain. I am grateful to Anthony Ellis for bringing this point to my attention.

Utilitarian value theory is the subject of a substantial and ongoing debate, where the main contenders for the content of that theory are (1) the experience of pleasure, (2) preference-satisfaction, or (3) some qualified preference-satisfaction view (for instance, the satisfaction of rational preferences). The preferred content for the value theory, in the present context of international relations, is the satisfaction of *basic* wants or *vital* interests. No doubt, a fully developed value theory would go beyond this minimum content, but for the purposes of international political philosophy in the contemporary context, there is good reason to restrict the focus of one's value theory in this way.

Utilitarian theory will here be considered not as an all-embracing theory of individual right action but as a justificatory apparatus for the performance of institutions. Let me make this point especially clear. Utilitarianism is often taken to offer a criterion of right action for individuals, but since my focus is on the institutions making up what I have called the international basic structure, it is only as a justificatory theory of these sorts of institutions that utilitarianism will be addressed here. Moreover, while pleasure or want-satisfaction have traditionally been the main options for the conceptualization of utility, I believe the special and limited case of global obligations should be content with a limited value theory, namely, a conception of the most important values of persons. My concern is with a consequentialist perspective that prioritizes the protection of the basic interests of individuals or the satisfaction of their basic wants. This view may be seen as a form of utilitarianism if in the place of 'utility' we substitute 'the meeting of basic interests'.[5]

The vital or basic interests of persons are those interests which every reasonable person would take to be the necessary conditions of a recognizably human life. These include interests in obtaining food, safe drinking water, clothing, shelter, a certain (though, across societies, variable) level of education, and access to basic health care. This choice of values to be maximized might be rejected on the grounds that it leaves out much that is worthwhile for human beings. It is of course true that most of what matters morally in our lives is not mentioned by the basic interest utilitarian. However, a theory of international ethics does well to keep the more ground-level desiderata in clear view, for the present arrangement of global institutions does not protect them. Thus it is reasonable to limit the demands of morality in this way when to attain their satisfaction would be a major achievement requiring substantial

---

[5] Gerard Elfstrom, *Ethics for a Shrinking World* (London: Macmillan, 1990), is a clear representative of what I call 'basic interests utilitarianism'.

change to the present system. If a utilitarian theory so circumscribed can justify substantial redistribution of wealth and resources from rich to poor countries, it will have achieved a great deal.

Restricting the scope of what counts as utility might still appear to be nothing more than an *ad hoc* move designed to produce particular conclusions to which the theorist is already committed. Since I want to avoid falling prey to this objection, I should point out in more detail exactly why utilitarianism as applied to global politics is best conceived as recommending the maximization of the protection of basic interests of persons.

The objection stems, in part, from a recognition that much of what is considered relevant to the happiness or want-satisfaction of individuals is left out by the basic interests utilitarian, yet there is no obvious reason, at the foundational level of moral theory, for excluding some aspect of utility from consideration. The 'basic interests utilitarian' (BIU) response to this charge is to deny it outright: if we focus, for convenience, on 'utility' as 'want-satisfaction', then it is clear that, contrary to the objector's claim, there are some wants that ought not to be satisfied. If someone wants to torture innocent children, the utilitarian who proposes to include *all* wants in his calculus will be required to include that want along with all the others. This is clearly unacceptable from a moral point of view. This point is sufficient to show that restriction of the range of wants to be maximized is perfectly acceptable. (Of course, I am then denying that want-satisfaction is intrinsically good, but I see no way around this denial. This presents a problem for those who take utilitarians to exemplify the approach that says 'the good is prior to the right'. Since 'the good' is to be maximized, on my view, only when it is subject to prior qualifications that rule out unfair treatment of persons, there is already a right-based constraint on the good to be maximized. Utilitarianism remains intact, then, only in its call for maximization of the *morally permissible* good. This is consistent with most contemporary attempts to defend utilitarianism, since those attempts generally include sophisticated construals of 'utility' in part designed to exclude evil desires from the counting procedure.)

But the objection might be not that it is wrong for utilitarians to restrict the range of wants in some way, but that it is *ad hoc* to exclude some *morally permissible* wants from consideration. The basic interests utilitarian answers that, in the international context, there are good reasons for these restrictions, and so focusing only on them is well-motivated. This is in part an acceptance of the objection, but only in so far as the objection pointed out the unreasonableness of excluding some classes of wants at the level of moral foundations.

I have said that, when considering international relations, there are good reasons for limiting theoretical and practical concern to the basic wants of persons. What are those reasons?[6] First, these are the wants that are generally valued most highly by people. Secondly, satisfaction of basic wants are necessary conditions for the satisfaction of any non-basic wants. The facts that people generally value their interests in obtaining food and physical security above their other interests (say, in obtaining the goods of culture), and that protection of these interests is a precondition for the protection of the others, are both ways of saying that basic interests are, morally speaking, very important. These two reasons do not preclude the possibility that a sufficient number of non-basic wants could tip the scales in the other direction, but it does make that possibility seem highly unlikely, especially when the following reason is considered. The third reason is that it is difficult to satisfy the non-basic wants of individuals in far-away countries, whereas it is relatively easy to satisfy basic wants in those countries. Consider the undeniable interest persons have in obtaining cultural goods. That interest is protected and promoted by ensuring that the distinctive cultures of different societies function effectively; but the functioning of a culture is in general best left to those who participate in sustaining it. This suggests that promoting this particular interest is best achieved by leaving cultural matters to insiders. Outsiders are more likely to misinterpret features of unfamiliar cultures, with the likely consequence of cultural impoverishment when they act on those misinterpretations. Promotion of basic interests, whose variation is much less wide-ranging across societies, is accordingly easier to achieve.[7] Moreover, the goal of creating and sustaining cultural goods will not

---

[6] Cf. Elfstrom, *Ethics for a Shrinking World*, 15.

[7] This is not to say that a simple redistribution of resources will succeed in bringing about significant changes to the meeting of vital interests. The World Health Organization's division of Intensified Cooperation (ICO), set up in 1994, has already had a marked effect in this regard, but its experience does not hold universally. For instance, this programme 'has achieved a higher rate of child immunisation in poor regions of Guinea-Bissau than in the US'. The reason for this sort of success is that 'much of its work focuses on helping governments to formulate their own health priorities and to channel resources to where they are most needed. At present, millions of dollars in aid go to waste because poor countries cannot use the money effectively and donors dictate the terms.' George Graham and Frances Williams, 'WHO and Baltimore Share Prescriptions', *Financial Times* (London, 16 Aug. 1995), 3. Even if basic interests are the only focal point of aid, the assistance is most effective when it is not tied to programmes designed to make profits for Northern transnational corporations.

be pursued properly unless vital interests are protected. Consequently, there seem to be good utilitarian reasons for not interfering in the *strictly cultural* matters of foreign countries; however, these considerations in no way warrant a policy of non-interference in the domestic affairs of other countries where those affairs concern matters relating to the vital interests of people in those countries.

A fourth and final reason for focusing single-mindedly on vital interests is that the utilitarian's ultimate aim of promoting human well-being might best be promoted by restricting our focus in this way. As Geoffrey Scarre puts it,

many of the positive things which do make lives go well, such as the forming of affections and relationships, the pursuit and attainment of goals, and the acquisition of self-respect and the respect of others, are things which an individual must largely secure for himself, others' capacity to assist him being mainly limited to the reduction of the obstacles (e.g. sickness, poverty, isolation, economic and social oppression) which stand in his way.[8]

The focus on basic wants or vital interests can be nothing more than a general recommendation, however, and nothing said here can rule out expansion of the class of globally relevant wants or interests in a particular case.

Basic interests utilitarianism is not susceptible to the objection that utilitarian theories fail to take proper account of needs. This criticism maintains that utilitarianism in all its variants focuses on desires and the maximization of *their* satisfaction, even when needs go unmet as a consequence of the maximizing process.[9] The objection does not touch those consequentialist approaches which focus on needs rather than desires, that is, those that stipulate for 'utility' or 'welfare' a more objective definition than the desire approach allows. Consequentialist theories which *do not* focus *exclusively* on desire fulfilment are not fatally damaged. Another way to think of basic interests utilitarianism is that it limits the desires which will count for the purposes of aggregation; it therefore imports some objective conception of what it is that people ought to want, even when they would disagree in some instances with what is included in that conception. Of course, the arguments generating the list of basic interests are closely tied to the facts about what people actually do want.

[8] Geoffrey Scarre, *Utilitarianism* (London: Routledge, 1996), 18.
[9] Onora O'Neill, in several of her works, has pressed this objection. See, for instance, 'Hunger, Needs, and Rights', in Steven Luper-Foy (ed.), *Problems of International Justice* (Boulder, Colo., and London: Westview, 1988), 69.

The connection is often complicated, however, in at least two ways. First, there are cases where some people do not want what they actually need to survive and live a normal human life. Such people—hunger strikers, for instance—might be motivated by ideals which lead them to forgo the requirements of existence in order to further some larger, perhaps collective cause. These people constitute a special exception for the basic interests utilitarian; the fact that they are clearly special cases, however, lends weight to the theory's applicability in standard cases. An alternative instance in which people do not want what they need is the existence of people who are psychologically handicapped in some way, and as a consequence are incapable of knowing what it is they need to survive. Here the objectivist character of the theory averts the difficulties such persons raise for wholly desire-based conceptions. Secondly, there are cases where lack of knowledge, on the part of those not mentally impaired in some other way, severs the link between needs and wants. For instance, most people want to be healthy and so also want to obtain adequate nutrition for themselves, but they may not realize that they need a certain vitamin intake to satisfy that want, hence they do not want what they in fact need. An objective concept of utility dissolves this problem of ignorance by shifting the focus to what individuals *would* want if they had adequate information about what was needed to protect their vital interests.[10]

2.2. THE IMPLICATIONS OF UTILITARIANISM FOR GLOBAL JUSTICE

Consequentialists writing about international issues defend a variety of practical recommendations. Onora O'Neill accuses utilitarianism of giving rise to directly opposed views about international obligations.[11] For instance, Peter Singer recommends, on utilitarian grounds, large-scale

[10] Brian Barry, *Justice as Impartiality* (Oxford: Clarendon Press, 1995), 140, distinguishes 'welfare' from 'utility' and says that, in ordinary usage, 'welfare is an objective concept rather than a subjective concept. Welfare corresponds roughly to the absence of harm (i.e., the presence of adequate food, clothing and shelter, freedom from pain and suffering, and so on).' If we accept this suggestion, the position outlined in the text could be renamed 'Basic Interests Welfarism', or even simply 'Welfarism'.

[11] See, for instance, Onora O'Neill, 'Transnational Justice', in David Held (ed.), *Political Theory Today* (Oxford: Polity, 1991), 283; or Onora O'Neill, *Faces of Hunger: An Essay on Poverty, Justice and Development* (London: Allen & Unwin, 1986), 56 ff.

redistribution from rich to poor irrespective of nation-state boundaries,[12] while Garrett Hardin (not to be confused with Russell Hardin), combining a broadly consequentialist view with a commitment to neo-Malthusian ideas about population growth, argues that, if the aim is to minimize suffering, there should be no redistribution whatsoever.[13] If utilitarianism does not generate a single policy recommendation, it lacks the determinacy which was supposed to have been one of its central virtues. Will Kymlicka argues that, as utilitarian theories have become more sophisticated in the face of the complexities of both empirical disagreement and moral reasoning, they have abandoned their heritage of radical critique, reformism and anti-traditionalism; 'utilitarianism does not immediately identify any set of policies as distinctly superior. Modern utilitarianism, despite its radical heritage, no longer defines a distinctive political position.'[14]

   While O'Neill and Kymlicka offer accurate assessments of utilitarianism as a family of approaches to political morality, their claims do not constitute a very telling criticism of any particular utilitarian view. For utilitarians can still (i) carefully outline a distinctive characterization of 'utility' that best suits contemporary global conditions, and (ii) assess the best available empirical evidence in order to develop policies for utility maximization. Disagreements within the utilitarian camp can then be adjudicated by evaluating both the theory of 'utility' and the empirical evidence. We should note that *any* ethical theory needs some account of the good, at least if it holds it to be desirable to do good, so lack of utilitarian unanimity on this point hardly constitutes a shortcoming unique to that particular school of moral and political thinking. Moreover, it is surely not a drawback for a theory of international ethics that it requires careful examination of the causes of suffering and the available means for overcoming it.

---

[12] Peter Singer, 'Famine, Affluence and Morality', *Philosophy and Public Affairs*, 1 (1972), 229–44. References will be to the version reprinted in Charles Beitz *et al.* (eds.), *International Ethics* (Princeton: Princeton University Press, 1985), 247–61.

[13] Garrett Hardin, 'Lifeboat Ethics: The Case Against Helping the Poor', *Psychology Today*, 8 (1974), 38–43. He addresses these same issues in *Living Within Limits* (Oxford: Oxford University Press, 1993). I do not deal with this issue at any length in this work, but I should note that his neo-Malthusianism is a non-starter, since Third World populations are expanding rapidly *even with the extreme poverty and neglect they are now experiencing.* So the 'do nothing' approach is no solution at all, because it *ensures* that there will be a catastrophe.

[14] Will Kymlicka, *Contemporary Political Philosophy: An Introduction* (Oxford: Clarendon Press, 1990), 47. Gerard Elfstrom, on the other hand, prefers utilitarianism to alternative approaches to international morality because it is more flexible, more sensitive to context. See his *Ethics for a Shrinking World*, 12.

Proceeding then to consider the implications of what I take to be the best version of utilitarianism as applied to the entire globe, we should first look at the facts of deprivation. Just as a sampling of a depressing story, consider the following. Approximately 750 million people go hungry every day because they are in extreme poverty.[15] One-third of the population of the world lacks clean water, a half of the world's population lacks sanitation adequate to prevent the imminent likelihood of the spread of disease, and millions of children die each year from diseases against which they could be immunized.[16] All of this coexists 'with over a quarter of the world's population living at material standards vastly in excess of anything required to meet their basic needs'.[17] Any satisfactory utilitarian theory (indeed any satisfactory theory, utilitarian or otherwise) must be sensitive to these statistics; in a world with such advanced productive, technological, and transporting capacities, the very existence of such miserable conditions is cause for concern. The massive scale of the crisis only serves to strengthen the case for addressing and attempting to overcome this predicament, so an adequate theoretical approach to these problems should accommodate and explain beliefs about the wrongness of this situation, beliefs which arguably form the core of most people's considered moral judgements.[18]

Basic interests utilitarians are of course especially sensitive to the failure to protect the vital needs of individuals, so they can easily register the harms the current international system either creates or allows to happen. Furthermore, such utilitarians recommend that—given the falsity of Malthusian views about population—large-scale redistribution of wealth and resources from rich countries to poor countries is morally required, since this is the only way to maximize the satisfaction of the basic wants

[15] Hans Binswanger and Pierre Landell-Mills, *The World Bank's Strategy for Reducing Poverty and Hunger* (New York: World Bank, 1995). For some parts of the world, the future is likely to be much worse than the present. Harry Walters, the World Bank advisor on food security in Africa, forecasts that the proportion of the world's seriously malnourished people in Africa alone is expected to rise from 20% in 1995 to 45% by 2010.

[16] Stephen Nathanson, *Patriotism, Morality, and Peace* (Lanham, MD: Rowman and Littlefield, 1993), 181, citing Ruth Leger Sivard, *World Military and Social Expenditures 1989* (Washington, DC: World Priorities, 1989), 24–35.

[17] Brian Barry, 'Justice, Freedom, and Basic Income', in Horst Siebert (ed.), *The Ethical Foundations of the Market Economy: International Workshop* (Tubingen: J. C. B. Mohr (Paul Siebeck), 1994), 75.

[18] Of course, utilitarians could not judge a state of affairs to be *wrong* simply because it is characterized by widespread suffering, for that suffering first has to be weighed against the positive side of the ledger (the numbers of people with their basic interests protected), and then compared to possible alternatives, before an overall assessment can be made.

of persons, their desires for the means to life itself and to the conditions for satisfactory functioning within one's society.

If the general cosmopolitan perspective is thought to be a reasonable one,[19] then this form of utilitarianism is a plausible view, not only for its consistency with a reasonable belief that suffering is bad, but also because it suggests a reformation of the international institutions which through their normal functioning have allowed this suffering to come about. Much of the empirical argument needed to justify this practical suggestion will be assumed for the present, for I want to assess 'basic interests utilitarianism' as a theory of international morality. Accordingly, I will allow that the facts and the best way to deal with them are as outlined above, and move on to evaluate the normative core of this form of utilitarian political morality.

2.3. TWO OBJECTIONS TO UTILITARIANISM

Utilitarianism has been criticized for so many alleged shortcomings that it is difficult to know where to begin. I propose two criteria for selecting objections. First, an objection should to go to the moral core of the theory, to what it is that makes the theory utilitarian. Secondly, we should be especially concerned with objections that arise most clearly in a global context. The two objections I consider satisfy both criteria. The first criticism says that utilitarianism asks of individuals and institutions what cannot be required of them. Maximizing utility, it is often said, would mean giving up the lifestyles and relationships we know and value, and these are demands that we should not have to meet. The second criticism says not that utilitarianism *demands* too much but that it *permits* too much: utilitarians fail to rule out actions and policies which should be forbidden, such as the sacrifice of some individuals for the sake of the greater overall good. Utilitarianism is thus taken to be too permissive.[20]

In the context of debates on international distributive justice, these criticisms take particular forms. For example, redistributing wealth and resources from the rich to the poor countries so as to promote the maximal satisfaction of basic interests is asking too much of the people

---

[19] Theories fundamentally opposed to cosmopolitanism are considered in Part II, Chs. 5–8.

[20] These objections are stated in many works on ethics. See for instance, Gilbert Harman, *The Nature of Morality* (New York: Oxford University Press, 1977), ch. 13.

in well-off countries (the overdemandingness objection); and promoting the consequentialist goal may result in the using of some individuals for the sake of the greater good, whereas (mere) maximization should not be the one and only criterion of decision-making (the 'too permissive' objection). I will argue that the overdemandingness objection can be deflected to a large extent, at least in its application to international justice. I will then consider the 'too permissive' objection, arguing that, while utilitarians need not support violations of rights, their reasons for not doing so fail to capture precisely what it is about rights-violations that makes them wrong.

Is Utilitarianism Too Demanding?

Considerations of diminishing marginal utility suggest that a distribution leading to the maximization of such wealth and resources as are needed for the protection of basic interests would be one much closer to equal shares for everyone in the world. Peter Singer's utilitarian argument, for the claim that we should prevent the suffering of the world's deprived people when doing so does not require us to sacrifice 'anything of comparable moral importance', leads to an egalitarian conclusion, but one which seems seriously burdensome for individuals in the rich countries, despite Singer's suggestion that the 'comparable moral importance' principle is relatively 'uncontroversial'.[21] Do we really believe we should be required to redistribute up to the point where further giving would reduce us to a condition below that of those to whom we are giving? Have we acted *wrongly* when we give anything less?

One response to the overdemandingness objection is to accuse it of begging the question.[22] Knowledge of what is too demanding depends upon a prior solution to the problem of what is morally required, and if we already know what is morally required the proper response to utilitarianism is not to accuse it of overdemandingness but simply to point out its incompatibility with the preferred criterion. But the accusations usually levelled against utilitarianism on this point do not say why it is that their anti-utilitarian view should be accepted. Hence James Fishkin makes an essentially empty claim when he says that some significant moral argument is advanced by citing 'the kinds of limits on moral demands we

---

[21] Singer, 'Famine, Affluence and Morality', 249.
[22] Brian Barry, *Theories of Justice* (Hemel Hempstead: Harvester-Wheatsheaf, 1989), 82–3.

commonly presuppose in secular Western moral culture'.[23] Fishkin claims, plausibly, that we assume the existence of a 'zone of indifference' which permits many of our actions to be directed toward ends which clearly are not utility-maximizing. In addition, the other side of this coin is that there is a 'cut-off for heroism', that is, individuals are not obligated to sacrifice themselves or their perceived interests beyond some (hazily specified) point.[24] These limits on what morality can require of us are merely stated, they are not defended; hence they ought not to deter the utilitarian, whose purpose is in this case to question received opinion. We want to know why the zone should not be restricted[25] and, similarly, why the cut-off point should not be shifted to render obligatory many of those actions and policies commonly thought to be heroic.

This *petitio principii* or circularity reply to the overdemandingness objection is not fatal, however. It would only be so *either* if no grounds could be offered for the commonly accepted limits *or* if such grounds as could be provided failed to show that what is wrong with utilitarianism is precisely that the amount individuals would be required to give up beyond those limits is more than those grounds permit. The question of demands becomes most important when we consider what persons, with the characteristic and perhaps unchangeable weaknesses we know them to possess, would be able to achieve while retaining their identities as individuals. We therefore need to ask whether people could live with utilitarian demands while continuing to live recognizably human lives.

When discussing the demands made on individuals and institutions, we need to clarify the point at issue by asking: 'Too demanding for whom?' *Any* system of moral requirements will be demanding for *some* group of people, for example, either the propertied or the impoverished. We are then, I think, led to ask which of the interests opposed to each other has greater moral force. In this case, the interests protected by the claims of private property are opposed to the interests protected by claims to subsistence. We must choose one set of interests over the other, since it

[23] James Fishkin, 'Theories of Justice and International Relations: The Limits of Liberal Theory', in Anthony Ellis (ed.), *Ethics and International Relations* (Manchester: Manchester University Press, 1986), 4.

[24] Fishkin claims that other liberal, non-utilitarian theories are guilty of the same crime, since—like Beitz's contractarian theory—they are 'systematically impartial' in their assessment of states of affairs. But utilitarianism is the most demanding of this group of approaches. I address this misconception of impartiality at some length in Ch. 5.

[25] On traditional accounts of utilitarianism, where utility is interpreted more expansively, the utilitarian claim would be that the zone of indifference should be eliminated altogether; but if 'utility' means 'protection of basic interests', there will likely be room for the pursuit of personal projects and the like, consistent with meeting the demands of the theory.

is not possible to accommodate both sets simultaneously. Viewed in this way, protecting the interest in subsistence begins to look more plausible because the urgency of the interest in subsistence is greater than the urgency of the interests protected by private property rights. Jeremy Waldron puts this point nicely:

In general, where resources are scarce relative to human wants, *any* system of rights or entitlements will seem demanding to those who are constrained by it. If an economic system includes provision for welfare assistance, it may seem overly demanding to taxpayers. But if it does not include such provision, then the system of *property rights* in such an economy will seem overly demanding to the poor, requiring as it does that they refrain from making use of resources (belonging to others) that they need in order to survive. As usual, the question is not whether we are to have a system of demanding rights, but how the costs of these demands are to be distributed.[26]

The general point about relative moral priority of rights was well-stated by Jeremy Bentham in his 'Principles of the Civil Code'. Bentham said that

the title of the indigent, as indigent, is stronger than the title of the proprietor of a superfluity, as proprietor; since the pain of death, which would finally fall upon the neglected indigent, will always be a greater evil than the pain of disappointed expectation, which falls upon the rich when a limited portion of his superfluity is taken from him.[27]

While these points are worth making, it none the less is true that the overdemandingness objection is generally put forward on behalf of the well-off, therefore it is the force of the objection so understood that I will assess.

Overdemandingness is a problem for a theory of international moral obligation in a way that it is not for simpler cases of actions requiring sacrifice on the part of persons. Peter Singer attempts to persuade his readers by starting with an uncontroversial example, namely, that it is right for any person to save the life of an innocent child who is drowning in a nearby shallow pool. There are many elements involved in this

[26] Jeremy Waldron, 'Rights', in Robert E. Goodin and Philip Pettit (eds.), *A Companion to Contemporary Political Philosophy* (Oxford: Blackwell, 1993), 580, emphases in original.

[27] Jeremy Bentham, 'Principles of the Civil Code', in John Bowring (ed.), *Works of Jeremy Bentham* (Edinburgh: William Tait, 1843), i. 316, cited in John Dinwiddy, *Bentham* (Oxford: Oxford University Press, 1989), 98. Bentham composed this work in the 1780s.

example,[28] but for our purposes the most important one is that it concerns an individual's duty to promote the good where individual actions can succeed by themselves in bringing about the desired result (in this case, saving the innocent child). In most cases saving the child's life would be considered a duty, even though it might require some sacrifice or risk on the part of the duty-bearer. But Singer argues by analogy that people in rich countries ought to do what they can to save the lives of those in poor countries who would die without their help. The problem with this argumentative strategy is that it is addressed to *individuals* in rich countries, and it is this feature which lends credibility to the overdemandingness objection. The problem is that solitary individuals in large-scale cases like this are unable 'to determine an outcome independently of the actions of others'.[29] This suggests that, even if Singer is right about the drowning child case, the complexities of international suffering will make that case importantly different, most importantly in that it introduces considerations of strategic interaction. Arguments by analogy only work when the two cases being compared are relevantly similar, but the 'drowning child' case and the 'starving millions' case are dissimilar in a way that makes the latter morally more complex.

In addressing only individuals, utilitarians run into the following problem. In so far as the aim of action is to maximize utility, it seems to follow that utilitarian individuals should give *even more* whenever others fail to give as much as they can. This is not only unfair but impossible, for, on the one hand, people should not be required to give more than an equitable share towards the bringing about of good outcomes, and on the other hand, it is true by definition that utility cannot be maximized when some are not doing what they can to contribute to this goal.[30] But

[28] For a detailed account of the relevant features of Singer's argument, including replies to some central criticisms and an overall assessment, see Brian Barry, 'Humanity and Justice in Global Perspective', in *Liberty and Justice: Essays in Political Theory*, ii (Oxford: Clarendon Press, 1991), 183–87 (1st publ. in 1982). Recently, there has appeared a very interesting book-length defence of a demanding duty of individuals to end avoidable suffering: Peter Unger, *Living High and Letting Die: Our Illusion of Innocence* (Oxford: Oxford University Press, 1996). Unger carefully distinguishes the various considerations relevant to determining the plausibility of such a duty.

[29] Hardin, *Morality within the Limits of Reason*, p. xvii.

[30] It might be objected here that utilitarianism does not require that utility be maximized; it requires that the agent do the action which, of those available to him, will maximize utility. Since, it might be thought, an individual *can* do that in this case—he can do that act which would produce more utility than would any other action he could perform—there is a sense in which it is not impossible that utility can be maximized in this case. In response to this point, I maintain that there is *no action* that the agent, *acting in isolation*, can perform here that would maximize utility; and if more utility could be produced by enforced

if we shift the focus to institutions, the problem faced by solitary individuals disappears, for compliance can be enforced by those institutions,
thereby bringing lazy or otherwise uncooperative persons into line in a
duty-sharing cooperative venture. I should note, however, that this appeal
to the need for institutional mechanisms to end avoidable suffering *does
not* provide any foothold for those who would invoke the claim that
'governments should provide the aid' as a means to getting themselves
off the hook for not making any *individual* contribution themselves, here
and now, i.e. when the institutional framework is not yet in place. When
many avoidable deaths can be prevented by individual acts of giving,
no one has a blanket excuse for giving nothing at all *simply because*
governments would prevent those deaths more efficiently.[31]

If one's aim is the utilitarian one of utility-maximization, institutions
will loom large in one's moral and political theory, since institutions 'can
help us achieve better results than we could hope to achieve through
individual actions, even well-intentioned individual actions'.[32] This point
coheres nicely with the requirement to understand and assess the international basic structure that I mentioned earlier.[33] Rather than attempt to
bring about good results by oneself, utilitarians (should) say that we should
endeavour to create and support good-promoting institutions. Moreover, if
such institutions are brought into existence, the demands utilitarianism
places on individuals will be significantly reduced. Or, more precisely, in
the absence of these institutions, it is, as we have said, literally impossible
for individuals to succeed at bringing about what utilitarianism requires,
for the limitations of isolated individual action render each person capable of only minor contributions to overall utility. Utility maximization
is possible, then, only when an institutional framework for doing so is in
place. It follows that utilitarianism imposes a duty on individuals to work
for the creation of that institutional framework, since this is a necessary
condition of the ultimate ethical end.

It might be thought that this move does not obviate the overdemandingness objection, for if it is true that such institutions will enable utility
maximization, then each individual should be doing all he or she can to
bring these institutions into existence. But this seems just as demanding

---

cooperation, the agent's duty is not to act on his own where that does some good but less
than could be produced by cooperative activity.

[31] Unger, *Living High*, 40, makes this point persuasively. Unger's overall position,
however, is more in line with Singer's 'individualism' than with the collective approach
urged here.

[32] Hardin, *Morality within the Limits of Reason*, 11.   [33] See Ch. 1.

as the requirement that each person give some significant proportion of his money to the badly off: everyone should *either* quit their job (if they have one) and work to bring about the necessary global institutional framework *or* donate a large proportion of their salary to the relevant lobbying organization. The point here is that shifting concern to institutions does not lessen the demands on the individual, it merely refocuses them. And, in addition, the problems of cooperation identified earlier would remain.[34] These points are persuasive to some extent, but they fail to recognize that the foundations of an international institutional framework are not entirely non-existent, so it is not as if each of us must start from scratch here. What is needed is likely only the alteration of activities by organizations which already exist, and if such alteration can only be brought about by constant lobbying, or by each of us paying a significant amount to fund such lobbying, then surely this is not too much to ask. I am assuming here, of course, that we think it important to eradicate the momentous suffering now endured by a very large number of human beings. Demanding such actions may well be, but not *too* demanding, given the expected benefits.

If it is now objected that the utilitarian criterion makes excessive demands on certain affluent *states*, since some may be required to give up more wealth and resources than otherwise whenever some states fail to live up to their commitments, the solution is to 'locate Government House in UN Plaza'.[35] That is to say, the theory recommends the setting up of an enforcement mechanism to ensure that individual states each contribute their fair share to the goal of maximizing the global satisfaction of basic interests.[36] International compliance with the requirements of utilitarianism would make it easier to meet the demands of the principle because the combined wealth of the rich nations is considerable, and so the amount required from any individual nation would be lessened. I should add, however, that if, say, 10 per cent of GNP is the amount necessary to do the job, no appeal to considered judgements about zones of indifference and cut-offs for heroism should deter the theorist—or the citizen—from accepting that amount as what is morally required.

---

[34] I am grateful to Anthony Ellis for raising these points.

[35] Robert E. Goodin, 'Government House Utilitarianism', in Lincoln Allison (ed.), *The Utilitarian Response* (London: Sage, 1990), 146. Here it looks as though moral cosmopolitanism requires, for its implementation, *institutional* cosmopolitanism, i.e. some global institutional framework with enforcement capabilities. The precise form of world institutional set-up needed to enforce the demands of cosmopolitan justice is not obvious, however.

[36] The point here might seem to be less a matter of overdemandingness, and more one of ensuring a just distribution of the costs of meeting vital interests around the world.

We should note as well that we are discussing 'basic interests utilitarianism', which is much less demanding than versions of the theory with more expansive conceptions of utility. This fact further weakens the overdemandingness objection. The charge of excessive strain on potential contributors to projects aimed at helping the badly off in distant countries can be deflected *if* there is reason to think that making contributions would not result in excessive impoverishment of contributors. And the combination of (i) international cooperation to protect the vital interests of individuals, and (ii) focusing only on *vital* interests, limits the demands of justice considerably.

In sum, the answer to the overdemandingness objection is as follows: the sacrifices required by utilitarianism are not excessive, at least not when three points are made clear. First, the theory focuses on basic want satisfaction. This diminishes the *number* of interests that require protection: it must be less demanding to satisfy a set of basic desires than it is to satisfy all the desires (or rational desires) of individuals, since the former is a subset of the latter. Secondly, the theory requires cooperative action as a necessary condition of the fulfilment of the duties of individuals. This rules out the possibility of large-scale avoidance of actions required by the criterion: public enforcement of duties to cooperate in schemes aimed at meeting the demand to protect basic interests makes it less likely that solitary individuals will have to shoulder the burden of self-sacrifice because others fail to contribute their fair share. Thirdly, the theory is concerned with public institutions. This limits the *agents* to whom the requirements of the utilitarian criterion directly apply: when asking about excessive sacrifice, we then look at the capacity of a set of institutions to achieve a given set of results.

Is Utilitarianism Too Permissive? History and Justice

In what way is utilitarianism meant to be too permissive as a theory of international moral obligation? I distinguish two ways. First, utilitarians wrongly permit historical or backward-looking considerations to be entirely discounted. Secondly, utilitarians are accused of permitting distributive injustices in the name of utility maximization. The second form of the objection is more serious than the first.

The first objection stems from the recognition that utilitarians are consequentialists. The question to be answered by the consequentialist is: are consequences the *only* thing that matter morally? The consequentialist claim is not simply that consequences matter, it is that consequences matter *and nothing else matters*, when deciding what course of action

would be right in the circumstances. An important criticism of the
forward-looking emphasis of consequentialists is the one stated by Stuart
Hampshire, what I call the *objection from historical consciousness*,
which emphasizes the ineliminability of backward-looking reasons in
the justification of political and social arrangements.[37] The value of con-
sequential calculation need not, indeed should not, be denied. However,
moral guidance can be provided equally well by reference to memories
of times past, and consequentialism fails to take proper account of the
importance of such reference.

But consequentialists have an answer to this objection. It is that, if
familial, national, and other communal considerations which include an
ineliminable reference to the past have a direct effect on the current desires
of individuals, then consequentialism *requires* such considerations to be
taken into account. Hence consequentialists cannot be accused of ignor-
ing them, except in cases where they are not thought important by the
individuals concerned. In such cases it would be bizarre to take account
of communal sentiments, for they are not valued by anyone (or at least
not by a significant number of persons).

I think this reply is successful as far as it goes, but that is not very far.
For both Hampshire's objection and this consequentialist reply, as I have
stated them, seem to accept the desires of persons as they are. So both
would have to find a place in ethical reasoning for the desires of racists,
for instance. Hampshire (or those whose position he is characterizing) would
be committed to this acceptance on the grounds that ethical argument
must find a place for 'the equal claims of memory and imagination to
supply moral direction, alongside the claims of the calculation of consequences'.[38] Imaginative association on the part of racists with racist
history and the needs of racists to retain a memory of great racist leaders
would require taking full notice of racist views, a controversial position
to say the least.[39] On the other hand, consequentialists who seek the

[37] Stuart Hampshire, 'Justice is Strife', Presidential Address to the American Philosophical
Association, Western Division, 1991. Further discussion of appeals to history to justify
moral claims are considered in Part II of this book, most directly in Ch. 6 on Nationality.

[38] Ibid. 26.

[39] I should emphasize here that Hampshire's own view identifies both the universal
and the particular as sources of morally legitimate considerations, and that the particular
(say, 'our' way of life) can be overridden by universalist appeals to justice or to the 'morally
repellent and destructive' character of the particular itself. This view would lead, of course,
to a rejection of racism. See Stuart Hampshire, *Morality and Conflict* (Oxford: Blackwell,
1983), 7. Nevertheless, Hampshire's reference to 'the equal claims of memory and imagination to supply moral direction' misleadingly suggests that he would always assign
normative force to appeals to history.

maximization of want-satisfaction would find a place for 'racists' wants' in their theory because they are committed to the equal consideration of the wants of all persons, even those (e.g. racists) who want some persons' wants to be denied satisfaction!

Consequentialist approaches which focus solely on the equal protection of vital interests are not susceptible to the above criticism, for the only wants they consider are those for the satisfaction of vital interests. Such desires are on the whole less controversial than the diverse desires conceivable on more inclusive accounts. But notice what the 'vital interests consequentialist' says in reply to Hampshire's objection from historical consciousness: if the protection of vital interests conflicts with a policy of recognizing the historical memories of communities, then so much the worse for historical memories. If a trade-off is to be made, it should favour whatever is more important to the living of a satisfactory human life, and since the protection of vital interests is plausibly taken to be a *necessary condition* for such a life, such protection takes priority.

Turning to the second objection under the 'too permissive' heading, the claim here is that utility maximization would entail sacrificing the interests of some persons in the name of the greater good, thereby allowing some persons to be treated as means to the larger, impersonal, aggregate end. I take this criticism to be exemplified by the *objection from justice*, which says that maximizing good consequences allows some to have their rights violated, but that the general good, or the good of the greater number, or the net increase in good produced, is not sufficient reason for imposing such costs on some individuals. Some interests of persons—for instance, the interests each person has in the basic requirements of a recognizably human existence, i.e. food, clean water, shelter, physical security, education to a level necessary to participate in the common activities of the society—are not to be traded off for the less important interests of others, even *many* others, even when such trade-offs maximize satisfactions or happiness.

There is nothing in utilitarian theory, *as traditionally interpreted*, to rule out neglecting the basic interests of one person in order to satisfy the relatively trivial interests of a lot of other people. One solution to this problem is to allow balancing of interests against one another, but only in cases in which the interests are of equal moral importance. So, where persons A and B each have an interest in obtaining shelter, there can be a conflict when, for reasons of scarcity, both interests cannot be satisfied simultaneously. In such cases some method of conflict resolution is needed.

To turn to a different case, A's interest in obtaining shelter should not be ignored or overruled simply because doing so would satisfy the interests of persons C, D, and E (whose access to adequate shelter is secure) in obtaining an extra amount of disposable income. The principle at work here is, 'The interests a person has which are of fundamental importance to a recognizably human existence should not be subject to a calculative procedure whereby those interests could be overruled by an aggregation of the less important interests of other persons.' Acting on this principle would rule out a utilitarian balancing which focuses merely on the satisfaction of wants regardless of content. We are thus led to consider other, more restricted versions of the theory, such as the basic interests utilitarian position.

We might ask: what would be the *point* of a 'just' distribution of goods if that distribution did not protect as many vital interests as could be protected by some alternative distribution? Some would say that there would be *no* point, at least if we carefully distinguish standard forms of utilitarianism (which seek to maximize want-satisfaction) from a consequentialist approach that seeks to maximize the satisfaction of persons' basic needs or to provide the most wide-ranging protection of their vital interests. Traditional 'want-satisfaction utilitarianism' fails precisely because it could leave some persons without their vital interests protected in cases where doing so is required by a distribution of resources that satisfies more wants than any alternative.

It is of course in the nature of the utilitarian criterion of right action that no particular type of act is ever ruled out of consideration as always wrong to do. Protections for individuals, say, in the form of rights, always admit of exceptions. This is a serious worry, since (as has often been pointed out) the protections provided to individuals by utilitarian reasoning are potentially very weak and uncertain. No doubt, utilitarian calculations will result in some—perhaps most—persons having the security provided by ascriptions of rights, but the problem is that the impartial perspective of justice requires that a distribution of goods is to be acceptable to *all* persons and from *each* point of view. But if a person has her basic rights violated, it will hardly be satisfying for her to be told that the distribution under which she suffers is utility-maximizing. To describe the rights assigned under utilitarianism as 'defeasible' or 'prima facie' is not sufficiently informative of the reasons utilitarians offer for overriding individual rights-claims. Defeasibility can obtain for different reasons: overriding of individual rights can be recommended either when (1) utility would be maximized by doing so, or (2) it is simply not possible to meet all equivalent individual claims, as in cases of extreme scarcity. Reason (2) still allows that rights may be overridden, but rights will be more secure in this case than in the utility-based rights-theory. Perhaps the permissiveness objection succeeds only given an implausible conception of utility such as the one we previously dismissed. If on the other hand 'utility' means 'basic interests', the objection might fail, for violating the basic interests of a person would then be recommended only when doing so is necessary for the protection of the *very same* interests of others. In some cases, it is simply not possible to protect the equivalent interests of everyone, so comparable vital interests will be susceptible to a trade-off procedure. But in the standard cases to which government policies are meant to apply, the general rule that basic interests should be accorded priority will provide all the protections it is reasonable to want.

But there is still a problem with utilitarianism, even in its most plausible, 'basic interests' formulation. For we can imagine cases which suggest that the justificatory power of the theory is questionable. Consider the following example. Resources are relatively scarce, and some people are not able, given their current shares, to satisfy their basic wants. (Note that this case is an accurate description of the contemporary world and not an 'imaginary' example in the bad, irrelevant sense.) Suppose that depriving a well-off North American or Western European of the means to life by withdrawing from him his resources can enable twenty badly off Central Americans or Africans to escape their condition of near-starvation. What do utilitarians recommend in this case?

A simplistic utilitarian response would be that, since twenty lives are worth more than one life, the wealthy North American should be stripped of his wealth. But that answer fails to consider the ill effects of implementing a *general policy* stating that individuals in wealthy societies may be sacrificed for the provision of resources for basic needs to a sufficiently large number of others. It is reasonable to believe that no such policy would in fact maximize utility. The rules that structure and define public institutions must speak the language of generality and eschew reference to particular cases.[40] Since rules requiring the systematic violation of people's basic interests will not maximize utility (in any sense of that term), utilitarian rules will exclude such treatment. Hence a better

---

[40] Goodin, 'Government House Utilitarianism', 148. For the idea that the utilitarian principle applies to institutions, see John Rawls, 'Two Concepts of Rules', *Philosophical Review*, 64 (1955), 3–32.

answer to the problem is that the well-off should not be victimized in this way as a matter of policy or institutional arrangement.[41]

This utilitarian reply coheres with widely held considered judgements about distributive justice, but it cannot explain crucial features of the problem of distributive justice itself. It is no good for a theory of political morality simply to be consistent with the requirements of justice; we want the theory to explain or account for the fact that we determine those demands as we do. Utilitarianism says that sacrifices should be limited *because* widespread sacrifice would not maximize utility. But an alternative, and better, explanation for restricting the sacrifices individuals should be required to make is that where possible no individual vital interest ought to be outweighed by a group of vital interests somewhere else.[42] The importance of vital interests might be lost in the aggregative procedure. This is not, however, to deny the point that sacrificing some interests for the sake of others is permissible in some cases.

Even if the reason for limiting sacrifices that utilitarianism provides is only somewhat unsatisfactory, a stronger objection to the justificatory power of the theory is that it does not correctly explain why in our example it is wrong to deprive the well-off North American or Western European. Most would agree that the advantaged person should not have his resources taken from him. But the wrongness of resource-stripping in this case lies in its unfair imposition of the *costs* of meeting the needs of the poor: in the example, one person is to bear the burden, whereas *ceteris paribus* this burden should be shared out amongst all those capable of providing the needed assistance. Resources can still be taken from our well-off person, but the amount taken must be adjusted. More equitable burden-sharing might, as a matter of fact, maximize utility, but its desirability is not accounted for by this fact.

---

[41] It is not true *in general* that one life may not be sacrificed for the sake of twenty others. As a counterexample to the general claim, consider a wartime surgeon who must choose between spending his finite time and resources on saving one person or, alternatively, passing over that person and saving twenty less seriously injured but still potentially terminal others. This example does *not* show, however, that it is always right to save twenty lives at the price of losing one, for it is wrong to kill a healthy person in order to use his organs to save the lives of those terminal others. For a discussion of this type of case, and its relevance to criticisms of utilitarianism, see James S. Fishkin, *The Dialogue of Justice: Toward a Self-Reflective Society* (London: Yale University Press, 1992), 20 ff.

[42] Where the numbers are large enough, say, where there are twenty opposing vital interests, and where *any* distribution will violate the vital interests of at least one person, the opposite conclusion is the correct one. In this sort of case, sacrifice is permitted, but only subject to considerations mentioned in the next paragraph.

The need for some qualification of the standard utilitarian view is suggested by the common-sense notion of the unfairness of leaving some individuals very badly off as a consequence of implementing a policy designed to maximize benefit. This point, along with much else relevant to our concerns, is clear from Jon Elster's interesting discussion of

the common-sense conception of welfare, [which] may be stated in four propositions, each of which modifies its predecessor. (1) Maximize total welfare. (2) Deviate from that goal if necessary to ensure that all achieve a minimum level of welfare. (3) Deviate from the requirement of a minimum level of welfare in the case of persons who fall below it because of their own choices. (4) Deviate from the principle of not supporting the persons identified in (3) if their failure to plan ahead and react to incentives is due to severe poverty and deprivation.[43]

Rather than the common-sense conception of *welfare*, we might see this as the outline of a conception of the requirements of justice. Its first proposition is utilitarian, and its first two propositions together roughly correspond to one understanding of the 'basic interests' version of utilitarianism. The third claim introduces the undeniable role of personal responsibility and choice within any satisfactory account of justice: persons should be held accountable for the predictable consequences of their freely made choices. But the fourth point renders the third largely irrelevant to the current global situation, since the deep poverty and deprivation of the world's worst-off people suggests that it would be both insulting and unjust to treat them as if their condition were the result of their own laziness, as if the blame for their suffering was all their own. (This is self-evident in the case of the world's starving children.) When extreme poverty has been eradicated, we can begin to consider the international implications of the choice principle (Elster's third proposition). Until then, there is much to be said for basic interests utilitarianism, if that view is understood as requiring the protection of basic interests as a qualification on the requirement to maximize interest-satisfaction.

Another point to make in this connection is that utilitarianism, considered as a *public* philosophy, involves adopting 'institutions and practices and policies [as opposed to particular actions], on a utilitarian basis; and those must, by their nature, be publicly accessible and relatively long lasting. . . . We must . . . adapt our choices to standard situations recurring across protracted periods, and do so in full knowledge that the

---

[43] Jon Elster, 'The Empirical Study of Justice', in David Miller and Michael Walzer (eds.), *Pluralism, Justice, and Equality* (Oxford: Oxford University Press, 1995), 97.

nature of our choices will sooner or later become common knowledge.'[44] The idea here is that using some persons as means to the achievement of the greater good cannot succeed *as a matter of policy*, and it is only as a matter of policy that such an approach is available to would-be utilitarian public officials. Yet another consideration, mentioned earlier, is that utilitarianism itself tends toward distributional equality (given diminishing marginal utility), thereby ruling out the prospect of singling out some group for especially bad (or especially good) treatment. Hence distributive injustices cannot issue from utilitarian public policies.

I think these points are plausible, but they only provide reasons for thinking that utilitarianism is not the monstrous philosophy it is sometimes thought to be; they do not sufficiently explain why it is that we think it is unjust at some fundamental level to leave some without access to the means necessary to meet their basic needs. I would maintain that utilitarianism is unable to explain this sort of injustice at any deep level because it cannot, at least at that level, rule out its implementation. What would normally be called violations of rights are generally rejected by utilitarians as well, but the utilitarian reasons for doing so—that they rarely, if ever, would maximize utility; that public policy must deal in generalities; and so on—seem to miss what it is about rights-violations that makes them morally offensive. The problem is not that utilitarianism cannot be rendered consistent with our considered convictions about justice, it is that its method of doing so is lacking as a moral explanation. It is as a response to this sort of problem that I have introduced basic interests utilitarianism, but it remains something of an open question whether or not this new variant of the theory is really rather a significantly different theory altogether, for it seems to prioritize basic interests protection even if doing so does not guarantee utility maximization. The question is open because one could argue on the one hand, as I have, that there are good utilitarian reasons for restricting the scope of 'utility' to basic interests alone, while on the other hand, one wonders why it wouldn't be preferable to adopt a moral perspective which provides guarantees for the protection of basic interests at the ground level, as does the basic rights theory outlined in the next chapter.

Perhaps some further light can be shed on these matters by briefly discussing some ideas of Jeremy Bentham, the great utilitarian thinker of the late eighteenth and early nineteenth centuries who explicitly addressed the problem of distributive justice in his civil or distributive law writings,

---

[44] Robert E. Goodin, *Utilitarianism as a Public Philosophy* (Cambridge: Cambridge University Press, 1995), 22.

'where he was concerned with what configuration of rights a utilitarian legislator would want to distribute in the interests of maximizing social welfare'.[45] In the 'Principles of the Civil Code', Bentham says that rights and obligations should be distributed in such a way as to bring about 'the happiness of the body politic'. And he continues: 'In inquiring more particularly in what this happiness consists, we find four subordinate objects—Subsistence. Abundance. Equality. Security. . . . The more perfect the enjoyment of all these particulars, the greater the sum of social happiness, and especially of that happiness which depends upon the laws.'[46] The two most important sources of utility, according to Bentham, are security and subsistence. So, on Bentham's account, the protection of the basic interests associated with subsistence and security are actually 'subordinate objects' with which the legislator is to concern himself as a means to promoting 'the sum of social happiness'. If rights to subsistence and security are *necessary conditions* of utility maximization, then there can be no danger of such rights being violated by utilitarian legislators. This raises the question of whether these basic rights really are necessary preconditions for a social framework that can be defended by clear-thinking utilitarians. If, on the other hand, it remains possible for there to be a utility-maximizing framework which does not give full-scale recognition to these rights, then the alleged link between utilitarianism and basic rights is severed. The link between rights and utilitarianism in Bentham has recently been defended by P. J. Kelly. The burden of Kelly's argument is to show that—at least in Bentham's civil law writings—there is an *internal* or *tight* connection between the subordinate objects and the primary goal of utility promotion. The tightness of this link seems to be ensured by Kelly's identification of subsistence, abundance, equality, and security as themselves 'sources of utility'.[47] However, one problem here might be that, while these can clearly be identified as universal sources of utility, we still need to be shown why it is that, say, subsistence for *some* (e.g. a majority) might not be part of a utility-maximizing institutional framework in which others (e.g. a minority) *lacked* subsistence rights.

A better approach would be to classify the sources of utility in order of moral importance. Taking this tack would lead, I think, to identifying security and subsistence as lexically prior to other sources of utility, such

[45] P. J. Kelly, *Utilitarianism and Distributive Justice: Jeremy Bentham and the Civil Law* (Oxford: Clarendon Press, 1990), 72.

[46] Bentham, 'Principles of the Civil Code', p. 302, cited in Kelly, *Utilitarianism and Distributive Justice*, 73.

[47] Kelly, *Utilitarianism and Distributive Justice*, 73.

as abundance, so that protection of security and subsistence must be universally guaranteed before going on to consider the less vital elements of utility. (Equality, the other subordinate object identified by Bentham, is of course a basic desideratum, but not in any literal sense that would require absolutely equal shares.[48] Rather, there is a fundamental equality of concern stemming from the characterization of the cosmopolitan point of view.) Maximization of utility is, then, to be pursued in stages, where each stage focuses on particular sources of utility whose moral significance is taken to be unquestionable. In practice, this amounts to a rejection of any simply utilitarian conception and an emphasis instead on the protection of vital interests as themselves sufficiently important to justify institutional protection regardless of the ultimate impact on general utility.

Shelly Kagan points out that even theories that constrain actions, say, by forbidding rights-violations 'might still lack more general permission to act nonoptimally—requiring agents to promote the good within permissible means'.[49] That is, even if it is admitted that there are *restrictions* on what may be done, it is still possible to maintain that, while recognizing those restrictions, there remains an obligation to maximize good or to produce the best consequences. Hence, even if the justice objection can be met—say, by recognizing (virtually) inviolable protections for the basic interests of all persons—one could consistently maintain that there is a general duty to produce the best consequences (while recognizing certain impermissible means of doing so, i.e. violating basic interests). My view is that, as a political and hence public morality, basic interests utilitarianism can deal with the overdemandingness critique, but it cannot make clear why it is we think it right to enforce restrictions on the demand to promote the good.

2.4. CONCLUSION

Because utilitarianism has an initial appeal and because several of its proponents are significant figures in the contemporary global justice debates, this chapter outlined and evaluated utilitarianism as a moral theory. We have seen that utilitarianism is a consequentialist ethical theory designed to maximize benefit for all those affected by the actions or policies open

---

[48] Bentham's own thinking here seems to have been influenced by his views on the diminishing marginal utility of money, which led him to believe—correctly—that policymakers aiming to maximize happiness should be *directly* concerned with distribution.

[49] Shelly Kagan, 'Does Consequentialism Demand Too Much?', *Philosophy and Public Affairs*, 13 (1984), 240.

to the agents in question. I argued that there are several good reasons for utilitarians addressing the global realm to limit their concern to the maximal satisfaction of the vital interests of persons, that is, interests in subsistence and security, liberty, basic education and health care. In addition, we saw reason to focus our concern on the *institutions* whose workings most significantly affect the life prospects of individuals world-wide, rather than simply on what each of us as isolated individuals can do to limit global suffering.

After outlining some relevant facts about global deprivation, I claimed that utilitarianism has quite radical implications for global social policy: it demands a significant redistribution of wealth and resources from rich to poor and, if necessary, supports institutional changes designed to ensure that the basic interests of everyone are protected, regardless of the citizenship of the individuals concerned. Nevertheless, utilitarianism has been subjected to a vast array of objections, and two of the most important were addressed and discussed in this chapter. In reply to the claim that the utilitarian demand maximally to promote utility asks too much of us, I attempted to defend the utilitarian position by pointing to the relevance of institutional coordination supported by public enforcement, and by urging an emphasis on the *basic* interests of persons to the exclusion of those interests less easily addressed by large-scale distributive policies. I then assessed two versions of the claim that utilitarianism is too permissive. The first version pointed to the relevance of backward-looking considerations in determining the requirements of justice, and my reply was that utilitarians can take these considerations into account in so far as they affect what people want here and now. More importantly, however, appeals to the past were demoted to a secondary ethical status when compared to claims for the protection of vital interests. The second version of the permissiveness objection focused on considerations of justice, and claimed that utilitarianism cannot rule out violating the rights of individuals in its pursuit of good maximization. I argued that utilitarianism, properly conceived, would not sanction such violations, but that it nevertheless does not provide the best explanation of why it is that these violations are wrong. If there is an alternative account of the fundamentals of morality that can *both* guarantee that no vital interests will be sacrificed to the overall social good *and* provide a plausible explanation of why this is so, then we should opt for that alternative to utilitarianism. The basic rights view outlined and defended in the next chapter satisfies both of these requirements.

3

Basic Human Rights: The Moral Minimum

> [T]here is one right which . . . I am confident [man] neither does
> nor can possess—a right to subsistence.
>
> (Thomas Malthus, *An Essay on the Principle
> of Population*, 190–1)

> The central and most obdurate problem in any theory that would
> appeal to human rights, or indeed to any moral rights whatsoever,
> is to establish the existence of such rights by specifying their grounds.
>
> (Carl Wellman, *Human Rights Quarterly*, 3 (1981), 144)

In Chapter 2 we looked at the utilitarian conception of cosmopolitanism
and found significant difficulties. We should therefore investigate the view
which promises to avert those problems and provide the rationale for a
defensible account of global justice. The view I have in mind is perhaps
the most popular form of cosmopolitanism in both academic and non-
academic discourse: the rights approach.[1] Rights-based theories require
social, political and economic arrangements to be consistent with the
recognition of a set of rights held by persons. A central feature of rights
is their functioning in arguments concerning such arrangements as
reasons of sufficient strength to effect a general shift of the burden of
proof on to those who would ignore or override them.[2] Hence any violation of a right will need to be accompanied by a justification that appeals
to relatively powerful moral reasons, if not other rights. The popularity
of rights-talk and the moral force of appeals to rights are undeniable, but

---

[1] Jeremy Waldron, *Nonsense upon Stilts: Bentham, Burke and Marx on the Rights of
Man* (London: Methuen, 1987), 155, points out that 'there is now scarcely a nation on earth
which is not sensitive to or embarrassed by the charge that it is guilty of rights-violations
. . . [and that this] new consensus on the political importance of human rights has been
reflected in political theory'.

[2] This is true even if rights are not always capable of 'trumping' competing moral con-
siderations. On 'rights as trumps', see Ronald Dworkin, *Taking Rights Seriously* (London:
Duckworth, 1977), p. xi, 90–4, and 364–8; Ronald Dworkin, 'Rights as Trumps', in Jeremy
Waldron (ed.), *Theories of Rights* (Oxford: Oxford University Press, 1984), and Ronald
Dworkin, *A Matter of Principle* (Oxford: Clarendon Press, 1985), 335–72.

that popularity is not necessarily coincident with the meaningfulness or argumentative power of such talk, nor is that moral force beyond question. So at least four important tasks are suggested: we need to determine, first, whether and to what extent the rights approach to global distributive justice is intelligible; secondly, what the substantive content of a defensible account of rights should be; thirdly, how particular rights-claims are justified, and the cogency of such justifications; and finally, what the main problems are with the project of conceiving global distributive justice in terms of rights. I propose to address these questions in this chapter by offering a defence of basic human rights which is plausible as well as useful in making sense of the most important rights-claims likely to be made by, or on behalf of, actors in global politics. My focus is on the right to subsistence, but rights to physical security and liberty also may be justified by using the framework provided here (although I do not provide any such justifications). The cosmopolitan character of the human rights approach should be obvious, for 'the whole thrust of human rights theories is that the boundaries of nations are not the boundaries of moral concern'.[3] Judging the reasonableness of such theories is therefore an important element in the assessment of cosmopolitanism.

I do not doubt that traditional societies lacked a conception of human rights, but I deny that in a modern context we can get along without such a conception. If we consider the historical background of political theorizing in the Western tradition, it becomes evident that human rights thinking in its properly modern form became possible only with the rejection of ascribed social status, so that universal equality of concern replaced the earlier emphasis on the social importance of birth as a determinant of an individual's life prospects. Hence human rights thinking is possible only with the falling away of a certain view of the social world. Moreover, theorizing about human rights is *necessary* in the modern context, where state power and the ever-increasing influence of institutional agents in the private economy (i.e. transnational corporations) suggest the need for countervailing individual entitlements and protections.[4]

The discussion in this chapter addresses some general philosophical questions about the nature and defence of rights, including the question of the relative priority of so-called 'positive' and 'negative' rights. I defer until Part II of this work a companion task, namely, to assess the

---

[3] Raymond Plant, *Modern Political Thought* (Oxford: Blackwell, 1991), 290.
[4] See David Beetham, 'What Future for Economic and Social Rights?', *Political Studies*, 43 (1995), 47.

limitations of a rights-based conception of international distributive justice in light of the case that can be made for nationalist, patriotic, or other community-based loyalties. In those chapters there will be further discussion of some central tasks for defenders of human rights, for example, the elaboration of duties generated by rights and the identification of primary and secondary duty-bearers.

3.1. CONCEPTUAL PRELIMINARIES

Defending the intelligibility of rights discourse requires the presentation of a compelling analysis of the concept of a right.[5] The brief analysis presented here is designed to pick out only the salient elements of the concept of a right in order to assess the prospects for a rights-based theory of global justice. My concern in this chapter is with minimum moral requirements, with the grounds for, and duties attaching to, the basic rights of human beings.[6] Basic rights will be claim-rights, that is, if a person has a basic right to something—to perform an action of some sort or to gain access to an object of a certain kind—then there is a claim on some other or others to ensure that the content of the right is obtained by the right-holder.[7] But this is getting ahead of ourselves. First we must ask the following question: what are the elements of the concept of a right?

There are four central elements of the concept of a (claim-)right: whenever a right exists there must be a specification of a right-holder, an addressee and a right-content, along with a statement (implicit or explicit) of the right's normative strength. First, there is the *right-holder*, the possessor of the right; the right-holders of most interest to us here are individual human beings. Secondly, there is the *addressee* of the right, or the right-regarder. In cases where rights give rise to duties—i.e. the sorts of cases we will be discussing—the addressee is the duty-bearer, the agent or agency assigned the duties generated by the right. Thirdly,

---

[5] See L. W. Sumner, *The Moral Foundation of Rights* (Oxford: Clarendon Press, 1987).

[6] This is the project embarked upon by Henry Shue in *Basic Rights: Subsistence, Affluence, and U.S. Foreign Policy* (Princeton: Princeton University Press, 1996), 2nd edn. (1st publ. 1980), a book to which I am much indebted.

[7] See Joel Feinberg, *Social Philosophy* (Englewood Cliffs, NJ: Prentice-Hall, 1973), 58. And see the discussions in Lawrence C. Becker, *Property Rights: Philosophic Foundations* (London: Routledge & Kegan Paul, 1977), 11, and James W. Nickel, *Making Sense of Human Rights: Philosophical Reflections on the Universal Declaration of Human Rights* (London: University of California Press, 1987), 23.

there is the *content* of the right, that which the right is a right *to*. We will be interested in one content in particular: subsistence, or the means to a minimally adequate standard of living. And fourthly, there is a statement of the *normative strength* of the right-claim, its capacity to override 'competing considerations'.[8]

There are several types of relationship that might exist between rightholders and addressees. I follow Wesley N. Hohfeld's treatment, but I will forgo prolonged discussion of the details and focus on only one of those relations, that which holds when a claim-right is linked with a correlative duty.[9] 'To have a claim-right is to be owed a duty by another or others.'[10] If rights are taken to be morally prior to duties, the existence of a right generates or gives rise to a duty or set of duties, and the question 'Why do these duties exist?', is answered by referring to the existence of the right. Duty-bearers are required to ensure that the rightholders are protected in their possession of the content of the right. In different circumstances there will be considerable variation in the duties attaching to different agents and agencies and in the actions and omissions required of duty-bearers.

The normative strength of a right-claim is always quite strong relative to other moral reasons, but it need not be absolute (i.e. it need not be necessarily dominant in cases of conflict with other moral norms). The relatively high normative force rights possess in moral debate stems from their function as protections for the basic interests of individuals.

The assertion of a right should be likened to the use of 'for', 'since', 'because' or other words and phrases used in rational discourse to signal the imminent presence of a reason or premise in an argument. The use of a reason-indicator, like 'since' or 'because', tells one's interlocutor that

[8] Sumner, *Moral Foundation*, ch. 2. James Nickel calls this element the 'weight' of the claim, noting that the weight 'specifies its rank or importance in relation to other norms'. *Making Sense of Human Rights*, 14.

[9] Wesley N. Hohfeld, *Fundamental Legal Conceptions as Applied in Judicial Reasoning* (New Haven, Conn.: Yale University Press, 1919). Hohfeld sometimes reserves the term 'right' for what I am calling a claim-right. He distinguishes four types of normative relations, all of which utilize the language of rights: liberties (privileges), claims, powers, and immunities. Hohfeld did not himself use the term 'claim-right'; rather, he referred to rights 'in the strict sense'. See Peter Jones, *Rights* (London: Macmillan, 1994), 13.

[10] Jones, *Rights*, 14. This way of defining claim-rights is superior to that proposed in Nickel, *Making Sense*, 23: '[a] claim right to A is matched by duties of the addressees to act in ways that will make A available to the rightholder'. The problem with Nickel's definition is that he makes it sound as though a claim-right always requires positive action on the part of duty-bearers. This is a substantive question, not to be settled by a definition.

a reason for some disputed claim is about to be given. Similarly, the use of a right-assertion, such as '*A* has a right to *x*', should tell one's interlocutor that strong reasons exist, whether or not they are made explicit, for believing the right-holder in question should be guaranteed the content in question by imposing duties on others. An arguer who, when asked why anyone else should believe some controversial claim he is putting forward, simply says 'Because!' is refusing to engage in rational argument. Similarly, someone who, when asked why subsistence should be guaranteed to everyone by enforcing duties on others, simply says, 'Because every person has a right to subsistence!' is, if he stops there, refusing to push forward the argument, since the questioner is asking for a reason to show that such a right exists or that we should agree to assign such rights to persons.[11] Rights-assertions are, in part, reason-indicators and therefore are not free-standing reasons. The confusion of these two candidates for the proper function of rights is one of the abuses noted by Jeremy Bentham, for whom the appeal to *natural* rights as premisses in moral and political disputes constitutes the fallacy of 'begging the question', of using as a premiss 'the very proposition which is admitted to stand in need of proof'.[12] Bentham further maintains that 'the language of natural rights . . . is from the beginning to the end so much flat assertion. . . . It lays down as a fundamental and inviolable principle whatever is in dispute.'[13]

When we come to discuss the right to subsistence, it will become clear that defenders of that right need not be unaware that justifications are required, beyond the mere assertion that such a right exists. So rights-discourse cannot stand on its own in moral and political discussion; any given right requires grounding in some morally relevant property or in an argument to the effect that something of special importance to individuals is at stake. But rights-talk may still prove useful in clarifying many of the relations between agents which have traditionally been the concern of political philosophy, for example, the relations between states and citizens. Other relations also become relevant to theorizing when

---

[11] 'Thus, specific "natural" or "human" rights are not the moral basis for demands in politics. Rather, they are the demands themselves, and the justification for the demand has to be forthcoming in each case.' Brian Barry, *Political Argument: A Reissue with a New Introduction* (Berkeley and Los Angeles: University of California Press, 1990), p. lv.

[12] Jeremy Bentham, 'Anarchical Fallacies' (1843), in Jeremy Waldron (ed.), *Nonsense upon Stilts*, 47. Bentham's critique was aimed at the French 'Declaration of the Rights of Man and the Citizen' (1789), and was written in 1795–6.

[13] Bentham, 'Supply Without Burthen or Escheat Vice Taxation', in Waldron (ed.), *Nonsense upon Stilts*, 74.

we focus our attention on the rights persons have; for instance, the links between one individual and another, the relations between states and foreign individuals (non-citizens), and the connections between non-governmental organizations (NGOs), states, and individuals.

As we have said, central problems with discussions of rights concern the normative force a right carries when it comes up against competing moral claims, including other rights. This force varies with the content of the right. For instance, a right to subsistence carries more normative weight than a right to periodic holidays with pay, other things being equal. To see why this is so, we must clarify what is meant by '*A* has a right to *x*'. My claim will be that human rights are best conceived as protections for the basic interests of persons, and that according to that conception no other right-content has moral priority over subsistence, although other contents may be no less important than subsistence. There are rights that do not protect basic interests, for example, rights persons have to the fulfilment of promises made to them. I assert here only that *human* rights are best understood as being ultimately grounded in basic human interests.

There is no sound argument—in the sense of an argument whose conclusion follows from true premises by way of a deductively valid inference—for the claim that there are human rights to the protection of vital interests. Three implications might be drawn from this fact (only one of which may be accepted at any one time): the first is human-rights scepticism, the second is human-rights fideism (implicit or explicit faith in human-rights claims), and the third—which demands an evaluation of the plausible arguments for and against human rights—is a suitably modest acceptance or denial of basic human rights claims. Let us briefly outline each of these moves.

First, it can be maintained that, since there is nothing to *compel* adherence to basic human rights, it follows that there are no such rights. We can call this human rights scepticism, since it denies that there are any human rights at all.[14] This view takes too seriously the notion that deductively valid arguments with true premises are, in general, very good

---

[14] Alasdair MacIntyre is not committed to the unrealistic criteria for argumentative success that is my present object of concern, but he does conclude that 'the truth is plain: there are no [natural or human] rights, and belief in them is one with belief in witches and in unicorns'. Alasdair MacIntyre, *After Virtue: A Study in Moral Theory* (London: Duckworth, 1985), 2nd edn., 69. And see ibid. 67. However, MacIntyre does not offer any detailed assessment of arguments that have been or might be given in defence of human rights, nor does he seem to be sufficiently aware of the important disanalogies between witches, unicorns, and rights.

arguments.[15] It fails to recognize that many other forms of argument are quite respectable. Moreover, in moral argument, it is likely that a good case can be made for a particular claim *even though* no one is compelled, on pain of contradiction, to accept that claim. This is especially probable in the case of disputes on moral and political subjects, where almost any conclusion one could imagine will be denied by someone. Since sound arguments (in the technical sense of the word 'sound'—true premises and valid inference) are not required, we are not justified in denying all human rights claims simply on the grounds that they cannot be defended by sound arguments.

A second move is to express *faith* in basic human rights claims, while admitting that logic does not compel us to accept them. I have called this position human rights fideism. 'There might not be undeniably good arguments for human rights', the fideist says, 'but I believe in human rights just the same.' This alternative suffers from the same drawback as human rights scepticism. The response to it, in short, is to point out that we should look for plausible reasons for accepting human rights, reasons that *could* be denied but that seem sufficiently credible to command assent from honest seekers after truth in moral matters. Expressions of faith and assertions of self-evidence are non-starters.

Thirdly, we can actually look at the most plausible arguments for and against accepting basic human rights and, having assessed these arguments, come to a considered position. I will follow this strategy. Specifically, I defend basic human rights by outlining arguments whose premises appeal to vital human interests.

3.2. QUESTIONS OF SUBSTANCE: RIGHTS AND INTERESTS

Clarifying the elements of the concept of a right goes no way toward defending the content of any particular right. There is no limit to the possible contents of right-claims, to the things persons can be said to have a right *to*. It is easy to announce that all human beings have a right to subsistence, but that is merely an announcement until reasons are offered

---

[15] Not all such arguments are good, however. Some, such as those with the form 'P, therefore P' are useless in the context of a dispute about P, despite their technically valid character. This argument form is valid because the conclusion must be true if the premiss is true. But no one ought to believe a disputed proposition P simply on the basis of P's being put forward by an interlocutor as evidence in its favour!

to support it. Justifying a right-claim is the difficult part of this sort of moral argument, and distinguishing the potential grounds for a right opens up the entire range of reasons adduced in moral theory generally. Hence a right may be justified by appeals to rational self-interest, to utility, to what would be agreed by contractors variously conceived, to the basic needs or vital interests of human beings, and so on. But no claim of right is any stronger than the strength of the reasons offered in defence of that claim.

One initially plausible thought about rights is that, although they may be used to justify the imposition of duties on individuals and collectivities, 'rights themselves need to be justified somehow, and how other than by appeal to the interests their recognition promotes and protects?'[16] On this view, the direction of justification is from an individual interest to the existence of a right. Thus, an argument for a right 'is an argument showing that an individual interest considered in itself is sufficiently important from a moral point of view to justify holding people to be under a duty to promote it'.[17] On this 'interest conception of rights', then, the role played by rights in normative discourse is to 'mark the way in which interests generate duties'.[18] So rights function as a middle ground between human interests on the one hand, and duties attaching to individual agents and collectivities on the other. Rights-talk is the language in which the connections between the two domains are made.

The attempt to understand the basic requirements of justice in terms of rights is familiar in recent political theory, but it is often confined to rights that can be recognized by nation-states. Global justice should not be restricted in this way. It may turn out that states are the primary duty-bearers when individuals claim their rights, but that conclusion awaits assessment of its grounds. When one takes a moral perspective, the set of right-holders cannot be restricted to citizens of particular nation-states:

---

[16] T. M. Scanlon, 'Rights, Goals, and Fairness', in Samuel Scheffler (ed.) *Consequentialism and its Critics* (Oxford: Oxford University Press, 1988), 74.

[17] Jeremy Waldron, *The Right to Private Property* (Oxford: Clarendon Press, 1988), 3. Similarly, for Joseph Raz to say that a person has a right to some content (e.g. free speech, subsistence, political participation) is to say that an aspect of that person's 'well-being (his interest) is a sufficient reason for holding some other person(s) to be under a duty'. Joseph Raz, *The Morality of Freedom* (Oxford: Clarendon Press, 1986), 166. Cf. Jeremy Waldron, *Liberal Rights: Collected Papers 1981–1991* (Cambridge: Cambridge University Press, 1993), 11, 212, 359. Raz, Waldron, and Neil MacCormick are the most prominent defenders of the interest conception. See also MacCormick, 'Rights in Legislation', in P. M. S. Hacker and Joseph Raz (eds.), *Law, Morality, and Society: Essays in Honour of H. L. A. Hart* (Oxford: Clarendon Press, 1982).

[18] Waldron, *Liberal Rights*, 214.

we are led, therefore, to a consideration of *human* rights. A human right always requires justification in terms of the 'interests which each individual is thought to have in common with every other'.[19]

A few questions naturally arise at this point. What are the interests which all individuals share? How do we determine exactly what those interests are? The most plausible conception of such interests ties them closely to the well-being of individuals; on this view, so-called 'welfare interests' are 'abstracted from actual and possible preferences'.

Welfare interests consist just in that set of generalized resources that will be necessary for people to have before pursuing any of the more particular preferences that they might happen to have. Health, money, shelter, sustenance, and such like are all demonstrably welfare interests of this sort, useful resources whatever people's particular projects and plans. . . . We can know what is in people's interests, in this most general sense, without knowing what in particular is inside their heads. Furthermore, at some suitably general level at least, one person's list of necessary basic resources reads much like anyone else's. . . . welfare interests are highly standardized.[20]

It is in someone's interests, therefore, to have access to those resources necessary for leading a recognizably human life. Without food, shelter, and a reasonable level of health maintenance, human lives are simply not possible. (The inclusion of money on Goodin's list of universally useful resources is perhaps incorrect, since it displays a kind of fetishism about the means of exchange which should be avoided by any theory of all *and only* vital human interests. Nevertheless, its inclusion in a list of currently applicable basic human interests clearly has some justification.) This analysis suggests the form of an argument for rights to these resources, and since 'subsistence' can be taken to mean 'the means to a minimally adequate existence', I will now assess the prospects for a right to subsistence.

3.3. THE HUMAN RIGHT TO SUBSISTENCE

It is often held that there is a certain minimum level of well-being below which no individual should be allowed to fall. One way of stating a commitment that no person should be permitted to starve or to live without the shelter necessary to lead a minimally acceptable existence is to assert

[19] Waldron, *Right to Private Property*, 90.
[20] Robert E. Goodin, 'Utility and the Good', in Peter Singer (ed.), *A Companion to Ethics* (Oxford: Blackwell, 1991), 244, 246.

a right on the part of persons to the contents in question, i.e. to food and shelter, clothing, minimal health care, clean air and water. A human subsistence right is a right of persons to the means necessary to meet these minimum requirements. It seems that the interest individuals have in continued, minimally comfortable existence should be sufficient, *if anything is*, to put someone or some collectivity under a duty.

Those who would base their theory of human rights on interests face the problem that interests are 'at most a necessary condition for having rights, since there would be an enormous and indeed unmanageable proliferation of rights if the having of any interest X were sufficient to generate a right to X'.[21] The focus on vital human interests overcomes this difficulty, since such interests form a manageable subset of the larger group of interests human beings have. In the case of vital interests, it is argued, we have both necessary and sufficient conditions for putting others under a duty. Of course, we must also take account of the *costs* involved in protecting a vital interest: for example, people do not have a right to *whatever is needed to keep them alive*, because that would commit us to the view that 'if a 75-year-old person would die without a mechanical heart, she has a right to a mechanical heart'.[22] The reason we rightly hesitate before assigning such rights to persons is that, at least under current conditions, the cost of meeting them is prohibitively expensive.

I will discuss two arguments for a human right to subsistence. The first is Henry Shue's argument and the second comes from Jeremy Waldron.[23] I will call them the indirect argument and the direct argument, respectively.

The indirect argument for a human right to subsistence is premissed on the claim that no right exists in the absence of a right to subsistence.[24] This strategy is aimed at convincing the proponents of a right to liberty that commitment to that right entails acceptance of a right to subsistence. If we assume for the sake of argument that a person's interest in liberty

[21] Alan Gewirth, 'Starvation and Human Rights', in *Human Rights: Essays in Justification and Applications* (Chicago: University of Chicago Press, 1982), 198.
[22] Henry Shue, 'Solidarity among Strangers and the Right to Food', in William Aiken and Hugh LaFollette (eds.), *World Hunger and Morality* (Upper Saddle River, NJ: Prentice-Hall, 1996), 113–32, at 116. Shue has correctly emphasized as well that, if an interest is to provide the basis for attributing a right to individuals, the interest must be not only *vital* but also *vulnerable*, in the sense that it is susceptible to regular threats against which individuals cannot generally protect themselves. See ibid. 114–15.
[23] Shue, *Basic Rights*; Waldron, *Liberal Rights*, ch. 1, where both arguments are discussed.
[24] Henry Shue offers an argument of this form in *Basic Rights*, 24–5.

is sufficient to ground a right to liberty, then, it is argued, we should be concerned to provide the necessary conditions of the exercise of liberty, most importantly, the meeting of one's subsistence needs. It is often noted that a right to liberty is of no use in the absence of the requirements for the liberty's enjoyment, those conditions necessary for making the liberty worth having.[25] John Rawls says that both Shue and R. J. Vincent[26] 'interpret subsistence as including certain minimum economic security, and both hold that subsistence rights are basic. One must agree with this since the reasonable and rational exercise of all liberties, of whatever kind, as well as the intelligent use of property, always implies having certain general all-purpose economic means.'[27] Shue maintains that no proposed right content is enjoyed *as a right* unless it is protected from 'standard threats'. So, for example, no one can truly claim the existence, on their part, of a right to free expression unless there are guarantees that, emergencies aside, they will have access to resources required to meet their subsistence needs. And since the guarantees amount to the recognition of a right to subsistence, it follows that no one has a right to free expression if they lack a right to subsistence. But this may fail to convince. It needs to be shown how the enjoyment of free speech as a right presupposes this basic subsistence right. The dependence of one right on the other needs to be demonstrated.

The first point of clarification is that malnutrition, lack of shelter, and the absence of protection from disease leave persons incapable of engaging in the autonomous activity the protection of which is often thought to justify concern for civil and political rights in the first place. But then, if rational agency is valued, its necessary preconditions ought to be valued as well. The argument is in part an appeal to consistency. Consequently, a commitment to a right to liberty presupposes, on pain of inconsistency, acceptance of a right to subsistence. This may still leave some sceptics unmoved, but the introduction of a second point settles the issue in favour of the defender of subsistence rights.

[25] See, for instance, the sensible comments in Robert E. Goodin, *Reasons for Welfare: The Political Theory of the Welfare State* (Princeton: Princeton University Press, 1988), 308: 'I can see no reason for championing or cherishing *worthless* liberties. If you care about liberty, you must also care about those elements that make that liberty practically meaningful. If you do not, I simply have to question the sincerity of your arguments for liberty in the first place.'

[26] R. J. Vincent, *Human Rights and International Relations* (Cambridge: RIIA/Cambridge University Press, 1986).

[27] John Rawls, 'The Law of Peoples', in Stephen Shute and Susan Hurley (eds.), *On Human Rights: The Oxford Amnesty Lectures 1993* (New York: Basic Books, 1993), 225.

The second point is that those in circumstances of severe need not only suffer from obvious harms (hunger, disease, and so on) but are also subject to a sort of dependence on the powerful which should concern the proponent of liberty rights. When people 'lack essentials, such as food, because of forces beyond their control, [they] often can do nothing and are on their own utterly helpless'.[28] The plight of such people contrasts with the victims of repressive regimes whose rights to physical security are violated: such people can often fight back against the regime or, if all else fails, attempt to escape. These options are not available to persons lacking subsistence rights, who suffer from a dependence amounting to subjection to the powerful. This shows that failure to recognize subsistence rights restricts liberties in a very real sense, since a lack of subsistence rights leaves non-state collectivities, other individuals, and especially governments free to deny people the means to the minimum requirements of existence and thereby to coerce the helpless (or potentially helpless). Therefore the absence of guaranteed access to subsistence renders individuals vulnerable in a way that threatens the credibility of any claim that *other* rights, such as civil and political rights, are protected.

I think the indirect argument for subsistence rights shows that there is a link between these 'socioeconomic' rights and the more traditional civil and political rights. Again, the relation is not a logically tight one in any technical sense, but it none the less makes it more difficult for Nozickian libertarians, or indeed anyone else, to fail to recognize subsistence as a right. Still, Shue's argument will not convince someone sceptical of *all* rights-claims, for it is premised on the acceptance of *some* right or other. The direct argument, on the other hand, makes no such assumption, so it is better able to address the rights-sceptic. And if rights-claims are simply assertions, then everyone should be a rights-sceptic until some persuasive case is made for accepting a particular right-claim.

The direct argument from subsistence needs to subsistence rights runs as follows.[29] Rights as we are conceiving them here are grounds for imposing duties, but rights themselves are justified by appealing to the interests individuals have in the contents of those rights. If we can find a highly important human interest, we have a strong premiss in support of a basic right-claim. The interests individuals have in meeting their subsistence needs, it is argued, are at least as important as any other interests one could mention. From a moral perspective, concern about

---

[28] Shue, *Basic Rights*, 25.

[29] See Jeremy Waldron, 'Liberal Rights: Two Sides of the Coin', in *Liberal Rights*, 10 ff.

'the primal necessities and vulnerabilities of human life' is of the first importance.[30] The effects on a person's life when she cannot find shelter or meet her nutritional requirements are, if anything, more serious than the results of denying her a right to, say, freedom of religion. This is not to deny the relevance of civil and political liberties for living a satisfactory life, but it should serve to bring out the role of subsistence rights in a theory of basic human rights. Onora O'Neill, despite her objections to a rights approach, notes the universal acceptability of the central premiss of the present argument: 'It is not controversial that human beings need adequate food, shelter and clothing appropriate to their climate, clean water and sanitation, and some parental and health care.'[31] If there are basic rights, then rights to meet one's basic needs as a physical and vulnerable being must be among them.

I understand this line of argument to reveal the importance of the contents of subsistence rights: food, shelter, health care, clean air and water, and so on. As R. J. Vincent has said, 'the right to life has as much to do with providing the wherewithal to keep people alive as with protecting them against violent death. . . . The right to life, if it exists at all, is a right to subsistence as well as to security.'[32] But now it might be objected that the importance of those contents was never in question. The case against a human right to subsistence does not deny that in standard cases everyone has an interest in such things; rather, that case stems from a number of points that arise *even if* the importance and universality of those human interests are accepted. By looking at these further objections to subsistence rights, along with the replies to those objections, we will be able to fill in the rest of the argument for holding those rights to be proper members of anybody's list of basic human rights.

3.4. BUILDING A CASE: OBJECTIONS AND REPLIES

The Negative–Positive Rights Distinction

The first objection to any human right to subsistence focuses on the well-worn distinction between negative and positive rights and uses that distinction to deny universal rights to aid. *Negative rights* are rights

---

[30] Waldron, *Liberal Rights*, 11.
[31] Onora O'Neill, 'Transnational Justice', in David Held (ed.), *Political Theory Today* (Oxford: Polity, 1991), 279.
[32] Vincent, *Human Rights and International Relations*, 90. Cf. ibid. 145.

requiring only omissions on the part of duty-bearers; for instance, if someone has a negative right not to be tortured, this requires merely that others refrain from torturing that person. Since recognition of negative rights requires of duty-bearers nothing more than avoidance, it is clearly possible that everyone can be asked to accept the duties those rights generate. *Positive rights*, however, are another matter. ('Positive' in this sense is *not* to be understood as 'institutional' or 'legal'.) When someone has a positive right to some content, omission is not sufficient to fulfil the duties generated by the right. Such rights are positive in the sense that positive action is required if individuals' access to the contents of the rights is to be protected. A right to subsistence is a positive right, for it may in some cases impose duties on others to provide aid to needy persons, thereby imposing a requirement for positive actions rather than mere omissions. But notice now that corresponding duties in such cases cannot attach to everyone, as with negative rights, since every person cannot be required to ensure that some particular person has her subsistence needs met. We are left with a purported right but no clear account of the duties with which it is associated, and this is a serious problem only for so-called positive rights. How should we respond to this problem?

The first thing to say is that there are two points being made by this objection and they must be distinguished from one another. First, there is a claim that negative rights can be clearly distinguished from positive rights, and secondly, there is an assessment of the moral priority of the two sorts of rights relative to one another, an assessment grounded in the need to assign duties to rights if those rights are to be protected. The upshot of the objection is that civil and political rights should be the only *human* rights because only they are correlated with duties it is reasonable to ask every person to bear. Responding to the objection, then, requires two replies, a short answer dealing with the positive/negative rights distinction and a longer answer telling a story about correlative duties. The story I will tell contradicts the supposed simplicity of right-duty relations embodied in the objection. Once both answers have been given, the first objection loses its appeal.

First, the short answer: the distinction between negative and positive rights is simply not an accurate rendering of the duties corresponding to any given right.[33] So-called negative rights, like the right not be tortured,

---

[33] The examples of rights to a fair trial, rights not be tortured, and rights to subsistence are discussed in Henry Shue, 'Rights in the Light of Duties', in Peter G. Brown and Douglas MacLean (eds.), *Human Rights and U.S. Foreign Policy* (Lexington, Mass.: Lexington Books, 1979), 65–81.

require both forbearance (the duty not to torture anyone) and positive action (duties to stop attempted torturing by others and duties to help victims of torture).[34] And if even supposed negative rights call for positive action, the objection—which depended on there being rights requiring only omissions on the part of duty-bearers—rings hollow.

Maybe a legitimate commitment to a right not to be tortured does demand that positive steps be taken. But is this the case for other rights? What about, say, the right to free expression? Can we not uphold this right simply by failing to stop people from speaking, that is, by allowing them to voice their opinions on matters of concern to them? The answer, again, is 'No'. While many people may recognize the required omission —not to interfere with expression of opinion—there may still be some who do not, and the right is not enjoyed *as a right* if some are allowed to avoid their duties of omission. On the contrary, a right to free expression is recognized only when a *set* of conditions is satisfied: obligations to omit restricting expression must be accepted, and when some individuals are actively restricted from expressing their views (as no doubt will happen) there is a further obligation to stop such restricting activity. And if there is a duty to stop those actions that restrict expression of opinion, it is reasonable to accept a distinct duty, namely, the duty to make arrangements to ensure that restrictive actions do not occur in the first place. Individuals do not have rights if there are no socially imposed safeguards protecting the contents of those rights; against those who would violate the right-holder's interests, the larger society must put in place protective measures. There is no one-to-one relation between rights and duties; rather, a given right 'generates waves of duties', such as those we have suggested here for the protection of the right to free expression.[35]

Once we have seen that the distinction between negative and positive rights cannot be maintained, there can be no simple dismissal of so-called socioeconomic or welfare rights. We can then look at the complete list of proposed human rights and ask what I take to be the most

---

[34] This may seem like mere assertion, since rights not to be tortured have been construed by some theorists as imposing only duties of forbearance. The remainder of this section is aimed at defending the claim that no right correlates simply with duties of forbearance.

[35] The phrase 'waves of duties' comes from Jeremy Waldron, 'Conflicts of Rights' in *Liberal Rights*, 211–12. Of course, one cannot be protected against *all* threats: if protection against all conceivable threats were required, then no one would have any right to anything. Accordingly, Shue correctly recognizes that rights require protection only against 'standard threats'. See Shue, *Basic Rights*, 13.

important question about them: *which of the interests these rights are intended to protect are the most important interests?* In other words, we should ask about the importance of human interests relative to one another, since there is no *general* argument for dismissing any right merely on the basis of its supposed correlativity to positive duties that some would take to be overly demanding or indeed impossible to meet. It therefore seems reasonable to prioritize rights by the basicness or importance of the interests they protect.

The longer answer to the objection that positive rights are especially problematic, in a way that negative rights are not, is to clarify the complexity of the duties corresponding to any right. We have seen that the distinction between negative and positive rights fails to capture the duties generated by such rights. But what is needed now is some idea of what those duties are. One promising way of characterizing the duties correlative to basic rights (for instance, the right to subsistence) is as always coming in three general forms and as attaching to different sorts of 'agents' in various circumstances. This is Henry Shue's characterization.[36] Briefly, these are:

(i) duties to *avoid* depriving right-holding individuals of the content of the right,

(ii) duties to *protect* right-holders from being deprived of the right-content, and

(iii) duties to *aid* deprived right-holders when avoidance and protection have failed.

Notice that both omissions and positive actions will be required in order to fulfil the duties generated by rights. A human right to subsistence, for instance, generates duties on others to aid those unable to obtain the means to subsistence for themselves. But it also requires precautions to be taken to ensure that the means to feed, clothe and shelter themselves is not likely to be beyond the reach of persons. And finally, actual right-violations must be avoided: for example, if Central American farmers are satisfactorily providing for their own subsistence, others should not take actions which will effectively force those farmers to give up

---

[36] Ibid. 51–64. This interesting analysis has not received sufficient attention amongst philosophers and policy-makers, though the recent publication of the 2nd edn. of Shue's book, sixteen years after its first appearance, might go some way toward correcting this problem. Shue now stresses that this typology is not set in stone, and that his main point was simply that theorists should focus on the duties that would implement a right rather than talking in terms of a simplistic dichotomy between allegedly 'positive' and 'negative' rights. See ibid. 160.

their present existence and become dependent on help from others simply to meet their own basic needs. This last point raises two issues. First, subsistence rights may require not only that others act in various ways but that they also forbear from acting in other ways. One of the correlative duties of the right to subsistence is the duty to avoid depriving persons of food, shelter, and health care. The second issue is the importance of picking out the duty-bearers whenever we discuss these different duties of avoidance, protection, and aid. This is *the problem of agency*: if there are duties generated by right-claims, to whom do they attach? This problem must be solved; otherwise no right, no matter how important the interest it is designed to protect, will be able to provide the guarantees necessary to ensure its proper recognition.

Assigning Duties

The problem of agency generates the second objection to a human right to subsistence. A complete justification of any right incorporates three elements: the importance of an individual's interest in some content must be shown, then the assignment of obligations generated by that interest, by way of the right-claim, must be justified. The second move requires both an outline of what the duties are and a statement of who will bear those duties. So the three moves are (1) justifying the importance of an interest; (2) defending the existence of duties necessary to protect that interest; and (3) justifying the imposition of those duties on particular agents (individuals, states, non-state groups). Rights-claims are adequately grounded *only if* the three lines of argument are made out: i.e. if the three cases are not made, the overall case for protecting the right is not complete. So duties must be stated, duty-bearers must be found to fulfil the requirements of rights, and reasons must be offered to show that the list of duties is correct and that those duty-bearers are the right ones for the job. The second objection to a human right to subsistence, then, is that there is no cogent line of reasoning capable of justifying the assignment of correlative duties to various agencies. If the objection succeeds, we will be left with mere 'manifesto subsistence rights', ambitiously asserted in documents such as the Universal Declaration of Human Rights (Article 25) and the International Covenant on Economic, Social and Cultural Rights (Article 11) but doomed to remain, practically speaking, in limbo because no duties are or can be assigned on their basis.[37]

---

[37] Joel Feinberg discusses 'manifesto rights' in 'The Nature and Value of Rights', repr. in Philip Pettit, *Contemporary Political Theory* (New York: Macmillan, 1991), 31–2.

Both Joel Feinberg and James Nickel make a useful distinction between claims *to* particular right-contents and claims *against* duty-bearing agents.[38] A justified right includes both a justified claim to some content and a justified claim against some duty-bearer. The type-identities of duty-bearers must be known before justifications can be attempted; otherwise we would have an argument with an incompletely described conclusion! So a response to the second objection will need to offer an outline of duty-bearers along with the sorts of reasons capable of justifying picking out just those agents as the right ones to fulfil the duties required to protect a given right. On the tripartite analysis of duties outlined above, we distinguished duties of avoidance, protection and aid. Duties to avoid depriving right-holders of the contents of their rights can be attached to every person, state, and non-governmental organization because these duties require only omission and it is possible to require that every agent *not* do something. So one set of duties generated by the human right to subsistence is the duty of everyone and every collectivity not to stand in the way of persons in their attempts to meet their subsistence needs. The problem of agency does not arise for these duties of avoidance; it is when we come to discuss duties to protect from deprivation and duties to aid the deprived that suitable agents need to be identified. We want to know, in the cases of such duties, who is required to do what, and why.

It is helpful to think about the duties arising from any right as lying along a spectrum ranging from negative duties to increasingly positive duties.[39] Negative duties require only that duty-bearers avoid acting in a particular way, or if one insists on phrasing duties actively we could say that what is required is avoidance-behaviour of a certain kind. Positive duties call for actions directed at protecting right-holders from deprivation or assisting those deprived of the contents of their rights. (The negative/positive distinction is helpful here, even though it failed to capture anything morally relevant about rights. The earlier trichotomy of duties relates to the negative/positive distinction in this way: avoidance of deprivation is a negative duty; protection and assistance are different sorts of positive duty.) While negative duties can be borne by all agents simultaneously, positive duties must be assigned selectively, so the grounds

---

[38] Joel Feinberg, *Social Philosophy* (Englewood Cliffs, NJ: Prentice-Hall, 1973), 59; and James W. Nickel, 'How Human Rights Generate Duties to Protect and Provide', *Human Rights Quarterly*, 15 (1993), 77–86. Justifying a claim-against requires identifying both duty-bearers and duties.

[39] Cf. Henry Shue, 'Mediating Duties', *Ethics*, 98 (1988), 689.

for such assignments will play a vital role in justifying a right-claim. Since people's resources are finite, duty assignment calls for careful work on our part.

I will not engage in any detailed analysis of the process of identifying duty-bearers here. Instead I hope to give some idea of the sorts of questions which must underlie any such analysis.[40] First, since 'ought' implies 'can', the assertion that a duty should be imposed on some agent or agency requires that the agent or agency is capable of fulfilling those duties. Is the proposed duty-bearer capable of meeting the requirements to protect and assist the relevant right-holders? Secondly, there must be a morally compelling reason to believe the duties in question are properly assigned to *these* agents or agencies, for capability alone does not justify an assignment. Is there some moral justification for holding some agents to have a particular set of duties? This second question can be subdivided into further questions. What is the relation of this duty-bearer to this right-holder in virtue of which there is thought to be a justified assignment of a duty? Are the duties too demanding for the agents to fulfil? All of these questions should lead us to assess the prospect not only of individuals but of states and international (state and non-state) organizations bearing duties.

We now have some idea of the individualist emphasis of basic rights such as the right to subsistence, for these rights attach to individual persons in so far as they are embodied, needy beings. But we have seen as well the potential plurality of the duties and addressees arising from basic rights-claims: individuals, nation-states, and other collectivities may all be duty-bearers, depending on the arguments adduced in a given instance. Still, there seems to be a danger of creating so many duties that there will be no way for the human right to subsistence ever to be satisfied, for there are desperately needy people not only within one's country but in foreign countries as well. But that problem can be avoided by assigning a subset of duties to particular agencies; in this way, duty-overload is not necessary, since the greater efficiency of coordinated activity carried out by institutions may render it unnecessary to spend all of one's time and energy attending to the subsistence needs of others. Individuals would then have duties to create institutions capable of respecting rights to subsistence.

To see in more detail the motive for moving beyond individuals as duty-bearers, we can ask the following question: how should individuals

---

[40] See also, Nickel, 'How Human Rights Generate Duties'.

respond to a situation in which they, acting alone, are unable to protect right-holders from being deprived of their rights and to provide aid to the deprived? Here, as we have said, there is good reason to require individuals to create collectivities with the relevant capabilities. I will now outline an argument for a duty of individuals to develop individual-duty-fulfilling institutions.[41]

This argument begins with the assumption that, where an individual interest is of sufficient importance, there is reason to believe a claim to the content of a right exists. But genuine acknowledgement of the claim to the content should motivate in others a search for ways to fulfil the duties generated by the right. And, given contemporary conditions, isolated individual action is not sufficient to fulfil the duties to avoid, protect, and aid suggested by the right. Organizational or institutional actions, on the other hand, *are* likely to enable such duty-fulfilment in contemporary conditions. Therefore, individuals have a duty to set up organizations and institutions, or to use such collectivities as already exist, to fulfil the duties generated by the basic right in question. Of course, this line of reasoning only sets out the beginnings of a case for the duty to set up duty-fulfilling collectivities. The difficult work still remains, namely, to show that the demands upon persons who must shoulder this duty will not be too great. To repeat, there is one important consideration which indicates that the danger of overburdensome duties is not excessively worrying: if the importance of an interest suggests the need to assign some duties to protect that interest, collective coordination of action—such as that carried out by institutions or other organizations—is best able to provide effective interest protection because it is more efficient than the actions of disconnected individuals.

Assertions of human rights such as those found in the Universal Declaration of Human Rights apparently assume that states are the main agents obliged to respond to those rights. This assumption makes such pronouncements more practical in one respect but wildly idealistic in another. The practical point is that there is no proposal calling for the creation of a world state as the proper protector and promoter of human rights, a proposal which seems unlikely to receive a hearing in contemporary global circumstances. Nation-states already exist and, moreover, they request and receive recognition from each other as sovereign

---

[41] For recent arguments along similar lines, see Henry Shue, 'Mediating Duties', 695 ff.; Jeremy Waldron, 'Liberal Rights', 17; Robert E. Goodin, 'The State as a Moral Agent', in Alan Hamlin and Philip Pettit (eds.), *The Good Polity: Normative Analysis of the State* (Oxford: Blackwell, 1989).

over both a territory and a collection of individuals. Human rights claims which accept these sovereign entities and then attempt to bring about extensions of their responsibilities have a much better chance of success than claims requiring for their implementation new bodies (e.g. a world government) which are unlikely to appear on the horizon.[42]

Despite this realistic assumption of human rights claims, there is perhaps a fatal flaw in the confinement of these claims to states as the correct addressees. Some states seem unable to meet the obligations required of them by an acceptance of basic human rights, and the capacities of those states to meet those obligations has in recent years declined. So it appears to be a utopian dream to expect all states to fulfil the duties generated by human rights; many cannot do so, nor is it plausible to believe they will be able to do so in the foreseeable future.[43]

Thus we are in the grip of a dilemma. Either we reject the view that nation-states are the bearers of duties arising from human rights claims (thereby accepting some unrealistic belief that a world state is likely to come into existence to enforce those claims), or we restrict the category of duty-bearers to nation-states (thereby ensuring that many, perhaps most, of those claims will go unrecognized in practice, since countless states lack the resources to meet them). I should say immediately that I think this is a false dilemma; it sets up two unsavoury alternatives and suggests that we must choose between them. But the options are not as restricted as the dilemma makes them out to be. A more or less obvious solution is to require nation-states with more than they can use to redistribute wealth and resources to other nation-states who have less than they need. In addition, avoidable activities which make it less likely that poorer states can meet their own citizens' rights-claims could be disallowed, thus enabling those states to fulfil their obligations with less positive aid from other states. This solution retains the positive features of the earlier options while excising the weaknesses. We can throw out the bathwater yet keep our baby: nation-states retain significant duties on this view,

---

[42] In Chapter 8, below, I question the normative force of sovereignty claims in the face of widespread global deprivation. And in the Conclusion, I argue against the assumption that a stark choice must be made between the present system of sovereign states on the one hand and a world government on the other.

[43] Regarding food provision, the inability referred to here seems not to be an unalterable empirical fact. Since in many cases sufficient food may be available (even within a famine-struck country), it is more reasonable to focus on individuals' legal entitlements to food, entitlements which may be subject to change by altering ownership laws. On this point, see Jean Dreze and Amartya Sen, *Hunger and Public Action* (Oxford: Clarendon Press, 1989), ch. 2.

hence no appeal need be made for the creation of a world state with unchallenged sovereign powers; and when some states lack the capacity to fulfil the duties generated by human rights, steps are taken to give them that capacity. This requires both positive steps (actions) and negative steps (omissions). If there are good reasons for recognizing human subsistence rights, then there is a motivation to look for capable duty-bearers. The assignment of increased duties to states, although not only to states, promises to meet the demands made by rights and in so doing makes it possible to *act* on the recognition that the interests which form the basis for rights are morally important.[44]

Let us look briefly at an example relevant to the problem of assigning duties to protect the human right to subsistence. Transnational food corporations are not designed to protect human rights, but nor are they exempt from duties not to bring about rights-violations. It is reasonable to hold that such transnational corporations (TNCs) have a duty not to advertise and sell products which, in contemporary Third World conditions, are likely to contribute to serious harm and even death. The notorious, and continuing, behaviour of the transnational corporations engaged in the production and sale of baby-milk powder is a classic instance of a violation of this duty.[45] A duty of avoidance on the part of corporations is clearly in order, but so is a duty, assignable to everyone and through them to their governments, to protect individuals in the developing countries by monitoring the activities of TNCs, whose behaviour is motivated by amoral reasons (having to do with profits and market share and the like) but may result in basic rights violations. The corporate duty of avoidance

[44] There are, of course, numerous possibilities for change within the global political and economic system, such as increased powers for the United Nations, the World Trade Organization or supra-state authorities like the European Union or ASEAN. I defer suggestions on these matters until the concluding section of this book.

[45] Antonio Cassese, in his excellent book, *Human Rights in a Changing World* (Oxford: Polity, 1990), 138–52, outlines the central considerations raised by this issue. In Third World countries, baby-milk powder is marketed and sold to impoverished mothers by nurses (who are also corporate representatives). But these (often illiterate) mothers are not always able to read the product's instructions, and in any case lack the education and the financial means to use the powder safely. (The water used in preparing the milk is inevitably polluted, and the mothers tend to use insufficient amounts of the powder in an effort to make it last longer.) In these circumstances the product's instructions are inappropriate, for they presuppose social conditions not present in much of the Third World. Consequently, many infants are undernourished and diseased. In short, without significant social and economic changes, advertising and selling these products is likely to contribute to serious harm and even death. Unfortunately, there is no binding obligation on any corporation to take the precautions necessary to reduce the likelihood that its products will be used in these ways.

cannot be met by corporate self-regulation, so duties might attach to governments to ensure that such rights-violating behaviour does not occur. Exactly how these government duties should be assigned is a difficult question. Should governments in the countries of the South, who might be thought to have the primary duties to protect their citizens' subsistence rights, be required to deal with TNCs based in other countries? There is a serious question concerning *capability* here: are such governments able to protect their citizens from corporate actions? The same question arises when we turn to the duties of states in which TNCs are based. In the case of Nestlé, that particular corporation has a larger annual budget than its home government (Switzerland), which suggests something about the relative power of the two parties. Perhaps, then, there is a need for an international body, such as the World Health Organization, to be assigned duties to protect in this case. Sadly, this move will not lead automatically to protection of subsistence rights, since the honourable WHO initiatives of recent years have not been binding on member countries. These initiatives could have effect only if they were backed by the coercive powers now held only by nation-states.

A different aspect of the problem of assigning duties arises in the attempt to identify every human being as, in the first instance, a duty-bearer. Human rights are universal moral entitlements, i.e. they are held equally by all human beings. And it is natural to assume that the duties to which such rights give rise are likewise held equally by everyone, regardless of race, sex, state membership, or national affiliation. But one might object that, in the case of *welfare* rights like the right to subsistence, the claims are properly made against some particular state (nation, community) and not, therefore, against everyone in the world or against the global community. These rights would then more correctly be described as rights of citizens (or of nationals, of community members) and not as universal *human* rights.

Responding to this criticism will enable us to clarify the relation between human rights and the duties to which they give rise. The first point to make is that, as a matter of fact, it is not only welfare rights that are claimed against some community or government: the traditional list of *civil and political* rights are also asserted in this way. Yet this should not stop us from interpreting civil and political rights as *human* rights which, if not recognized within a given local jurisdiction, should generate international protest and action designed to protect the victims of such injustice. In short, people in other communities are not exempt from duties generated by basic rights, and if all rights are understood to be citizens' rights, that should not blind us to the (implicit) need to call upon non-nationals whenever co-nationals fail to live up to their obligations.

Perhaps rights are claimed against co-citizens only because doing so is the most effective means of protecting basic interests in reality.[46] If so, there can be little quarrel with such a practice, but where this kind of 'duty-localization' fails to protect basic human interests across the human population, there is good reason to adopt a different means. Moreover, it seems clear that this failure to safeguard vital interests, a failure created by duty-localization, is a feature of the world as we know it. Therefore, unless there is some good reason to place greater ethical value on local persons as against those further away, duties should be shared equitably amongst the human population.[47] In current circumstances, this would demand redistribution of wealth from those most easily able to pay, i.e. (the majority of) citizens of the rich countries, to those most in need of help, i.e. mostly (the vast majority of) people in the poor countries.

One way of averting this conclusion is for each nation to assert 'national rights' to the resources and wealth of their own nation-state. The two most significant problems with this move are, first, that *wealth-generation* is never confined within the boundaries of any one state, and secondly, that the location of the world's valuable resources is a matter of brute luck, so that it seems patently unfair that some people should flourish while others languish simply as a consequence of the differential control of such resources.[48] The implication of these two points is that national rights to wealth and resources, however commonly they are asserted, lack any coherent moral basis. What seems particularly evident is that the beneficiaries of national rights are thoroughly undeserving of the special benefits they receive.

Is Subsistence Sufficiently Important?

Let us now move on to a third objection to a human right to subsistence. The present claim is that the human interest in subsistence is not

---

[46] See Robert E. Goodin, 'What is So Special about Our Fellow Countrymen?', *Ethics*, 98 (1988), 663–86, for an attempted justification of special duties in terms of their efficient fulfilment of our general duties to humanity.

[47] In Part II, Chs. 5–8, I examine arguments for showing greater concern for those close to us than for those farther away.

[48] For the claim that the distribution of the earth's natural resources is morally arbitrary, see Beitz, *Political Theory and International Relations*, 136–43, and Brian Barry, 'Humanity and Justice in Global Perspective' (1982), in Brian Barry, *Liberty and Justice* (Oxford: Clarendon Press, 1991), 182–210, at 198.

sufficiently important to justify the recognition of a human right to it. This may seem a bizarre assertion, but it stems from an important and compelling belief, namely, that where persons *choose* not to meet their subsistence needs their choices should be respected and others should not impose upon them some alternative conception of what is in their interests. The proper reply to this claim is to point out, first, that in the overwhelming majority of cases the choices of individuals will be to meet their subsistence needs and, in the remaining cases, persons may be allowed to choose otherwise—say, to build a monument to their God rather than feed themselves. If someone chooses to sell his allotment of food in order to build such a monument, there are no *additional* enforceable obligations to give yet more food. Acceding to the objection in this way will not change the implications of the human right to subsistence in most cases, for the interest in subsistence really is that important to people. In the end, however, if people choose to use resources to which they are entitled for purposes other than their own subsistence, that is their right.

The second move in reply to this objection is to note that, while it is conceivable that individuals might, in certain circumstances, choose to forgo guarantees that their subsistence needs will be met in order to further some other interest they have (say, in political emancipation from autocratic rule), it does not follow that *subsistence is no longer in such a person's interest*. The latter point is supported by reminding ourselves that even brave and inspiring opposition to dictatorial regimes will falter if rebels fail to feed, clothe, and shelter themselves. Moreover, one powerful reason for opposing dictators in the first place is to overcome the arbitrary discretion such rulers maintain over crucial policies, including the institutional guarantee that subsistence needs will be met. The interest in subsistence does not disappear when some individual prefers, say, to further the cause of a political or religious group rather than meet his subsistence needs: this is a case in which two interests conflict, not where one potential right-content ceases to be in the interest of the person. Since, whenever interests are considered, such needs are never very far from the surface, and since subsistence is a permanently present concern of the world's poor, subsistence rights are plausible candidates for basic human rights.

Side-Constraints

A fourth objection to a human right to subsistence leads us back to the distinction between negative and positive rights and to considerations of agency. We can call it the argument from side-constraints, and it is motivated by the conception of rights favoured by Robert Nozick.[49] Earlier we answered the objection that duties to protect and duties to aid are not readily assignable, and that, therefore, no right requiring such duties can be recognized. That objection failed to take on board the point that *any* right requires duties of protection and aid, so we are obliged to look for possible assignments: there is nothing in principle which rules out the possibility of finding duty-bearers. Nozick claims, on the contrary, that rights are side-constraints on action and nothing more; hence we need not bother with the attempt to find bearers of duties to protect and to aid, since the only duties are duties of avoidance. One simply cannot rule out a conception of rights by definition, but this is exactly what Nozick appears to be doing here. He defines rights as side-constraints on action, thereby eliminating the possibility of conflicts of rights by accepting only those corresponding duties which can be accepted simultaneously by every-one. It follows from his definition of rights that there cannot be a right to assistance of any kind, but this offers a definition where there should be an argument. Nozick appeals to the importance to each individual of living a meaningful life, and argues that side-constraints are neces-sary if individuals are to shape their lives for themselves. But once we recognize that outright denial of positive duties of justice will have terrible consequences for many people, Nozick's argument loses its appeal. We would do better to consider carefully the words of H. L. A. Hart: 'Except for a few privileged and lucky persons, the ability to shape life for oneself and lead a meaningful life is something to be constructed by positive marshalling of social and economic resources. It is not some-thing automatically guaranteed by a structure of negative rights.'[50] In addition, Nozick's view falls foul of the point made earlier that rights call for institutional protection: even Nozick's minimal state would require a police force, courts, jails, and a tax system to protect his favoured list of rights. Therefore it is quite misleading to claim that there are *negative* rights that require only forbearance on the part of duty-bearers, for countless positive actions will be necessary to support any state we might attempt to justify. This might be seen as another way of saying that the negative/positive rights distinction cannot withstand scrutiny.

---

[49] Robert Nozick, *Anarchy, State, and Utopia* (Oxford: Blackwell, 1974), 28–35.
[50] H. L. A. Hart, 'Between Utility and Rights', in Alan Ryan (ed.), *The Idea of Freedom* (Oxford: Oxford University Press, 1979), 85.

With respect to Nozick's particular defence of negative rights, there is one more worry to be noted. It looks as if Nozick's theory is *duty-based* rather than rights-based: on his view, no one can ever violate their duty not to violate the (negative) rights of others. But it is by no means obvious that, in difficult cases, it might not be best to violate some rights in order to ensure greater rights protection or the preservation of more important rights. If there are duties to be assigned, why is it not more plausible to adopt the strategy of the present chapter, namely, to identify the most compelling interests at stake and aim to adopt the framework that best protects those interests? In short, 'utilitarianisms of rights' and 'egalitarianisms of rights' are not unreasonable views, and opposition to them which focuses on the agent's absolute duty not to be a rights-violator looks to be more concerned with the agent and her duties rather than with the recipient and her rights.[51]

Perhaps these replies will be seen as exemplifying a failure to engage honestly with Nozickian libertarianism; after all, the notion of self-ownership from which Nozick's account begins can seem plausible to defenders of liberal rights.[52] But the idea of self-ownership does not necessarily imply that no one can be obligated, by force if necessary, to help the needy. In this context, we should recall the views of Nozick's seventeenth-century predecessor, John Locke, whose theory of property rights also started with the idea that we are all self-owners.[53] Locke made certain qualifications upon what is now known as the 'full' or 'liberal' conception of ownership, according to which owners have rights to exclusive control of a piece of property, rights to all of the benefits accruing from the thing owned, rights to consume or waste the thing, and rights to give, exchange, or bequeath. David Lloyd Thomas has pointed out that 'Locke's view of a natural right to property departs from this conception of ownership in a number of respects. Both of the first two elements of ownership [exclusive control, benefits] are qualified

---

[51] Cf. Jeremy Waldron, *Right to Private Property*, 74–7. In fact, Nozick notoriously avoids the question of whether 'side constraints are absolute, or whether they may be violated in order to avoid catastrophic moral horror'. Nozick, *Anarchy, State, and Utopia*, 30. But this is not a topic one *can* avoid if one desires to give an adequate account of rights.

[52] For investigation of the claim that self-ownership is the foundation of Nozick's theory of rights, along with a vigorous set of replies to Nozick and others, see G. A. Cohen, *Self-Ownership, Freedom and Equality* (Cambridge: Cambridge University Press, 1996).

[53] 'Though the Earth, and all inferior Creatures be common to all Men, yet every Man has a *Property* in his own *Person*. This no Body has any Right to but himself.' John Locke, *Two Treatises of Government*, ed. Peter Laslett (Cambridge: Cambridge University Press, 1988), 287, *Second Treatise*, paragraph 27 (1st publ. in 1689).

by Locke to take account of the countervailing right of the needy to a share in the surplus of the owners.'[54] My point is not to invoke Locke as some sort of authority on the proper implications of the right of self-ownership; I introduce his view here simply to show that the premiss of self-ownership can provide the basis for conflicting positions about the legitimacy of enforceable positive duties to help others. Consequently, the proponent of self-ownership cannot maintain that the defender of duties of assistance falls foul of individual human rights.

Overdemandingness

A fifth objection to subsistence rights says that recognition of such rights is too demanding for the relevant duty-bearers and, therefore, no one is required to recognize those rights. I think this is an important claim, but the main elements of the response to it have been given in Chapter 2, where we discussed basic interests utilitarianism. Having said that, there are a few more points worth making on this general theme. This objection is related to the point about positive and negative rights, and is partly answered by pointing out that someone does not cease to have a right to something simply because it is impossible for everyone to ensure that he enjoys that thing. As we said above, only an oversimplified account of corresponding duties allows one to take that point seriously. Once potential duties are outlined, progress can be made on the problems of protecting people's rights. Unreasonable demandingness requires supporting argument, it cannot be shown by making a conceptual distinction; nevertheless, this objection deserves to be taken seriously. While I believe it is accurate to characterize a human right to subsistence as one part of the moral minimum, this does not imply that accepting this right's existence will not entail substantial changes either at the individual or the institutional level, or at both levels. Recognition of the right is a fundamental part of a minimally adequate theory of justice, and as such there are going to be restrictions on action and requirements to perform

---

[54] D. A. Lloyd Thomas, *Locke on Government* (London: Routledge, 1995), 95. Locke's view is that 'he that hath, and to spare, must remit something of his full Satisfaction, and give way to the pressing and preferable Title of those, who are in danger to perish without it'. These qualifications are well-motivated by Locke's own belief, stated in the same paragraph, that natural rights are themselves ultimately derived from the fundamental law of nature, which says that 'all, as much as may be, should be preserved'. John Locke, *Two Treatises of Government*, ed. Peter Laslett, 391, *Second Treatise*, paragraph 183. See also *First Treatise*, paragraph 42, where it is claimed that the needy have a right to the surplus of others.

certain actions, both of which are likely to be demanding. Evidence suggests, however, that existing resources and technical knowledge are capable of achieving universal rights-protection in the not-too-distant future.[55]

One point bears repeating: even though appeals to vital interests provide the justificatory force of basic human rights, the meeting of these rights need not consist primarily in the performance of positive duties by others. Persons have basic rights to whatever is needed to protect their vital interests, but we cannot say that their claims to those things—for example, their claims to food, potable water, personal security against intentional attack, basic housing, and health care—automatically call forth actions by others. In many cases, people will be able to protect these interests simply by being left to their own devices. Of course, in contemporary circumstances, in which claims on resources are the outcome of market transactions, people whose share of resources ensures that their own vital interests are not threatened will be required to give up some of the wealth they have amassed on the market, but that is simply to recognize that unrestricted markets will generate states of affairs in which many people lack protection for their vital interests. If markets are deemed necessary, then the protection of basic rights demands redistribution of market-generated wealth; but this should not lead us to interpret such redistribution as a demanding drain on the wealthy, since they lacked a legitimate right to that wealth in the first place.

Perhaps the overdemandingness objection refers to a distinct issue. Could the worry be that defenders of human rights to subsistence show *too much* concern for others or, rather, that such concern would be misplaced because it fails to distinguish between the deserving and the undeserving? Would implementing human subsistence rights unfairly benefit some who deserve no unconditional guarantees? The criticism here is that the sorts of guarantees required by institutionalized protections for subsistence rights would benefit everyone when, in fact, there would be countless cases in which some—most notably, able-bodied persons who choose not to contribute any useful labour to the community—would not deserve to be benefited. Is it not too much to ask of the hard-working persons that they should give up some of their earnings to provide subsistence for those who could have provided for themselves but chose

---

[55] See, for instance, any of the recent annual reports of one of the main multilateral institutions concerned with financing and development assistance: United Nations Development Programme, *Human Development Report, 1995* (New York: Oxford University Press, 1995).

not to do so? We can grant the importance of vital interests, it seems, while denying that these interests merit protection even when a person's own irresponsibility has produced his current needy condition.

The reply to this criticism requires us to augment some remarks made in section 2.3 above. Even if we admit that free-riding on the part of able-bodied individuals would constitute exploitation of contributors, this objection does not apply to (i) *children*, who can in no clear sense be said to have made a choice one way or the other on the question of willingness to work, and (ii) *the destitute*, i.e. the hundreds of millions of people who lack the means properly to feed and shelter themselves and whose plight is not the result of their having made any choice not to work. Once these classes of people have been removed from their desperate situation, by enabling them to provide for themselves and/or by providing them with whatever they cannot themselves produce, then we can address the objection that the industrious are victims of exploitation. As things now stand, however, the objection is a red herring for hundreds of millions of potential claimants to the conditions of a minimally satisfactory existence. On the whole, *any* proposal on this matter will have at least *some* undesirable consequences, so we should look for the option with the best overall record when measured against our desire to protect the vital interests of human beings. Even if the objection has some force, perhaps our uneasiness can be tempered by appealing to the relevance of the actual numbers involved: if we can go a long way towards eliminating poverty with a relatively small cost in lost labour supply, the cost might well be worth accepting.[56]

Further support for my position can be found in the following quotation:

I also do not want to prejudge the issue of whether healthy adults are entitled to be provided with subsistence *only* if they cannot provide subsistence for themselves. Most of the world's malnourished, for example, are probably also diseased, since malnutrition lowers resistance to disease, and hunger and infestation normally form a tight vicious circle. Hundreds of millions of the malnourished are very young children. A large percentage of the adults, besides being ill and hungry, are also chronically unemployed, so the issue of policy toward healthy adults who refuse to work is largely irrelevant.[57]

To sum up Shue's argument here: the exploitation objection depends upon the truth of three distinct points, each of which is rebuttable. First,

[56] See Goodin, *Utilitarianism as a Public Philosophy*, 24–5 and ch. 14.
[57] Shue, *Basic Rights*, 23.

it requires that the exploiters be *adults*. But if hundreds of millions of the world's hungry are children, the objection does not apply to hundreds of millions of people. Secondly, it assumes that the adults are *healthy and able to work*. However, the vast majority of hungry people—something like a billion human beings—suffer from the diseases that all too often accompany malnutrition (with its correlation with increased susceptibility to disease). So, again, the objection has no application in this case. And finally, it requires that the healthy adults confront an employment market within which there is significant demand for work. But the chronic unemployment in Third World countries renders this third assumption untrue. In sum, the exploitation objection is irrelevant to the case of the plight of the world's hungry.

Is Rights-Talk Merely Egoism in Disguise?

In 'Supply Without Burthen or Escheat Vice Taxation', Jeremy Bentham registers a potentially devastating objection to those who would defend framing their moral and political views in terms of rights. Consider the following:

> When a man is bent upon having things his own way and giving no reason for it, he says: I have a right to have them so. When a man has a political caprice to gratify, and is determined to gratify it, if possible, at any price, when he feels an ardent desire to see it gratified but can give no reason why it should be gratified, when he finds it necessary to get the multitude to join with him, but either stoops not to enquire whether they would be the better or the happier for doing so, or feels himself at a loss to prove it, he sets up a cry of rights.[58]

The point of the above-quoted passage is that 'a cry of rights' is simply a means by which people demand things for themselves without any good reason for doing so. Two distinct problems with such cries may be noted here: first, that they allegedly *replace* reasons in moral argument and therefore constitute rhetorically powerful but irrational and unreasonable features in debates whose importance demands a rational and reasonable approach. Secondly, that rights-assertions are made by those who are 'bent upon having things [their] own way', or those who have 'a political caprice to gratify' but do not care whether the multitude 'would be the better or the happier for' agreeing with them. The idea here is that cries of rights exemplify a selfish concern on the part of those doing the crying, in

---

[58] Jeremy Bentham, 'Supply Without Burthen or Escheat Vice Taxation', in Jeremy Waldron (ed.), *Nonsense upon Stilts*, 73–4.

the context of a debate about morals, that is, a subject-matter in which resolution of disputes demands that egoism be set aside in favour of an equal concern for each agent whose interests might be affected.

Bentham's first point, that claims of rights are irrational and unreasonable, has already been addressed: so long as we realize that reasons must be forthcoming, this potential weakness in rights-talk is not a problem. The language of rights is indeed the language of assertion, but it is *merely flat assertion* only when those who use it fail to develop any arguments in support of their assertions.

But we need to address the second point Bentham seems to be making: that rights exemplify a species of egoism that has no place in moral debate. Interestingly, versions of this objection were made not only by Bentham but by Edmund Burke and Karl Marx as well.[59] Do theories of rights overlook *responsibilities*? Though the answer to this question is that they need not do so and that any defensible account of rights will require an explicit emphasis on responsibilities, the popularity of the positive answer to the question is perhaps understandable, for prominent rights-theorists such as Robert Nozick reach conclusions that permit people to amass and retain large amounts of wealth while others are left with less than they need. Such conclusions appear to violate common-sense views about our moral responsibilities to one another, therefore supporting the view that rights-based accounts underemphasize responsibilities.

To return to the objection, it seems to run as follows: the focus on individual rights will lead to social divisions between persons which, in turn, will make it impossible to sustain even the type of community favoured by defenders of rights. I think this notion, that there can be no such thing as a 'rights-based community', is generated by a fundamental misunderstanding of what rights are and what social frameworks it is necessary to support if rights are to be protected. No right is properly recognized unless the duties to which it gives rise are themselves acknowledged in practice; hence a rights-based community fosters social bonds of a very specific kind. It should be noticed that this type of community

---

[59] See the excerpts from these thinkers contained in Waldron (ed.), *Nonsense upon Stilts*. In Waldron's view, '[t]he great and recurring theme in all three of these attacks is that the rights of man embody as the be-all and end-all of politics a demand for the immediate and unqualified gratification of purely selfish and individual desires'. *Nonsense upon Stilts*, 44. Burke, for instance, believes that, 'by having a right to everything, [men] want everything'. Edmund Burke, *Reflections on the Revolution in France*, ed. Conor Cruise O'Brien (Harmondsworth: Penguin, 1968), 151.

is quite clearly preferable to a so-called 'community' in which social ties are founded, not on the recognition of the equally legitimate claims of each person as a moral being, but on some traditional conception of the proper place of each person in a social hierarchy. If communities are to recognize the importance of each and every relevant individual, they would do well to take rights seriously by making honest commitment to the community conditional upon the background protections rights provide.

In other words, the egoism objection seems to say that rights serve to *isolate* people from one another, thereby interfering with noble attempts to build communal solidarity. But the idea of a 'community' whose members lack rights is the idea of a community open to serious ethical criticism, either for its potential for mistreatment of some members (who lack recourse when mistreated) or for its exclusion of some people from the community for no good reason. On the other hand, a community of rights-holders is a legitimate candidate for the honorific label of 'community', since its members recognize the legitimate interest of one another and, moreover, acknowledge the dignity of each other by considering claimants as equal members of the group of rights-holders. We should be careful to distinguish *selfishness*—a tunnel-visioned regard for one's own good, regardless of the costs this might impose on others—from a perfectly uncontroversial *self-concern* that characterizes every human being in so far as they pursue ends they identify as their own. And once we understand what it means to accept universal human rights, we can see that selfishness is ruled out and that self-concern is acceptable so long as it coexists with a recognition of the equal claims of everyone else.

One of the best replies to the egoism objection has been stated by Alan Gewirth, and it is worth quoting at length:

[H]uman rights, which are universally distributed moral rights, require of each person that he act with due regard for other persons' interests as well as his own. For since, in principle, each person has human rights against all other persons, every other person also has these rights against him, so that he has correlative duties toward them. The concept of human rights thus entails a reciprocal universality: each person must respect the rights of all the others while having his rights respected by all the others, so that there must be a mutual sharing of the benefits of rights and the burdens of duties. The human rights thus involve mutuality of consideration and, thus, a kind of altruism rather than egoism. By requiring mutual aid where needed and practicable, the human rights make for social solidarity and a community of rights.[60]

[60] Alan Gewirth, 'Rights', in Lawrence C. Becker and Charlotte Becker (eds.), *Encyclopedia of Ethics* (London: Garland, 1992), 1108.

The egoism objection, therefore, goes wrong by focusing on only one half of the story. It quite properly notices that any person has rights against all others, so that in my own case I am entitled to demand that everyone respect claims made on my own behalf. But this would constitute morally objectionable egoism only if it were not also the case that *every other individual* is in the same position as me. For any human being, the claim being made by the defender of human rights is that she or he may demand that her or his rights are respected by all other members of the rights-holding community. Consequently, rights theories are characterized by what Gewirth aptly calls 'reciprocal universality' and 'a mutual sharing of the benefits of rights and the burdens of duties'. Seen in this light, rights actually require a significant amount of concern for the interests of others on terms equal with one's own interests. Rights thus embody in a striking way the cosmopolitan commitment to impartiality, and that commitment can in no way be confused with egoism.

3.5. CONCLUSION

In this chapter I outlined the conceptual elements of a claim-right and defended a specific conception of human rights as grounded in vital human interests. After showing the plausibility of recognizing a human right to subsistence, I addressed six of the most substantial objections to rights-talk in general and to subsistence rights in particular. Let us assume that I have presented the beginnings of a plausible case for the existence of subsistence rights for all human beings, along with a reasonable, rough estimate of the obligations necessary to recognize those rights, and a suggestion of who will be charged with fulfilling those obligations. We may still ask, however, whether this goes far enough. Is the protection of subsistence rights, along with the changes required in the present international system in order to implement them, all that can be justified as required of a commitment to universal human rights? Isn't the focus on guaranteeing persons minimal protections too narrow?

This challenge assumes an optimistic view about the prospects for satisfying rights-claims in the international political realm. Nevertheless I agree with an assumption the challenger makes, that subsistence is not the *only* content of a legitimate human right. But the problems constituting the contemporary global predicament really are so serious that honest argument is forced to address their seriousness head on. Faced with the injustices of the world, we should ask ourselves which are the most morally urgent and which we might be in a position to alter. Hunger and homelessness, both near and far, rank at the top of this list, and if individuals, governments, and other agencies can act to eradicate such injustices then we should look for ways to require them, within reasonable bounds, to do so. Recognizing a human right to subsistence, and allocating correlative duties, is a necessary condition of the protection of any other rights; so, as an argument identifying the lowest rung on the ladder of individual and collective moral responsibility, the defence outlined in this chapter is the proper first step in any rights-based argument for global distributive justice.[61]

Nevertheless, there is still an important cosmopolitan position to be investigated. In Onora O'Neill's Kantian approach, we have not only a powerfully argued defence of cosmopolitanism but a direct challenge to human rights theories. Consequently, we should not finish our assessment of cosmopolitan justice without evaluating the Kantian emphasis on universal obligations.

---

[61] Moreover, I think it is plausible to maintain that protection of basic subsistence rights, and more substantial rights as well, should be a central concern even for those, such as modern-day Aristotelian perfectionists, whose sights are set on the heights rather than the depths. Thomas Hurka puts this point well: 'Think . . . of our modern Western societies. Their more prosperous members are doing fine with their university studies, their interior decorating, and their business careers. What cries out for attention is the plight of those millions of people, both within the industrialized world and outside it, whose material condition prevents them from acquiring any organized knowledge or achieving any truly stretching goals. While others have more than they need for valuable activities, these poor are denied any substantial exercise of their essential powers. This is what Aristotelian perfectionism finds most appalling and what it most wants to see altered.' Thomas Hurka, *Perfectionism* (Oxford: Oxford University Press, 1993), 189.

4

O'Neill and the Obligations of Justice

4.1. INTRODUCTION

Onora O'Neill has made several interesting contributions to the debates on international distributive justice, in her 1986 book, *Faces of Hunger: An Essay on Poverty, Justice and Development*[1], in at least a dozen articles published over the last two decades, and in her most recent work, *Towards Justice and Virtue: A Constructive Account of Practical Reasoning*.[2] My aim in this chapter is to give an outline of O'Neill's Kantian strategy for tackling the moral problems of international poverty and to defend a human rights approach against her objections. I begin, in section 4.2, with an overview of O'Neill's Kantian theory of international morality, showing how the categorical imperative functions to test the maxims of individual and collective agents, and pointing out the respects in which O'Neill's version is different from, and superior to, traditional Kantian accounts. In section 4.3, I state O'Neill's main objections to a welfare rights theory of the sort defended in Chapter 3 above, and then respond to these objections, in the process presenting an original line of argument to show that O'Neill's own premises commit her to such rights. And in section 4.4, I canvass some other objections to O'Neill's Kantian approach, dismissing specific claims of Thomas Nagel and Partha Dasgupta, and arguing that the Kantian strategy might be thought of as an alternative route to the conclusions reached earlier in this book. There are, however, seemingly fatal problems with the Kantian approach that render it—to put it mildly—less useful than a rights-centred strategy for justifying judgements about global justice.

---

[1] London: Allen & Unwin, 1986.
[2] Cambridge: Cambridge University Press, 1996.

4.2. TAKING OBLIGATIONS SERIOUSLY: O'NEILL'S MAVERICK KANTIANISM

I begin my outline of O'Neill's theory with a recognition of its Kantian character. The basis of O'Neill's approach to international ethics is the Kantian *categorical imperative* (or CI, for short), 'Act only according to that maxim by which you can at the same time will that it should become a universal law.'[3] The test embodied in the appeal to the categorical imperative is a test of maxims, and a maxim is a subjective policy or rule on which an agent acts. For instance, a famous example of a maxim, obviously relevant to our project, is given by Kant himself: 'Let each man be as happy as heaven wills, or as he can make himself; I will not take anything from him or even envy him; but to his welfare or assistance in time of need I have no desire to contribute.'[4] To assess the moral permissibility of an agent's maxim, one determines whether it is possible for all others to act on that maxim as well. As O'Neill puts it, 'The central conception of Kantian ethics is that a maxim should not be acted on if it *could not* (not *should not* or *would not*) be acted on by others. Here obligations are a matter of refraining from action whose fundamental principles others cannot share.'[5] If a principle could not be adopted by everyone, because such adoption would lead to the injury of some, then that principle should be rejected.[6]

The Kantian moral theory developed by O'Neill is clearly cosmopolitan, since it holds that all human beings are part of a single moral universe, in virtue of their shared capacity for rationality.[7] In so far as we are all rational agents, we all require equal consideration. Impartiality is demanded by the Kantian test for maxims of action: people are not allowed to make exceptions for their own case; what one proposes to do must be what any other agent could also do in those circumstances.

While O'Neill develops a Kantian cosmopolitan theory, there are some important ways in which her approach branches out in new directions. These innovations are, in my view, improvements on the original Kantian

---

[3] Immanuel Kant, *Foundations of the Metaphysics of Morals*, 2nd edn., tr. Lewis White Beck (London: Collier Macmillan, 1990), 38 (Prussian Academy pagination, 421). This version of the categorical imperative is widely known as the Formula of Universal Law (FUL).

[4] Kant, *Foundations of the Metaphysics of Morals*, 40 (Prussian Academy pagination, 423).

[5] O'Neill, *Faces of Hunger*, 134, emphases in original.

[6] See O'Neill, *Towards Justice and Virtue*, 164.

[7] Cf. Thomas Donaldson, 'Kant's Global Rationalism', in Terry Nardin and David R. Mapel (eds.), *Traditions of International Ethics* (Cambridge: Cambridge University Press, 1992), 144.

approach. I will mention two respects in which O'Neill's perspective differs from traditional Kantianism, and explain why I think her amendments are helpful.

An important element in O'Neill's theory of international justice is her emphasis upon the claim that human beings are embodied creatures with material and psychological needs.[8] Kant of course recognized this fact as well, so O'Neill's perspective is not entirely original, but what *is* new—as against the traditional Kantian approach—is the emphasis on the centrality of the needs of physically limited, partially rational persons for considering the acceptability of acting on maxims that affect the interests of others. If human beings are to act at all, they require food, water, protection from attack, and some basic skills. Accordingly, maxims which deny access to such necessities could not possibly pass the universalizability test and therefore are morally impermissible. As we will see, maxims which deny obligations to provide aid to those in need are non-universalizable maxims, and are therefore not permissible from a moral point of view, however much they may seem appealing from a purely self-interested standpoint.

It is important to note that O'Neill's emphasis on human weakness and vulnerability brings out what can be found in Kant's own work. As Roger J. Sullivan says, Kant believes that to engage in moral deliberation,

. . . we need to be aware, for example, that we are dependent physical beings with needs to be met with the help of our reason. We need to know we are emotional as well as rational beings, so that we have to take an interest in something before we will act so as to attain it. . . . We need to recognize that we are only contingently rational and do not always act intelligently even in prudential matters.[9]

Thus empirical facts about human beings are straightforwardly relevant to the project of understanding our moral lives as both agents and recipients of the actions of others. But the fact that

the application of the Categorical Imperative to human life requires us to *take into account* features about human beings that we can learn only from experience does not mean that Kant's theory is therefore *based on* experience or anthropology. His theory retains its objectivity because it remains an analysis of what it means to act as a rational agent, albeit now an agent who is contingently rational, dependent, physical, emotional, and so on.[10]

---

[8] O'Neill, *Faces of Hunger*, 135.

[9] Roger J. Sullivan, *Immanuel Kant's Moral Theory* (Cambridge: Cambridge University Press, 1989), 160.

[10] Ibid., emphases in original.

So the traditional Kantian emphasis on the requirements of rational action remains, but arguments about what constitutes rational or consistent willing must take full account of embodied, vulnerable, partially rational human nature.

O'Neill's second development of the traditional Kantian ethical approach is her explicit introduction of the idea that the CI can serve as a test for the maxims of *both* individual agents *and* social agencies. When proposed maxims remain at the level of individual interaction, there is little hope that anything relevant will be said about global issues such as world hunger and poverty. Thus the reasonable way to proceed is to assess the maxims on which influential collective agencies act (i.e. nation-states, transnational corporations, powerful non-governmental organizations like the World Bank and the International Monetary Fund), thereby undertaking a moral assessment of the activities of those bodies most liable to have a lasting effect on the plight of the world's hungry people.

The categorical imperative test for maxims is akin to one type of contractarian test for proposed rules of action. Both tests judge rules or policies permissible whenever each person affected is taken into consideration and when none could reasonably veto what is being proposed. When a maxim of action passes the universalizability test, that maxim can serve as a law for everyone. Let us look at the way the Kantian categorical imperative test for maxims of action works in the context of a particular case.

Consider a transnational corporation, intent on increasing its shareholders' return on their investments and on increasing its market share. These corporate goals will affect the maxims on which the corporation may be taken to act in specific circumstances. Now imagine that this corporation offers to set up a factory in a poor country which is desperate for investment and, aware of this fact, the corporation successfully pressures the government of the poor country to offer extremely attractive terms (viewed from the corporation's perspective) in return for setting up shop there. If the poor nation accepts corporate investment on terms no relatively wealthy nation would accept, there is reason to believe that the gulf in bargaining power between the two parties has led to coercive imposition upon the poor country of an agreement on the terms of investment.[11] Let us assume that the maxim on which the corporation acts is as follows: 'When we can best pursue corporate goals by investing in a relatively

---

[11] In the following paragraph I give reasons to think that what is happening in this example is not best understood as coercion.

poor country, paying low wages and avoiding taxes, then we will do so, even if such investment coerces others into accepting our preferred terms.' Now to determine whether this maxim is morally permissible we ask whether it is possible for all agents to act on such a maxim. For the purposes of evaluation, the important point about this maxim is its general form, which is its claim that the agent will pursue a course of action even when doing so involves coercion. We next perform a thought experiment in which all agents act on a maxim involving coercion, and we are led to see that no such maxim is universalizable because one cannot simultaneously will (i) that I achieve my ends by coercing another, and (ii) that everyone achieves their ends in this way. As O'Neill says, '[p]rinciples can be universally acted on only when others' agency is respected, and the core of respect for agency is not to destroy or override it'.[12] The contradiction is clear: there is no possible world in which I can coerce others and in which everyone else does so as well, for I would then be in a world in which I *both* freely act *and* am unable to act freely.[13]

I should say that *if* coercion is going on in this sort of case, then it is impermissible for that reason, but it is not clear that coercion *is* occurring at all. What happens, rather, is that the differences in bargaining power of the two parties have a significant effect on the content of the agreement reached. But if one means by coercion 'threatening somebody (or some group) with being *worse off* if they do not do what you want them to do', then it is unclear whether the poor country is coerced when it agrees in this case. In the example under discussion, the poor country is made better off by accepting the deal; the problem is that the corporation takes unfair advantage of its bargaining power.[14] Again, one can consistently

---

[12] Onora O'Neill, 'Hunger, Needs and Rights', in Steven Luper-Foy (ed.), *Problems of International Justice* (London: Westview, 1988), 80.

[13] Of course, coercion in some instances will be justified, as in cases where individuals are imprisoned for crimes they have committed. But the Kantian claim is that coercion cannot function as a *fundamental* principle of an agent, and the permissibility of coercing criminals can be shown by considering that everyone could adopt a principle of justifiable coercion in response to criminal acts. Since coercion, according to this picture, is recommended as a *response* to some injustice, it is accordingly not recommended as a fundamental principle.

[14] It is standard to say that threats coerce but offers do not. However, there is no uncontroversial solution to the problem of whether the corporation *threatens* the country or merely makes it an *offer*. If we say that '*A* makes a *threat* when *B* will be worse off in relation to some relevant baseline position if *B* does not accept *A*'s proposal, but that *A* makes an *offer* when *B* will be *better off* in relation to some relevant baseline position if *B* accepts *A*'s proposal', then judgements about coercion will depend on inevitably controversial claims about the relevant baseline. See Alan Wertheimer, 'Coercion', in Lawrence C. Becker and Charlotte Becker (eds.), *Encyclopedia of Ethics* (London: Garland, 1992), 172–5; quotation from 173.

will that everyone makes offers that people freely accept, so the Kantian test does not capture the core problem here: that problem is simply one of taking unfair advantage. The severely deprived are easier to manipulate than any better-off group, since their overriding concern is simply to remain alive, to keep their heads above water. They are in no position to organize themselves and give voice to their claims in such a way as to have some noticeable effect on their interlocutors. People can be treated unjustly even when they are not coerced. One takes justice seriously by rejecting certain agreements because they are unfair to one or other of the parties, even when those agreements were freely accepted by those unfairly treated.

On the basis of the above sort of argument, O'Neill concludes that every agent has an obligation not to coerce or deceive in their dealings with other agents. I have rejected O'Neill's specific claims here, but I agree that, in the absence of special circumstances, coercion and deception are morally impermissible. On the Kantian view, noncoercion and nondeception are perfect obligations, i.e. there are no circumstances in which agents can fail to recognize and act upon them.[15] But there are also important imperfect obligations, or duties to perform actions at least some of the time for at least some others. One of these imperfect obligations was hinted at earlier, when we mentioned the maxim, 'Let each man be as happy as heaven wills, or as he can make himself; I will not take anything from him or even envy him; but to his welfare or assistance in time of need I have no desire to contribute.'[16] That there is an obligation to help those in need, and that it is a different kind of obligation from the obligation not to coerce or deceive, is shown by performing the universalizability thought experiment for this maxim. In this case one's maxim tells one to take no account of people who need help whenever coming to their aid conflicts with other goals or interests one has. Now imagine everyone acting on such a maxim. While we can conceive of a world of universal indifference to the suffering of

[15] An obvious difficulty with taking noncoercion and nondeception as perfect obligations is that agents then seem to be precluded from coercing or deceiving others even in emergencies or extreme cases. Notoriously, Kant believed that one should *never* lie, even when a madman intent on murder asks you to tell him the whereabouts of his would-be victim. Immanuel Kant, 'On a Supposed Right to Lie from Altruistic Motives', in *Immanuel Kant: Critique of Practical Reason and Other Writings in Moral Philosophy*, ed. and tr. Lewis White Beck (New York: Garland, 1976), 346–50. (Kant's piece was originally published in 1797.)

[16] Immanuel Kant, *Foundations of the Metaphysics of Morals*, 40 (Prussian Academy pagination, 423).

others,[17] we run into a contradiction when we attempt to *will* that such a world should exist. To will something is to commit oneself to taking the necessary means to bring it about. Human beings are not self-sufficient, therefore, as a human being, I cannot rationally will that I refuse the help of others when I am in distress, since such refusal would be a straightforward denial of a means to some of my ends. But at the same time, in the imaginary world created by our thought experiment, I would also be willing that no one helps anyone in distress. Hence I would be attempting to bring about *both* that I get the assistance of others when I am in need *and* that no one helps others when they are in need. This is a contradiction in willing, and so the maxim is morally impermissible. This type of contradiction is not as immediate as the contradiction in conception which generated the perfect obligations not to coerce or deceive; contradictions in willing generate imperfect duties, in this case the duty to help some others some of the time. One cannot act on a maxim that one should never assist the needy. This duty to assist those in need applies, of course, to individual agents and collective agencies as well.

I will not discuss Immanuel Kant's own international theory in any detail, but I should at least note an important difference between Kant and O'Neill. In *Perpetual Peace*, Kant argued for a federation of free states and, with respect to the treatment of *individuals*, he believed that 'cosmopolitan right shall be limited to conditions of universal hospitality'.[18] O'Neill's Kantian theory of international relations—correctly in my view— defends more far-reaching obligations towards individuals on the part of the citizens of foreign nation-states and of those states themselves.

We have before us, then, the outlines of O'Neill's revised Kantian approach to international justice. It proposes to use the categorical imperative to test the maxims of important collective agencies, and such a test must determine whether the proposed maxim could be acted on by all agents, individual and collective. Moreover, it is to be kept in mind that individual agents (i.e. human beings) are not the disembodied rational entities to be found in the works of some moral theorists; rather, individuals are physically and emotionally needy, only partially rational, and vulnerable to the coercive and deceptive practices of more powerful agencies.

---

[17] As Kant says, not only can we think of such a world, but in such circumstances the plight of the human race would be an improvement upon 'a state where everyone talks of sympathy and good will or even exerts himself occasionally to practise them while, on the other hand, he cheats when he can and betrays or otherwise violates the right of man'. *Foundations of the Metaphysics of Morals*, 40 (Prussian Academy pagination, 423).

[18] *Kant: Political Writings*, ed, Hans Reiss (Cambridge: Cambridge University Press, 1991), 105.

4.3. O'NEILL'S CRITIQUE OF RIGHTS-BASED COSMOPOLITANISM

O'Neill presents her neo-Kantian theory as an alternative to the two other main contenders in the global justice debate, utilitarianism and rights-based theories. As we have seen, my approach is based on a conception of basic human rights (Chapter 3), and it is a conception which is in many ways similar to an (admittedly unorthodox) utilitarian theory (Chapter 2). My strategy, therefore, is to outline O'Neill's objections to rights-based cosmopolitanism and to defend that view against those objections.[19] In the following section of this chapter, I offer some other criticisms of O'Neill's Kantian approach, in part defending that approach against popular but misguided criticism but ultimately rejecting her account in favour of a strategy that argues for human rights by directing our moral gaze to the vital interests of persons.

It should first be noted, however, that O'Neill does not believe rights-based theories to be completely misguided, so long as we carefully distinguish between libertarian rights theories (which, in her view, are wholly mistaken) and welfare rights theories (which are in part correct). The arguments of Alan Gewirth and Henry Shue are based on basic human rights, and O'Neill admits that these arguments are persuasive and important. The main strength of such arguments, according to O'Neill, is their recognition that there *is* an obligation to help those in need, that contrary to common opinion it is not simply an optional act of charity to come to the assistance of someone in need of help. The rights theorist puts this point by saying that each individual has a right to have his or her vital interests protected, hence there is an obligation of some agents or agencies to ensure that the means to such protection exists. O'Neill wants to assert that there is an obligation to help, but to deny that this obligation corresponds to a human right to be helped.

This is the first respect in which rights-based theories are mistaken, according to O'Neill. The obligation to help those in need does not correspond to any *right* on the part of the needy to the help they need. Consider the position of Immanuel Kant on this matter. For Kant, rights are attributed to persons when the maxim of a proposed action cannot be *conceived* as a universal law.[20] Contradictions in conception generate

[19] Some of O'Neill's main objections to utilitarianism were dealt with in Ch. 2.
[20] Immanuel Kant, *Metaphysics of Morals* (Cambridge: Cambridge University Press, 1992), originally published in 1797, Prussian Academy pagination, 218–21.

perfect obligations and counterpart rights. Hence a right again seems to be one side of a coin whose other side is a perfect obligation; rights exist simply by virtue of our coming to see that a proposed maxim cannot be thought as a maxim for everyone. But it follows from this account that there could not be *rights* to be helped when in need, for a maxim of not helping *is* thinkable; the problem with such a maxim is that it is not *willable* simultaneously by everyone, hence there is an imperfect obligation to help, an obligation which does not correspond to any right. Helping those in need is an obligation, but it falls into the realm of virtue, not of *Recht* (right or law).

O'Neill argues against the human right to food (one of the basic human rights, on my account) by taking seriously the distinction between positive and negative rights. Those who use this distinction generally deny that there are any positive rights, and this is how I interpret O'Neill's argument. She says that someone has a right only if 'others have an obligation to respect or fulfil that right. If nobody has such obligations, there just is no right at all.'[21] So, on this account, a necessary condition of a right ascription is that obligation-bearers can be identified. A person can have a right not to be assaulted only if others have an obligation not to assault. O'Neill believes the right to food is problematic in a way that the right not to be assaulted is not. My response to this claim, which has been more or less covered in the previous chapter, is that the two cases are much more similar than she suggests. For in both cases the corresponding obligations include both actions and omissions, whereas O'Neill implies that the right not to be assaulted correlates with nothing more than a duty not to assault. On the contrary, I believe that a person can have a right not to be assaulted only if all others have an obligation not to assault *and* all others have a *collective obligation* to provide the protections necessary for ensuring that those individuals who are inclined to overlook their obligation not to assault are deterred from failing to act upon that obligation. This second, collective obligation requires some *positive action* on the part of others; moreover, the right not to be assaulted is not properly recognized unless and until *both* obligations are met. It is important to notice as well that acting on one's obligations in this way may be very costly—police forces, judicial and prison systems are not cheap, and a relatively poor society will find it difficult to pay these costs. But this is presumably no reason for denying that there is a right not to be assaulted.

[21] O'Neill, 'Hunger, Needs and Rights', 70.

This argument applies to the right to food as well. This right gives rise to obligations on all others not to deprive anyone of the food they need to survive. But it also generates collective duties upon all others to ensure that, within the limits of scarcity, each person can obtain for themselves the requirements of subsistence. It is misleading to interpret the right to food as requiring simply the provision of food to those who need it. The reality is more complex. If the right to food generates a range of obligations, from the duty not to deprive others of necessary food, to the duty to protect individuals from having their food sources taken from their control, to the duty to provide for those still needy even when the first two types of duty have been acted upon, then it is not obvious that the right to food will be any more difficult to recognize and enforce than the right not to be assaulted.

O'Neill says that there is no human right to food because we cannot show 'that there is a counterpart obligation to provide that food to which everybody has a right'.[22] She asks, 'Who has the obligation to supply food to all those who need it?' and I answer, 'All of us'. The obvious fact that no one person can ensure that everyone can meet their subsistence needs does not imply that those needs lack strong claims to be met. O'Neill's strategy is to argue for imperfect obligations to meet the needs of others, obligations to which there are no counterpart individual rights. But it is equally plausible to hold on to the idea that persons have rights to the protection of their vital interests, in which case an alternative strategy presents itself, namely, to ensure that the obligation we all share to protect vital interests is fairly met by everyone, and this in turn means that, *ceteris paribus*, the obligation should be met by everyone equally. The importance of O'Neill's argument is that it forces rights theorists to take seriously the need to give an account of the agents and agencies with the counterpart obligations, in order to preclude merely announcing a set of 'manifesto rights' with no corresponding duties. However, she does not show that no such account can be given, and the classification of duties into duties of avoidance, protection and aid provides a plausible framework for that account.[23]

A related strategy O'Neill uses to show that there are no universal human rights to welfare is to point out that allocation of *duties* cannot be universal and that this restriction of duties transfers over to the correlative rights as well. As she puts it:

---

[22] O'Neill, 'Hunger, Needs and Rights', 70.
[23] This classification of duties comes from Henry Shue, *Basic Rights*. I discussed it in more detail in Ch. 3.

Advocates of welfare rights [such as Henry Shue] face the problem that allocation *cannot* here be universal and thus remains undetermined. Some have argued that this raises no problem once we address the institutionalization of rights. All rights, even liberty rights, can be enforced only by allocating specific powers and obligations to particular agents and institutions. In this respect, there is nothing special about welfare rights. However, we cannot move on to questions of enforcement until we know what human rights there are. For we would not know what should be enforced.[24]

The last two sentences of this quotation constitute O'Neill's objection to Shue's institutionalization point. O'Neill's claim is that enforcement of rights is a secondary matter, to be dealt with only after it has been determined which human rights exist. But is her objection sound? I think not, for two reasons. First, if we start from the claim that each person has basic interests, and that these interests give rise to legitimate claims to have those interests protected or satisfied, then 'we know what human rights there are' in the sense that we know what is important from the perspective of recipience. The next task is to look for ways to meet the interest-based claims in the world as we know it, and this will be a matter both of determining the extent of material scarcity *and* of the fair sharing out of the obligations to meet those claims (assuming that scarcity is not so extreme as to render impossible the attempt to meet *all* such claims). So we can conceive of better and worse reasons for attributing rights to human beings, and for assigning so-called positive rights to them. And on that basis we then try to discover which of those supposed rights can be protected in the world of scarcity and conflicts of interest. However, this is to say that an answer to the question of what can be enforced is directly relevant to the question of what rights there are. Secondly, if no one can be said to have a right unless others have correlative duties, enforcement becomes a primary consideration, and the statement of a right is incomplete unless it includes an outline of the correlative duties that need enforcing if that right is to be protected adequately.

O'Neill rightly points out that human beings are not disembodied rational agents; on the contrary, we are only partially rational and we have material, social, and psychological needs. Specifically, she mentions the needs for security and subsistence as the most basic needs we have, for they 'are needed for any sustained life involving autonomous action'.[25]

[24] O'Neill, 'Hunger, Needs and Rights', 76–7. Cf. O'Neill, *Towards Justice and Virtue*, 131.
[25] O'Neill, *Faces of Hunger*, 143.

But if these needs are so important, it is odd just to conclude, as O'Neill does, that individuals and collective agents have obligations to meet only some of the needs of some others and only some of the time.

The relationship between needs on the one hand and autonomous action on the other is brought out by an important passage in *Faces of Hunger* in which, I maintain, O'Neill seems committed, despite herself, to human rights to the satisfaction of basic needs. O'Neill claims that

> . . . the specific policies and institutions which might be just in actual human situations must do more than rule out a limited range of coercive and deceptive forms of action that undermine any sort of rational agency. The details of human justice must take account of the most basic needs that must be met if other human beings are not to be fundamentally deceived or coerced. Any just global order must *at least* meet standards of material justice and provide for the basic material needs in whose absence all human beings are overwhelmingly vulnerable to coercion and deception.[26]

O'Neill points out an important implication of a recognition of the perfect duties of nondeception and noncoercion, namely, that people should have their basic 'material needs' met because failure to meet those needs renders people susceptible to the coercive and deceitful practices of the powerful. I will not discuss here the oddity of the claim that the reason why people should have, say, enough to eat is to avoid coercion and deception, since my aim is merely to show that, even if we accept O'Neill's central claims, there is a right to subsistence.

As O'Neill suggests, there is in fact a correlation between (i) serious-ness of material deprivation, and (ii) vulnerability to deception and coercion. An individual who lacks food necessary for her survival, or the means to produce that food, will 'consent' to 'offers' of assistance which are contingent upon her 'agreeing' to some conditions set out by the provider. But 'consent' and 'agreement' lose their normal senses in this context, for the cost to the individual of failing to accept the offer is so high that consent will likely be given come what may. As refusal of the offer is not a live option, we lack the possible alternative that is present in standard contexts, where consent *can* be given freely. In short, the worse off a person is, the more vulnerable she will be to coercion by the better off; and when the deprivation is sufficiently severe, such con-sent as may be given takes on the character of a surface phenomenon, shrouding the unfreedom created by severe material need.

---

[26] O'Neill, *Faces of Hunger*, 141, emphasis in original.

Up to this point, then, I am in complete agreement with O'Neill. But I maintain that the coercion/deprivation connection strengthens the case for subsistence rights, while O'Neill denies that there are such rights. From her perspective, the claims to food correspond to *imperfect* duties to feed some others at least some of the time; hence these claims cannot be rights. However, there is a more or less obvious argument available to the rights theorist in reply to this move.

The argument runs as follows. If each individual has a right not to be coerced, and if any person is overwhelmingly vulnerable to coercion whenever their basic needs remain unmet, then every individual should have a right to the satisfaction of her basic needs, in order to ensure that the right to noncoercion is protected adequately. Hence access to food *is* a matter of justice and not merely a requirement of beneficence. O'Neill seems to acknowledge this point when she asserts that the meeting of basic needs must be part of an account of 'the details of human justice'.[27] But she seems not to see the significance of this line of argument for the advocates of basic subsistence rights.

O'Neill maintains that positive obligations to assist others fall into the realm of beneficence rather than justice. 'The central demand of Kantian justice is negative: that action, policies and institutions not be based on or conform to fundamental principles of coercion or deception.'[28] However, if my argument above is sound, justice cannot be purely negative, for justice can never be done where agents merely keep their slates clean in the ways O'Neill recommends. Of course, noncoercion and nondeception are necessary conditions of justice; my point is that, contrary to O'Neill's claims, they are not sufficient. Accordingly, a commitment to human rights to noncoercion and nondeception entails a parallel acceptance of basic human subsistence rights.

O'Neill's objections to rights-based strategies can hold up only if there is a clear distinction between obligation-based and rights-based approaches, but it can be argued that the difference between the two is merely superficial. Kant's first formulation of the categorical imperative centres on the standpoint of the agent; the second formulation, on the other hand, the Formula of the End in Itself (FEI), shifts the focus to those on whom the agent impinges when she acts. The FEI says: 'Act so that you treat humanity, whether in your own person or in that of another, always

---

[27] O'Neill, *Faces of Hunger*, 141. Cf. 'A just global economic and political order [has] to be one designed to meet material needs.' Ibid. 149.
[28] Ibid. 146.

as an end and never as a means only.'[29] Hence we have a formulation of the Kantian categorical imperative which focuses on those at the receiving end of action and which might even be glossed as claiming that every one has a right not to be treated merely as a means. Notoriously, Kant claims that the different formulations of the categorical imperative are equivalent to each other, so on these grounds we could conclude that a recipient-based conception of just action is not only to be found in Kant but that such a conception is merely another way of stating the criterion of right action which, in its first formulation (the Formula of Universal Law) centres on agents. We are thus given Kantian grounds for a rights-based theory of justice.

Of course, it is highly controversial to take at face value Kant's claim that the different versions of the categorical imperative are equivalent to one another. However, two points can be made to answer suspicions on this score. First, we can at least make intuitive sense of the supposed equivalence claim. To say that a maxim could not be willed by everyone is clearly similar to saying that at least some people could not consent to the maxim, and the latter claim is akin to the view that acting on a maxim to which not everyone could possibly consent is to treat some persons merely as a means. Secondly, O'Neill herself uses the FEI version of the categorical imperative in some of her work, most elaborately in 'Ending World Hunger',[30] so if this version of the CI makes the same moral point from the perspective of the recipient rather than that of the agent, O'Neill can hardly deny the relevance of my claim here that there is no deep moral difference between obligation-based and rights-based Kantian theories.

Moreover, violations of the FEI version of the categorical imperative can also be understood as instances of inconsistency, as forms of irrationality. Using other people for one's own ends involves denying that they are also ends themselves, and this contradicts one's (perhaps implicit) recognition that others are in fact ends. Someone who (merely) uses other people treats them like things, yet cannot deny that others have perspectives,

---

[29] Immanuel Kant, *Foundations of the Metaphysics of Morals*, 46 (Prussian Academy pagination, 429). One might maintain that the focus of this formulation is on the quality of the act, that is, on whether the act treats those affected by it merely as a means. But my view is that one may sensibly view this imperative as telling us to consider directly the interests of recipients.

[30] Onora O'Neill, 'Ending World Hunger', in Tom Regan (ed.), *Matters of Life and Death*, 3rd edn. (London: McGraw Hill, 1993), 235–79.

aims, and plans just like he has. So he treats them as something other than what he takes them to be, and accords himself a status and importance he cannot honestly affirm.[31]

Rights are the correlatives of obligations, so it is just not possible to offer a coherent argument for a human right without presenting a case for the counterpart obligations. Thus, contrary to O'Neill's claims, rights-based arguments do not fail to address the powerful, since it is precisely powerful agents and agencies which will be the bearers of the obligations in question. O'Neill presents no reasons why ethical argument cannot address *both* recipients and agents. She argues that rights-talk is rhetorically powerful but cannot be ethically basic, since it does not address those who have the power to do something about international injustice.[32] But the correlativity of rights and duties, and the necessity of finding duty-bearers to protect rights, means that those with the power to ensure that rights are recognized will be required to do so. Moreover, by beginning with the moral relevance of vital human interests in food, water, health, and education, a rights-based theory enables us to see why certain kinds of activity and inactivity are morally condemnable; therefore we are provided with strong reasons for viewing a particular state of affairs as unjust. If one begins the justificatory process with obligations, on the other hand, the moral force of one's arguments may gain credence only by way of an implicit appeal to the very interests which provide the backing for human rights claims. In that case, the rights approach and the Kantian obligations strategy are two sides of one coin, and there is therefore no reason for denying that the former method is equally reasonable, if not more so. The most plausible reason for saying that we have obligations in a given instance is that those obligations protect or promote the interests of those affected by the actions under consideration; but then the explanation for the duty is that it is required for interest-protection, so interests—and the rights they generate—are morally prior to, and explanatory of, obligations.

[31] For a discussion of this Kantian strain of thought, which points out the inconsistency of failing to treat others as ends, see A. John Simmons, *The Lockean Theory of Rights* (Princeton: Princeton University Press, 1992), 41–2. Simmons believes that the inconsistency in question here is weaker than the sort Kant concerned himself with, but my view is that this description of violating the formula of the end in itself is, at the very least, compatible with the Kantian understanding of what is wrong with using other people. I reserve judgement on Simmons's point that these ideas are to be found in John Locke's moral theory.

[32] O'Neill, *Faces of Hunger*, 119–20.

4.4. CRITIQUE OF O'NEILLIAN INTERNATIONAL DISTRIBUTIVE JUSTICE

A proper appreciation of O'Neill's account of international distributive justice will bring out both its strengths and its weaknesses. I begin with the strengths. O'Neill's account stresses the ideas of obligation and need; both ideas are necessary to any satisfactory theory of global moral relations. The claims of the needy must be a central concern of those who would address world poverty, and a good theory will outline the duties, and duty-bearers, necessary to meet those needs. My disagreement with O'Neill, as we have seen, is mainly with her claim that there is something to be gained by eschewing the notion of basic rights.

We have already canvassed some objections to O'Neill's theory, but there are others, some of which are ultimately unconvincing, but which nevertheless might have undue influence. It is therefore important to deal with them here.

One objection to the Kantian universalization test for maxims is that it fails to generate any positive duties, and so cannot justify obligations to help those whose vital interests need protection in the form of positive action. In answer to this objection, it simply has to be pointed out that positive duties to help the needy stem from a double negation, a denial of a denial. If someone attempts to deny that he has a duty to help others, the CI test shows that the denial is wrong because it cannot be universalized. But then it follows that it is wrong *not* to help others, or alternatively, that it is right (in the sense of required rather than simply permitted) to help others. If it is not permissible to avoid a course of action, then it is required that the course of action be performed. Hence positive duties can be derived from the Kantian test of maxims.

Another objection with which I disagree is Thomas Nagel's claim that rich people can reject the beneficence maxim. Let us reconsider the maxim of denying needy others the help they need. Nagel reasons as follows:

But here is the main problem. Because the situation involves a conflict of interests, *any* maxim on which a person proposes to act would, if universalized, conflict with what he would want for himself in at least *one* of the hypothetical positions he might occupy under it. The principle of no mutual aid, to be sure, contradicts what he would want if he were destitute. But a positive principle of charity contradicts his antecedent preference for keeping his money for himself. Even a destitute person, testing the universalizability of a principle of charity, would have to acknowledge that it requires some sacrifices by the better off— sacrifices which he would prefer not to have to make were he among the better off. So why doesn't *every* maxim one might propose in such a situation fail to satisfy the categorical imperative, by generating a contradiction in the will when one tries to will its universalization?[33]

Nagel purports to show that any maxim involving a conflict of interests (in this case, the conflict is between the destitute person's interest in receiving help and the wealthy person's interest in keeping his money) will fail the CI test. But Nagel's argument fails. While a human being could not rationally will that no one helps him when he is destitute, he can quite easily will that some of his excess income be taken from him in order to provide for those who are unable to meet their basic needs; therefore, on grounds of universalizability, there is an important difference between the perspectives of the rich person and the poor person. I think Nagel's reasoning fails to convince because it does not consider the relevance of a deeper discussion about the relative importance of the interests in conflict and the reasons why contradiction arises in the universalizability of some maxims. Once we compare the importance of these interests, we can see that, while the rich person would not be irrational to deny aid to the poor person, such denial would none the less be unreasonable, because any argument for keeping excess wealth would come up against the trumping counterclaim that desperate straits merit moral priority. The fact that giving up some of his wealth is a sacrifice that 'he would prefer not to have to make' hardly constitutes a reason for denying that one has any obligation to make the sacrifice. Nagel seems to have missed the point of the universalization test. The uncharitable maxim is morally impermissible not because there is at least one perspective from which one would want to veto it; if that were the case, then, as Nagel points out, *no* maxim concerning charitable giving would be permissible. The impermissibility of acting on a maxim of failing to help those in need is shown, rather, by considering the hypothetical world in which one both wants to be helped and where everyone denies needed help to others. A similar thought experiment will show that a maxim of helping the needy is indeed possible to will consistently as a universal law, for one would will both that one helps those in need and that when one is in need one obtains the help of others. Despite what Nagel suggests, the simple truth that every person has a perspective does not show anything about the Kantian test one way or the other. What matters is whether one's particular perspective is one that could be *the*

---

[33] Thomas Nagel, *Equality and Partiality* (Oxford: Oxford University Press, 1991), 42–3, emphases in original.

perspective of everyone simultaneously; on these grounds, charitable giving is required while refusal to give to those in need is forbidden.

Another objection to O'Neill's project is voiced by Partha Dasgupta, who reasons as follows:

[O'Neill's *Faces of Hunger*] is an exploration of our obligations towards the alleviation of hunger in distant lands. . . . O'Neill rejects both rights-based and beneficence theories, on the grounds that they are not helpful for her purposes, and pursues instead an obligation-based theory derived from Kant. Unfortunately, the implications she is able to draw from her own analysis are singularly weak, to wit that agencies like the World Bank and the International Monetary Fund should not be deceitful in their dealings with poor countries, and that they should not coerce them into pursuing policies not in their interest. I find it difficult to think that we need an elaborate ethical structure if this is all we conclude. The World Bank, for example, was created explicitly to help countries reconstruct and develop. Duties of international organizations are written into their charters, and they are forbidden to deceive and coerce. That they both may have practised deceit and coercion is not the point here, and no high-powered ethical theory is needed to be invoked to condemn them if they have.[34]

Simply stated, Dasgupta's objection is that O'Neill's theoretical apparatus is unnecessary for the derivation of her conclusions about institutional practices around the world. Her main conclusions are that major institutions have perfect duties not to deceive or coerce vulnerable countries in their dealings with them. It is true, as Dasgupta says, that we do not need a Kantian universalizability argument to show that deception and coercion are not options, for this sort of objectionable behaviour is ruled out by the very charters which define the purposes of these institutions. But I think O'Neill could properly reply that the charters could have been different, for instance, they might not have ruled out certain forms of coercion as a means of bringing about desired states of affairs. In that event, O'Neill's arguments can be introduced and used to show that, in spite of what the charter happens to say, deception and coercion are immoral practices and hence can form no part of the purposes of institutions engaged in international (or domestic) activity. If Dasgupta's point is that O'Neill's Kantian apparatus is unnecessary because duties not to coerce and deceive are rather obvious, then we should agree about the obviousness, but deny that reasons are not necessary in support of the obvious. It is important to seek defences even for those ethical positions we can hardly imagine rejecting, because we should try to discover *why* we take

---

[34] Partha Dasgupta, *An Inquiry into Well-Being and Destitution* (Oxford: Clarendon Press, 1993), 27.

such positions and because the rationale we develop might lead us to recognize the unacceptability of other practices we now accept.

O'Neill can make another, different response as well. It is that Kantian reasoning does not reveal merely that there are duties not to deceive and coerce, it also shows that there are positive duties to help poor countries (even though, on O'Neill's account, those duties do not correlate with rights).[35] Again, Dasgupta is correct that it is, in one sense at least, unnecessary in the present context to point out that these duties can be justified by appeal to a Kantian argument, since the World Bank *already has* duties to help poor countries. However, Dasgupta is mistaken here, for something like O'Neill's argument is in fact necessary; the reason for its indispensability is that we need some line of moral reasoning to justify the obligations to which we can (as it happens) otherwise appeal simply by pointing to charters. In the absence of an argument along these lines, one can have no reason to object to proposed changes in the charter of the World Bank, apart perhaps from an appeal to stability and the value of settled expectations, for one is, on this view, content to stop arguing at the level of mere appeals to existing documents. (I do not claim that Dasgupta believes that justification should be restricted in this way; I only maintain that his dismissal of O'Neill's approach is too quick because it implies that this restricted conception of justification is adequate.)

I now turn to two further objections to the Kantian account of international obligations. The first weakens that account considerably, while the second seems to render it deeply unsatisfactory. O'Neill sees that the second objection is serious, but her attempt at answering it does not silence doubts about the question-begging nature of the Kantian test for the moral acceptability of maxims. Accordingly, O'Neill's project lacks a satisfactory defence of its core idea.

There is a criticism of O'Neill's theory that says it suffers from a debilitating indeterminacy concerning the obligations to provide assistance to those in need, and therefore cannot properly guide the agencies in a position to help. O'Neill's arguments generate clear duties of non-coercion and nondeception for agents and agencies operating within countries and across borders. But isn't the theory too vague about the amount of *positive help* these agencies are required to provide? We are correctly advised that helping is a moral requirement and not an optional extra or an heroic sacrifice, but if the duty to relieve suffering says

---

[35] I say that O'Neill can respond in this way, despite the fact that she is less than explicit (most of the time) about the existence of these more positive obligations.

nothing more than that we should provide aid on some occasions, leaving it to the agents to decide in what way aid should be given and how much help to give, then the theory's implications are importantly indeterminate. Now this indeterminacy could be seen as a positive feature of the theory, since it accords with the common-sense idea that there should be some room for agents to decide for themselves both when and to whom to provide assistance. But this indeterminacy is neither unavoidable nor acceptable, for an adequate account of international obligations will mention specific positive duties which thereby rule out some options left open by O'Neill's account. If one's goal is to help needy individuals, then if one is rational one will take the most efficient means to that goal, and that entails ensuring that properly accountable collective agencies exist (or are brought into existence) whose purpose is to help those in need. To leave it open to individuals to discharge their duties of aid merely by uncoordinated individual actions is, it seems, to allow some needy people to undergo avoidable suffering. This seems like straightforward prudential irrationality, and this is directly relevant here, since both Kant and O'Neill properly require maxims to pass two tests, one for prudential rationality (the hypothetical imperative test) and one for morality (the categorical imperative test).[36]

I now come to the most important objection to O'Neill's project. A serious problem for the Kantian test of the acceptability of maxims is that *some nonuniversalizable maxims seem to be morally permissible*, in which case the Kantian criterion would condemn acceptable practices. Allen Wood gives an illustration of a maxim of this sort: 'I will occasionally accompany others through a doorway, and on those occasions I will always go through the door last.'[37] One's maxim is simply one of showing consideration for others, but it seems that Kantians would be led to judge this maxim impermissible because its universalization yields a world in which no one goes through a doorway (or that one is obligated to be sure to be alone when one does so)![38] This example shows that passing

---

[36] See Jerome B. Schneewind, 'Autonomy, Obligation, and Virtue: An Overview of Kant's Moral Philosophy', in Paul Guyer (ed.), *Cambridge Companion to Kant* (Cambridge: Cambridge University Press, 1992), 320, for a helpful account of the two-test strategy.

[37] Allen Wood, *Hegel's Ethical Thought* (New York: Cambridge University Press, 1990), 157.

[38] If politeness is indeed the agent's motivation in this case, one should be wary of the possibility of forcing others to be impolite by refusing to go first oneself. So a more reasonable, and universalizable, maxim would be: 'I will always offer to go last, but I will not insist on it if the other person strongly prefers to go last.' Nevertheless, if the maxim is as Wood says it is, the objection still applies.

the universalizability test is not a necessary condition of a maxim's moral permissibility: the politeness maxim is not universalizable and yet the maxim is permissible, therefore a maxim can be morally acceptable even though it fails the CI test. This point weakens considerably the utility of that test as a method for determining global obligations, since some activities may be permitted though the Kantian criterion rules them out.

O'Neill's reply to this criticism appears to be that it does not focus on the 'fundamental principles' on which an agent acts, and so mistakenly takes a maxim to be nonuniversalizable when in fact it can quite easily be universalized without contradiction. In the specific case of an agent's maxim that he will go through a door last (when others are accompanying him through a door), the maxim as we have stated it is too specific and therefore fails to pick out what it is about the agent's proposed action that guides him. We get a better idea of what the agent's maxim is by asking what reason he has for proposing to act as he does, and in this case the reason would mention his plan to be courteous to others. However, if one's maxim is, 'I will show others consideration and respect', then the universalizability test will be passed with flying colours.

But how do we tell how specific or general a maxim should be? The decision to interpret the maxim in the foregoing case in one way rather than another seems to gain its plausibility from an appeal to our considered judgements about what is morally acceptable: it is pretty clearly permissible to let others go through a door first when one is accompanying others through a door. But then it is our moral intuitions which are doing the work in this case, and not the universalizability test. Why, in short, should we accept the claim that the fundamental principle on which the agent acts in this instance is that one ought to be polite and considerate to others, and not that one ought to go through doors last when others are going through the same door? What could a Kantian say to someone who stubbornly maintained that his maxim made essential reference to the necessity of going through doors last?

And for that matter—and this is a general problem with this entire approach to moral argumentation—what are we to do when it is unclear what the maxim is on which an agent acts? One reply is that this may present problems of interpretation, but we can still argue about what the maxim in question actually is, or what our best guess is as to its content; and in this way grounds for the assessment of maxims, and therefore of actions, are provided. None the less, there presumably will be cases in which a maxim *can* be identified and yet, despite its evident permissibility, it fails to be universalizable and hence is judged by the Kantian test to be forbidden.

These should be familiar criticisms to those versed in the debates about Kantian moral philosophy, but they are not therefore less compelling. The main point to take from this discussion is that nothing in O'Neill's original contribution does anything to quell the doubts one has about some of the traditional problems with the Kantian enterprise. O'Neill's Kantian strategy fails, despite its being on the right track. It fails because some permissible maxims are not universalizable, so a maxim's moral acceptability cannot be equated with its capacity to be universally conceivable or universally willable without contradiction. Nevertheless, the idea that permitted maxims of action should be subject to a veto on reasonable grounds is an important notion for moral and political theory. A better strategy than O'Neill's, deriving from this same idea, is simply to compare, in cases of conflict of interests, the values in conflict and to favour the more important value. In this sort of case, no right is absolute, including the right not to be coerced; therefore, even for cases in which O'Neill would claim that human beings have rights, those rights can be put aside in emergencies, in favour of the more fundamental interests persons have, such as meeting their basic needs.

O'Neill appears to countenance this sort of move—again, despite herself—in her penetrating discussion of problems of population growth and their relation to issues of global justice. She allows that, though coercion should be avoided, it may be permissible where engaging in it is necessary to protect each person's basic interest in satisfying her or his material needs or, in other words, where it functions to protect against the deeper, more 'fundamental coercion of widespread destitution and hunger'.

. . . the prospects of population growth (and the methods of population control appearing in some parts of the world) are alarming enough to raise the question of coercion. If noncoercive public policies fail to reduce population growth, would more coercive measures be unjust? Kantian justice rejects *fundamental* reliance on coercion or deception, but in harsh circumstances lesser coercion might be the only way to avoid fundamental coercion. If it was clear that the fundamental coercion of widespread destitution and hunger could not be avoided without limited coercion of procreative decisions, a case might be made for limited coercion. However, the case could only be plausible when other less coercive ways of avoiding or averting fundamental coercion and deception had been exhausted.[39]

---

[39] *Faces of Hunger*, 158, emphasis in original.

Policies designed to check population growth in a noncoercive manner can be effective, but 'if such policies fail, and just productive and redistributive measures too cannot meet needs, direct coercion of procreative decisions would not be unjust'.[40] Hence if there are rights not to be coerced, empirical circumstances can justify overriding these rights; but then rights to noncoercion are indistinguishable in this respect from subsistence rights, for which the same overriding conditions apply.

4.5. CONCLUSION

In her more recent work, O'Neill characterizes justice in a slightly different, and perhaps more helpful way. Justice is seen now, not in terms merely of the absence of coercion and deception, but in terms of a *principle of the rejection of injury*: 'The core of injustice is action on principles which if universally acted on would forseeably injure at least some; the core of justice is rejection of principles whose attempted universal adoption would forseeably injure at least some.'[41] This view seems to be consistent with my own position, since my view is that individuals should have their vital interests protected and that failure on this score constitutes an injury or harm to those whose interests are neglected. To dovetail the later O'Neill with my rights perspective, one needs to add the claim, which I also accept, that injury exists where someone is not secure against physical attack, and where she lacks food, water, and health care at a basic level. O'Neill's rejection of injury, then, amounts to a defence—in very general terms—of basic interest protection. However, her continuing focus on universalizability has problems of its own and, in any case, does not add much to the general rights approach defended in these pages.

In summary, then, I have applauded O'Neill's version of Kantianism as a clear and in many respects reasonable account of ethics. However, I have also demonstrated its inferiority to a human rights approach, and have even shown that where O'Neill's view is most persuasive it actually collapses into a rights account. Another point made in this chapter is that, while many objections to Kantianism are misleading, O'Neill's maverick Kantian approach is insufficiently maverick to answer the most telling objections to the more traditional accounts of Kant's ethics.

[40] Ibid.
[41] O'Neill, *Towards Justice and Virtue*, 164. On O'Neill's revised view, coercion and deception are still unjust, of course, but they are understood to be so because they are forms of injury.

We have reached the end of Part I of this work, and we have seen in some detail the pros and cons of three central cosmopolitan theories of justice: utilitarianism, human rights theories, and O'Neill's maverick Kantianism. The preliminary conclusion I want to assert here is that a theory of basic human rights is a plausible approach for the cosmopolitan to take to the problems of international distributive justice. However, there are several approaches to these issues that point to the value of communities of smaller scale than the entire human race, so the communitarian approach to global justice needs to be assessed before we can reach any considered judgement on the plausibility of the case for basic human rights. Can cosmopolitans account for the ethical value of ties to particular groups of persons? Does cosmopolitanism unacceptably override the ethical claims that can be made on behalf of nations, or nation-states, or sovereign states more generally? In Part II, I will outline and assess some of the central communitarian approaches to international ethics, concentrating especially on their capacity for dealing with the obligations of distributive justice.

II

Communitarianism

5

Patriotism and Justice

5.1. INTRODUCTION TO PART II

Part II of this work investigates various challenges to the universalist ambitions of the arguments defended in Part I. In general, we can understand the topics discussed in Chapters 5 to 8 as being concerned with several sorts of *limitation arguments*, that is, arguments designed to show that, contrary to the conclusions of defenders of universal human rights, there are good reasons for limiting the scope of the obligations of justice to some *subset* of humanity. A limitation argument is designed to prove that the pretensions of cosmopolitans are illusory, incoherent, overridden by some morally more important considerations, or otherwise wrong-headed. Constitutive theorists, whose leading representatives are discussed in Chapter 8, maintain that, while there are perhaps good grounds for recognizing the claims of human beings *qua* human beings, cosmopolitans fail to take proper account of the value of what we might call certain *intra-species collectivities*, most importantly, sovereign states. Since sovereignty is a value, and since cosmopolitan arguments appear to ride roughshod over the sovereignty of states, it follows that the sort of moral universalism embodied in the basic human rights approach (my favoured version of cosmopolitanism) overlooks a value of great significance—at least in contemporary circumstances and for the foreseeable future—and is consequently mistaken in its conclusions. Relativists, one of whom is considered in Chapter 7, hold that justice, and morality in general, are subject to community-relative standards that make cross-cultural comparisons impossible. Hence, universal claims to justice make no sense. Defenders of nationality are my main focus in Chapter 6, where I look at the best attempt to base substantive conclusions on the ethical value of the 'nation', and to claim that distributive justice can be discussed properly only within the context of a given national community. On this view, justice can gain no footing in the absence of some group whose members experience various sentiments toward each other on the basis of their shared history, language, and territory.

In other words, there is no such thing as cosmopolitan justice; there is only what we might call *national justice*. In the present chapter I assess the views of patriots, who emphasize devotion to one's country as a primary moral virtue, and conclude that such devotion, in practice, entails favouritism for compatriots and, therefore, at least potentially, the denial of some of the claims of non-compatriots. If such a view requires the denial of the full force of human rights claims, then patriotism conflicts with cosmopolitanism.

In the main, I deny the claims of constitutivists, relativists, nationalists, and patriots in their strong forms. Yet we will see that there are distinctions to be made that might make it possible to hold on to some forms of each view. There might be ethically defensible forms of patriotism, nationalism, and constitutive theory, yet they do not in any way permit violations of the rights of foreigners, non-nationals, or non-citizens of one's state. And there might even be a plausible version of relativism, but it is not sufficiently strong to rule out the sort of moral universalism that I defend. In this chapter, then, I begin my investigation of limitation arguments by analysing the merits and demerits of patriotism.

5.2. EXCLUSIONARY PATRIOTISM, COMPATRIOT FAVOURITISM, AND MORALITY

Two important questions, for our purposes, are: (i) Is there an ethically defensible form of patriotism? And, if there is, (ii) What does patriotic loyalty imply about duties of justice to non-compatriots? I will first assess competing conceptions of patriotism, arguing that patriotism need not be an overtly immoral doctrine—it can be consistent with a defensible account of morality. However, I find no airtight arguments in favour of a blanket version of what I will call *compatriot favouritism*. Supposing, for the sake of argument, that patriotism can be ethically justified, I then propose to look at the status of international justice in light of the legitimate patriotic commitments persons may accept.

Patriotism is love of one's country and one's compatriots, and patriotic loyalty is the species of loyalty that requires devotion to one's country and a willingness to sacrifice one's own interests to some degree for one's fellow countrymen or countrywomen. Hence the patriot is someone who believes that he is justified in extending greater concern to some

persons (compatriots) than to others (non-compatriots or 'foreigners').[1]
Beyond this very basic characterization of patriotism, opinions diverge,
and it is the inclusion or exclusion of additional features that generates
competing conceptions of patriotism.

Patriotic special duties are a species of what are known as 'associative
or communal obligations'. These are special duties connected with membership in groups of various kinds (families, neighbourhoods, political communities), duties that appear to be recognized without having been chosen
by members. For Ronald Dworkin, people who have associative obligations must see those obligations as forms of special, personal concern
for particular others, and such concern must be expressed equally for
all members of the group in question.[2] Dworkin has defended associative obligations, but, as A. John Simmons has pointed out, such local-
ized duties are binding for Dworkin only when they meet standards of
justice that apply both to insiders and outsiders alike. In that case, we
want to know why the local group should be ethically prior when 'other,
foreign associations . . . may be better (more just) or more in need of
support'.[3] There is, therefore, a basic difficulty with defending patriotism in the face of global injustice. We shall return to this problem later
in this chapter, but in the mean time we should keep in mind that it
seems plausible to assert that patriotic special concern must not ignore
the condition of those in the wider world.

The wider world is ignored, however, in the following case. I have
said that additional features, beyond special concern itself, produce specific
versions of patriotism. The first extra characteristic that some writers
include as constitutive of patriotism is the view that one should concern
oneself *only* with the well-being of one's own compatriots. To say that
patriots 'extend greater concern' to compatriots is, on this reading, to say

[1] In this chapter, I focus on the general question of heightened concern for one's
compatriots, understood here as co-citizens of a nation-state. I therefore place no special
emphasis on the distinction between co-nationals and co-citizens. Since the differences
between these two types of group are potentially of great ethical importance, I turn in
Ch. 6 to the issue of *nationality* as an ethical value for persons as distinct from the value
of shared citizenship, and to the relation between nationality and global justice.

[2] Ronald Dworkin, *Law's Empire* (Cambridge, Mass.: Harvard University Press, 1986),
195–216, at 199–200.

[3] A. John Simmons, 'Associative Political Obligations', *Ethics*, 106 (1996), 247–73,
at 261. For an additional, related criticism of Dworkin's approach, accusing it of risking
circularity by presupposing the justice of certain types of favouritism, see Simon Caney,
'Individuals, Nations and Obligations', in Simon Caney, David George, and Peter Jones
(eds.), *National Rights, International Obligations* (Oxford: Westview, 1996), 119–38, at
133.

that non-compatriots fall outside the sphere of ethical concern altogether. This implies that 'foreigners' count for nothing, morally speaking, and we can therefore label this view *exclusionary patriotism*. This total exclusion of outsiders from consideration is no doubt an element in the set of commitments of some real-life (so-called) patriots, but I think it is uncontroversial to conclude that such a form of patriotic concern is not ethically defensible, for the simple reason that it could legitimate any action or policy done in the name of one's country *without taking any account of non-compatriots*. One need not be a moral cosmopolitan—i.e. a defender of impartialist, egalitarian individualism—to reject the idea that citizenship is the sole criterion of moral considerability. One odd consequence of accepting exclusionary patriotism is that it would seem to commit one to the belief that gaining membership in a country would somehow have the effect of turning one into a subject of ethical concern (from the perspective of those who are already members). This would lead, in turn, to our attaching monumental significance to immigration procedures![4] But this bizarre implication is not the real reason why we should reject this view. For, more simply put, on this conception of patriotism, patriots are those who believe that they are justified in pursuing policies that, from their own perspective, further the interests of their country, even though they do so only by enslaving or killing persons in other countries, because these exterior effects *count for nothing* in the moral assessment of the legitimacy of such policies. If this is patriotism, then it should be rejected outright.[5] Even if we conclude that a country is in general a proper object of its citizens' loyalty, there are limits to the sorts of actions and policies it is legitimate to pursue in its name, and part of the rationale of those limits is that non-compatriots should count to some extent.

Some versions of 'realism' in international relations theory and practice are indefensible in part for the reason that they exemplify the exclusionary approach to inter-country interactions. If individual egoism is unacceptable because persons are required to recognize the interests of *other persons*, then by similar reasoning state egoism or national selfishness is

---

[4] Of course, I am not denying that the granting of citizenship to immigrants can be, and often is, an extremely important matter, both for the admitting country and the applicants. My point is simply that its importance is not what it would be if, as the exclusionary patriot maintains, the granting of citizenship to a person were *at the same time* the recognition of that person as a moral subject.

[5] Stephen Nathanson, 'In Defense of "Moderate Patriotism"', *Ethics*, 99 (1989), 538, similarly rejects what he calls 'extreme patriotism', whose defining feature is its wholesale exclusion of non-compatriots from ethical concern.

not credible, since states—which are made up of individuals each of whom has obligations to consider others to some extent—must recognize that there are other states with interests similar to their own. So *wholesale renunciation of duties* to other states is not plausible. Brian Barry has asked some questions that reveal the weakness in exclusionary patriotism: 'Is there anything magical, after all, about one particular grouping— a nation-state—that can dissolve all wider moral considerations? Why should this one level of association be exempted from moral constraints that apply to all others?'[6] The realist might maintain that a state's concern for other states in an anarchic world is tantamount to irrationally leaving oneself open to exploitation by other states not naive enough to act in such an altruistic fashion.[7] But this claim is surely exaggerated, since concern for states other than one's own is compatible with the continued existence of one's state. Moreover, while we can debate just how much concern for other states is warranted, the realist claim (unless it is based on a wholesale moral scepticism) *does* in fact accept that non-compatriots count for something; the argument, as I understand it, is that the best way for every state to protect its own interests is to eschew concern for other states. But this line of reasoning is meant to apply to the leaders of *all* states, and it is unclear why one would offer such an argument if one thought those in other states were unworthy of any consideration.

Fortunately, a better conception of patriotism is available. According to this alternative view, patriots express their love of their country by showing greater care and concern for their country and compatriots than they do for other countries and non-compatriots, though the latter also count for something. By 'greater care and concern' here it is allowed that some concern should be shown to non-compatriots, but the level of concern will be less than that accorded to compatriots. The patriot, then, believes that, ethically speaking, 'compatriots take priority'.[8] I will call this view *compatriot favouritism* (or CF, for short). Now our question is whether there is a sense in which this sort of favouritism is ethically defensible.

---

[6] Brian Barry, 'Can States be Moral? International Morality and the Compliance Problem', in *Liberty and Justice: Essays in Political Theory*, ii (Oxford: Clarendon Press, 1991), 165.

[7] See Hans Morgenthau, *In Defense of the National Interest: A Critical Examination of American Foreign Policy* (New York: Alfred Knopf, 1951), 35–6. I am grateful to Simon Caney for pointing out this realist strategy to me.

[8] Henry Shue, *Basic Rights: Subsistence, Affluence, and U.S. Foreign Policy* (Princeton: Princeton University Press, 1980), 131–2. Shue is not himself a defender of compatriot favouritism.

One reason why we might think not is that, on the face of it at least, compatriot priority flies in the face of certain pervasive features of common-sense morality. For instance, it is commonly thought that adopting a moral perspective involves looking at any particular conflict of interests from a neutral position, and thereby exempting oneself from viewing matters from the particular perspective of any *one* of the parties to the conflict. The reason why this abstraction from any one viewpoint is considered to be justified is that it enables one to judge the dispute without favouring one party's interests over those of any other. In short, morality seems often to require *impartial* concern and the consequent non-accordance of priority to any particular individual or group. Consider, on the other hand, the vice known as bigotry, 'the groundless downgrading of some selected subset of humanity'.[9] Priority for one's compatriots can seem like the flip side of this coin: compatriot favouritists appear to *upgrade* groundlessly some selected subset of humanity. How can this be justified?

The challenge to cosmopolitanism that compatriot favouritism represents is to show, not that morality can apply beyond nation-state boundaries, but rather that these boundaries do not constitute a legitimate point at which to *decrease* somewhat the pull that generates a person's moral obligations. Cosmopolitans must, that is, give some account of the special ethical relationships compatriots are alleged to share. In doing so, they must aim to resolve the difficulty represented by the claim that some persons, those identified as compatriots, are due greater concern than others, a claim that on the face of it seems to contradict a root idea of cosmopolitanism and of much moral philosophy and common-sense moral thinking as well, namely, the idea that all persons are due equal moral consideration. Of course, the idea that compatriots take priority also has good common-sense credentials, so we cannot simply appeal to common sense to settle this dispute; we need to dig deeper.[10]

Let us be clear about what is at issue here. There is a contradiction, at least on the face of it, between:

[9] Samuel Gorovitz, 'Bigotry, Loyalty, and Malnutrition', in Peter G. Brown and Henry Shue (eds.), *Food Policy* (New York: The Free Press, 1977), 133.

[10] One might think that it is only the *patriot* who needs to give some account of the moral character of compatriot relationships. However, my view is that both sides have an interest in developing such an account, since there are strong conflicting intuitions both for and against impartial concern *and* compatriot priority. Moreover, in order to evaluate their own position, cosmopolitans need to discover whether patriotism has powerful moral credentials.

(i) a dominant moral tradition according to which each person is the moral equal of every other person and so merits equal consideration, and

(ii) the demands of patriotic commitment, which say that compatriots legitimately count for more than non-compatriots.

This conflict needs to be resolved, and there are several possible alternative resolutions. First, one could deny that morality requires impartial concern for each person. This is not a realistic option. Impartiality is an important moral value, since it requires us not to make an exception of ourselves when deliberating about what it is right to do. We should retain the idea that morality forbids deliberative processes that take account *only* of the subject of deliberation, or make that subject 'special' in such a way that general rules governing judgements about the acceptability of human behaviour do not apply to him. Moreover, when interests conflict, a stable resolution is not likely unless it is possible to abstract from one's own particular perspective and see the potential legitimacy of the interests of all sides to the dispute; but it is just this sort of abstraction that impartiality requires.[11] A second possible resolution would be to deny that compatriot favouritism is ethically acceptable. This is a real option, although it would mean rejecting a widely held belief. Thirdly, one could attempt a reconciliation of (i) and (ii), thereby holding out the possibility of retaining them both in some form. Defenders of this third option might effect this move by distinguishing different *levels* at which morality applies to our lives: at one level, preferential treatment can be justified, while at a second level we must take up a perspective of impartial consideration of competing interests. The trick is to show that one of these levels has moral primacy and that, from that level, taking up the supposedly conflicting attitude can be defended (though only at its proper level).[12] This resolution of the apparent conflict allows impartial concern to coexist with special ties to compatriots, within the limits imposed upon the actions those ties may legitimately generate. The most important such limits are that basic rights-violations are not permitted in the name of acts done in support of one's compatriots. It should be emphasized, however, that this reconciliation of compatriot favouritism

---

[11] Stephen Nathanson, *Patriotism, Morality, and Peace* (Lanham, Md.: Rowman and Littlefield, 1993), 67.

[12] Cf. Marcia Baron, 'Patriotism and "Liberal" Morality', in D. Weissbord (ed.), *Mind, Value and Culture* (Northridge, Calif.: Ridgeview, 1989), 269–300. I have also been influenced here by what is now the best discussion of the partiality/impartiality dispute: Brian Barry, *Justice as Impartiality* (Oxford: Clarendon Press, 1995), part iii.

with impartial concern shows only that the two are *compatible*, not that there are any independent reasons to be a compatriot favouritist in the first place. The third option, if successful, would have shown only that compatriot favouritism is consistent with the impartial concern required of conscientious moral agents; this is not to say that compatriot favouritism is independently plausible.

We can put the problem in the form of a set of claims, one of which must be rejected if the others are to be maintained.

1. The version of patriotism known as compatriot favouritism (CF) permits and often even requires persons to accord higher priority in their ethical deliberations and actions to the interests and needs of compatriots than to the similar interests and needs of non-compatriots.

2. Adopting a moral perspective involves abstracting from any particular individual's (or group's) interests, thereby viewing matters from an impartial standpoint.

3. From the impartial standpoint of morality, it is impermissible for the interests and needs of any one individual or group to be accorded any ground-level priority; each party is thereby shown equal consideration.

From these three claims it follows that CF permits or requires deliberation and action which is ruled out from the viewpoint of morality. The priority claim pressed in (1) is disallowed by (3) (which elaborates on (2)). Hence it looks as though we will have to give up either (1) or (3). We can call the present objection *the purported immorality of compatriot favouritism*. But is it an accurate portrayal of the options to say that we must choose between priority for compatriots on the one hand and commitment to morality on the other?

One thing seems certain: there is no across-the-board conflict between morality and special obligations. Some reason for admitting special ethical relationships into one's picture of an acceptable account of morality can be seen if we consider an objection one sort of impartialist might make to compatriot favouritism. This objection is a generalized version of the criticism we have been considering, since it questions compatriot favouritism by rejecting special duties as an entire class. This is the *special relationships objection*. The argument is that, since impartial moral concern requires equal consideration of everyone affected by an action or policy, special relationships that require unequal consideration, in the way of special concern for some people rather than others, are incompatible with morality.

With special reference to patriotism, the argument says that patriotism is immoral because, first, it consists essentially in a form of special concern for some circumscribed group of people and, secondly, such special concern for some others is inconsistent with a proper moral consideration of each person equally. This line of reasoning is ultimately unacceptable because its second premiss, although it is both relevant to and (along with the first premiss) sufficient to generate the desired conclusion, is, as stated, too strong and is therefore implausible. To accept the second premiss, we must believe that *no form of special concern for some particular person or group of people is ever morally justified*. This would require us to believe that the desires and actions constitutive of parent–child relationships, for instance, are in fact lacking any sound moral justification. While I will not here provide any extensive explanation of why such desires and actions are morally legitimate and indeed morally required, I can safely say that any theory that mandates their abolition is deeply flawed in some way. Compatriot favouritism might not be, in the end, an acceptable view, but the fact that it is an instance of the view that special consideration for some others is morally legitimate is not sufficient to show that it is a morally unacceptable view. In fact, the reality is quite the opposite. We tend to think that the special duties parents owe to children, for instance, are morally *required*, not merely permitted.[13] None the less, the patriotic version of special ties is not necessarily defensible simply in virtue of the plausibility of its familial analogue.

To see this last point more clearly, I will mention briefly one type of argument for special concern for compatriots that works by appealing to the meaning of the relation in question. Compatriot favouritism might be taken to be reasonable because the relationship co-citizens bear to one another necessarily involves special duties. I think this is an unsatisfactory way to defend special duties to compatriots, but it is important to see how the argument might proceed and where it goes wrong. Some special relationships are necessarily associated with particular obligations. As Samuel Gorovitz points out, '[t]o be a friend is to have certain obligations in regard to the object of one's friendship; to reject such obligations is to reject participation in that form of association known as friendship'.[14] To be a friend is to assume certain duties towards one's friend, and the rejection of such duties means that the relationship itself does not hold: these

---

[13] Nathanson, *Patriotism, Morality, and Peace*, 27.
[14] Gorovitz, 'Bigotry', 135.

obligations are definitive of the friendship relation. It would be implausible to say that A is a friend of B even though A would not 'put himself out' for B any more than A would for anyone else. Unfortunately for compatriot favouritism, the obligations of citizenship are importantly different from the obligations of friendship. The whole question of what is required of compatriots is debatable, and it has changed over the past few hundred years—where paying taxes for the funding of a substantial, national welfare state, for instance, is now usually thought to be acceptable where once it was not—to such an extent that we are unlikely to find any uncontroversial duties that are defining of the special relationship compatriots share. And even if there were widespread agreement in some contemporary state as to the content of those duties, that would legitimize those duties only if we accepted the implausible claim that people have obligations simply because they believe themselves to have them. Consequently, it seems that compatriot favouritism cannot be defended by reference to an appeal to what the compatriot relation definitionally requires.

In response to this last argument, we can say that what is required of friends and family members has likewise changed over time, though this does not show that friendship and family relationships are not, of necessity, forms of group favouritism. We can admit that there are different conceptions of citizenship, friendship and families, while consistently maintaining that *any* such conception will be a form of favouritism. This response is important, but it fails to show that compatriot favouritism is a *morally justified* version of special concern. This result is unsurprising, for we should not have expected the patriot's justificatory task to be performed successfully by simply appealing to a definition.

We should consider some of the other arguments relevant to the acceptability of patriotism. I take up this task in sections 5.4 and 5.5, but we should first consider the claim that compatriot favouritism will be fatally flawed if it cannot respond to the problem I have called *the purported immorality of compatriot favouritism*. In the next section I turn to a solution to this problem.

5.3. IS PATRIOTISM CONSISTENT WITH IMPARTIAL CONCERN?

Patriotic loyalty demands that persons deliberate in a partial manner, according moral priority to compatriots. But a dominant strand of common-sense moral concern demands that no one should specially privilege their own interests or those of people with whom they have special ties. We have seen that the rejection of special relationships as a class cannot be successful, but we have also noted that this does not necessarily help compatriot favouritism. If we take seriously *both* the particularist understanding of community co-member relationships *and* the universalist claim that everyone is morally entitled to treatment as an equal to anyone else, we are led to a contradiction. On the one hand, people are permitted, and sometimes required, to show special concern for their compatriots, but on the other hand, people are obligated to show equal concern for any person, regardless of the citizenship of either one. If this contradiction cannot be overcome, we will have to give up one of these claims, both of which have evident appeal. Fortunately, we can make a distinction that dissolves the supposed conflict and allows us to retain, in a suitably qualified form, both compatriot priority and impartial concern for all persons.

The resolution of the conflict is achieved in a manner described by Alasdair MacIntyre (though MacIntyre does not himself think the resolution is successful). MacIntyre says that 'patriotism and all other such particular loyalties can be restricted in their scope so that their exercise is always within the confines imposed by morality. Patriotism need be regarded as nothing more than a perfectly proper devotion to one's own nation which must never be allowed to violate the constraints set by the impersonal moral standpoint.'[15] The idea is that patriotic deliberation is often permissible or required; we can legitimately reason that we want to pay an extra tax to benefit our compatriots, or support a particular cause, even a war, against another country, but we must also be prepared to acknowledge that deliberation and action of this type is defensible for citizens of other countries in circumstances similar to our own. That is, from an impartial or impersonal second-order perspective, I must see that first-order thoughts such as 'This is *my* country!' can figure in the legitimate ethical thinking of any person. Defensible partiality, then, is partiality that anyone can admit is justifiable for anyone else to act upon. If it is all right for me to act from the reason that it is my country whose interests are at stake, then I must also believe that it is all right for non-compatriots to act for that very same reason with reference to *their* country, when circumstances are similar.

Distinguishing levels of moral deliberation, beginning with first-order thinking and adding the crucial perspective of second-order thinking about

[15] Alasdair MacIntyre, 'Is Patriotism a Virtue?', Lindley Lecture (Lawrence, Kan.: University of Kansas, 1984), 6.

the reasoning that goes on at the first-order level, dissolves the supposed incompatibility between patriotic special concern on the one hand and impartial consideration of the interests of all persons on the other.

One response to this argument is to deny that its acceptance of impartiality goes far enough: why not be a *first*-order impartialist? The short answer to this question is that first-order impartialism is a version of fanaticism, for it embodies a misunderstanding of the role impartial considerations should play in ethical deliberation and action.[16] In this context, it might be helpful to consider a classical discussion of this issue. I also include here my own contribution to this debate, namely, an example designed to show that compatriot favouritism is a clearly distinguishable species of the genus 'special ethical concern', and that its appeal cannot ride on the back of more intimate relationships between persons.

The classic case I have in mind is the *Godwinian fire dilemma*. William Godwin describes a scenario in which someone is confronted with the choice of saving only one of two people who are trapped in a burning building. One of these unfortunate individuals is an Archbishop, the other is the Archbishop's valet, who is perhaps 'a brother, father, or benefactor' of the person who must save one of the two people.[17] Godwin, the impartialist fanatic, opts for saving the person who is likely to produce more benefit for humankind; in this case it is presumed to be the Archbishop. Hence, according to Godwin, one should not save one's own father if one can produce more overall expected benefit by saving someone else. This is a version of first-order impartiality.

Godwin's position exemplifies a confusion about the role of impartiality in moral thinking. He correctly recognizes that the ultimate justification of moral principles must be carried out from a perspective that regards each person equally. Moral justification about basic principles must not allow a person's particular likes and dislikes any fundamental importance. However, Godwin mistakenly assumes that impartiality, understood as lack of special concern for any identifiable individual, is the way of life required of persons endeavouring to be morally upstanding. In short, the proper response to Godwin is to say that impartiality as a

---

[16] By using the word 'fanaticism' here I do not mean to engage in argumentative bullying. In the following paragraphs I go on to show why the word is justified in this case. That is, I think that first-order impartialists are overly enthusiastic about the admittedly important idea that the virtue of impartiality is central to a defensible account of morality, and their enthusiasm blinds them to the further distinctions it is necessary to make.

[17] William Godwin, *An Enquiry Concerning Political Justice and its Influence on Morals and Happiness*, 3rd edn., 1798, in *Political and Philosophical Writings of William Godwin*, ed. Mark Philp (London: William Pickering, 1993), iv. The attentive reader will recognize my debt to the discussion in Brian Barry, *Justice as Impartiality*, ch. 9.

necessary condition of legitimate reasoning about basic moral principles should be distinguished from impartiality as a way of life, and that the latter sense of impartiality is very unlikely to be defensible from the impartial deliberative point of view.[18]

Bernard Williams discusses another version of Godwin's problem, in which the choice is between saving one's wife and saving a stranger, both of whom will drown if nothing is done.[19] Abstracting from Godwin's utilitarianism, it seems clear that first-order impartialism would require that one cannot appeal to any ground-level reason for favouring one person over the other. Williams believes not only that the impartialist conclusion is incorrect, but that the whole idea that there is a need for a general, reasoned justification for saving one's wife is mistaken. My view is that both Godwin and Williams reason incorrectly.[20] Godwin is wrong because, though he rightly acknowledges the value of impartial concern, he applies his particular brand of utilitarian reasoning to each individual's particular context of action,[21] and he conflates two distinct senses in which impartiality is an option for us. As we have seen, partiality in such contexts is consistent with an overall commitment to impartial consideration of the equal claims of all persons. Williams, on the other hand, is wrong because he thinks there is no scope for reason-giving in contexts like the fire dilemma and the drowning spouse predicament. I think he is correct to say that it is obvious that a man should save his wife rather than a stranger—even an important stranger whose utility-producing potential is judged to be quite high (and much higher than his wife's potential in this regard)—however, I also believe, contrary to Williams, that it is necessary to understand that 'in situations of this kind it is permissible to save one's wife'.[22] The fact that one does not offer such a

---

[18] See Thomas E. Hill, Jr., 'The Importance of Autonomy', in Eva Feder Kittay and Diana T. Meyers (eds.), *Women and Moral Theory* (Lanham, Md.: Rowman and Littlefield, 1987), 129–38, at 131–3. As Hill says, the idea that 'we should live with our eyes fixed on abstract, impartial principles seems quite the opposite of what autonomous [i.e. impartial] moral legislators would recommend' (p. 132).

[19] Bernard Williams, 'Persons, Character, and Morality', in *Moral Luck: Philosophical Papers 1973–80* (Cambridge: Cambridge University Press, 1981), 1–19.

[20] I should make it clear that I disagree with Andrew Belsey, 'World Poverty, Justice, and Equality', in Robin Attfield and Barry Wilkins (eds.), *International Justice and the Third World: Studies in the Philosophy of Development* (London: Routledge, 1992), 40–2, who thinks that favouring one's wife in this case is necessarily a veiled form of selfishness.

[21] See Barry, *Justice as Impartiality*, 219.

[22] Williams, 'Persons, Character, and Morality', 18. Just for the record, I think it is probably a moral requirement of a husband in such a case to save his wife (or for a wife to save her husband). My substantive conclusion would then differ from both Godwin (who says wife-saving is in this case forbidden) and Williams (who says wife-saving is in this case merely permitted).

justification before acting does not mean that it does not make sense to think that there are good reasons for so acting. After all, if we could give no reason at all, even in a cool hour sometime after the fact, would we not have grounds for suspicion about the ethical status of the act?[23]

We can of course offer some very good reasons why 'partner-saving'— i.e. wife-saving, husband-saving, long-term co-habitator-saving—is justified in fire dilemma cases. Sincere and committed participation in these sorts of close relationships fosters other virtues in a person, such as honesty and concern for another person's general well-being. This sort of concern may even be a necessary condition for having the capacity to sympathize with the suffering of people in faraway places. If these are the relations through which we become moral beings, we can hardly deny the moral obligations they involve. Intimacy is important in the living of a meaningful life, and it generates a need—as a means to ensuring that intimacy retains its authenticity—for dispositions to act in certain ways in particular contexts: the fire dilemma case is one such context; in fact, we can now see that if we take seriously the importance of intimate relationships, there is no dilemma after all. One should regret that both persons cannot be saved, but this does not entail that there is not a correct answer to the question of which one *should* be saved.

There is an interesting point to be made about compatriot favouritism in connection with the Godwinian fire dilemma. Imagine a similar case, with a burning building and two helpless individuals, only one of whom one can save. But now imagine that one is a compatriot and the other is a non-compatriot. Whom should you save? I think that one thing that becomes obvious as soon as one thinks about this sort of example is that any conclusion one might reach is *very much* less obvious than in the standard Godwin–Williams example, in which one of the potential rescuees is a father, mother, or wife. At least with respect to the conclusions reached in the traditional case, Godwin is obviously incorrect and Williams is just as obviously correct (although he gives an unsatisfying account of the reasons for his choice). In the compatriot dilemma case, on the other hand, one could perhaps think of reasons for saving

---

[23] Perhaps Williams would agree that calm, reasoned justification is indeed necessary, in which case I have no quarrel with him. The problem of interpretation here stems from a fundamental lack of clarity as to whether or not reasons are thought to be necessary in the decision-making situation itself *and/or* in the relative calm of one's study, when one is considering what it would be right to do if one were faced with such an unpalatable choice. I am here interpreting Williams as saying that reasons are unnecessary in either case. Thus interpreted, Williams and I disagree.

one's compatriot before saving the non-citizen, but those reasons would not come anywhere near securing widespread agreement for their proposed recommendation for action. The simple yet vital point is that the traditional case and the compatriot case would not appeal to similar reasons, since the most important grounds for preferential treatment for one's partner are the intimacy of this relationship and the importance of intimacy in living a meaningful life. But, of course, intimacy and its justificatory power cannot be wielded on behalf of compatriot-saving, for most compatriots are strangers to us, just as most foreigners are as well. The fact that compatriots are slightly less 'strange' strangers hardly counts as a powerful reason, certainly not in the way intimacy counted in the traditional case. If intimacy is indeed part of the best supporting argument for partiality towards loved ones, then compatriot favouritism must appeal to different sorts of reasons from those appealed to in the cases of friends and family: intimacy can ground obligations only towards intimates, not towards people one has never even met.

There are two upshots of this discussion. The first, general one is that first-order impartiality is not a reasonable view. The second is that compatriot priority cannot be justified in the same straightforward way that we justify priority for intimates. The latter conclusion in turn suggests that we should look for other reasons for adhering to compatriot favouritism.

5.4. COMPATRIOT FAVOURITISM: FURTHER CLARIFICATION

I have just said that compatriot favouritism (CF) cannot be defended in precisely the same way that we justify favouritism for, say, our children or parents. But the defence of compatriot priority can be *structurally* the same as the defence of familial priority; this is because, as we have seen, both are forms of ethical particularism and there is no *general* reason for eschewing ethical particularism. There is no general objection to ethical particularism, understood as special ethical commitment to some person(s) rather than others, because *some* forms of particularism can be universalized. It is perfectly acceptable to show special concern for one's own children, but one must admit that others are justified in showing such concern for *their* children and that they need not show the same interest in your children as you do. Notwithstanding the structural similarity between different species of particularism, we still need to discover some more positive considerations in support of compatriot favouritism, along with the main objections to which it is subject. Sections 5.4 and 5.5 set out on this path of discovery. First we should say something more about the form taken by compatriot favouritism, my label for the form of patriotism that might turn out to be defensible.

As we have seen, CF says that people are justified in showing greater concern for compatriots than they do for non-compatriots, though non-compatriots must also be subjects of moral consideration. And we have shown that such a view can be consistent with a defensible overall account of morality. One feature of any plausible account of CF is especially important to mention: defenders of CF agree that no person should be accorded any *ground-level priority* over any other or others.[24] That is, CF does not accord ground-level priority to any person or group of persons. Rather, it accepts that each person is ultimately on a moral par with every other. But it urges us to take account of the implications for our ethical obligations of the existence of certain public institutions in which we participate with a limited number of others (i.e. our compatriots). Some compatriot favouritists might point out that ground-level moral equality does not rule out superstructural special concern grounded in the conduct of some but not others. This point is akin to the general claim that *what people do* affects how they should be treated.

It is crucial to note, however, that the CF version of the 'conduct affects proper treatment' claim does not justify special treatment for compatriots. One argument in defence of CF might say that the fact of sharing a commitment to a set of mutually beneficial institutions can render special concern for other, similarly committed persons legitimate. But this argument has several problems. First, it looks as though its defender would respond to an 'outsider's' claim to 'our' resources or 'our' concern by pointing out that it is only *insiders* (i.e. fellow citizens) who have contributed to the institutions in question and to the production of benefits those institutions have spawned. This may or may not be true empirically, and if it turns out to be false—say, where a country's GNP has been substantially enhanced by the contribution of foreign labour— compatriot favouritism lacks a defence. Moreover, even if we accept that it is only the citizens of a specific country who share the wealth they create by contributing to a public framework for generating co-citizen benefits, some of those citizens will not have contributed to the production of those benefits. Most interestingly, this will be true of the severely

---

[24] See section 5.2, the third of my three mutually incompatible points.

disabled citizens who none the less are usually thought to have a legitimate claim to help from compatriots. Yet the compatriot priority thesis itself
would seem to provide no grounds for excluding non-contributors and
explicit reason for *including* them. After all, handicapped compatriots
are still compatriots. What we can call the *contribution requirement*—
the demand that only those who have contributed to the production of
general benefits have a claim on those benefits—is therefore not the key
to understanding who does and who does not merit help from a set of
public institutions.[25] The second difficulty with this argument is the general oddity of its strategy for grounding special duties. If persons A and
B enter into some group and gain the benefits of co-membership, while
C lacks these benefits because he was not included in that group, why
should A and B get not only the advantages of membership but also the
additional benefit of having stronger claims on one another's services
than C has on the services of either one of them?[26] One might think that
if people derive advantages from belonging to some collectivity, their
obligations to those excluded from membership without their consent
would be *greater* than their obligations to co-members, since exclusion
can lead to increased vulnerability. In so far as the argument for compatriot favouritism depends on something like the contribution requirement, it provides no justification for special obligations.

Another important feature of compatriot favouritism is its *conditionality* upon the characteristics of the state in question.[27] It can never
be true that someone rightly has special obligations to his compatriots
simply because both he and they share a common citizenship. Consider
the implications of denying this claim. Someone who held that shared
citizenship is alone sufficient to generate ethical priority for another person would have to accept that German citizens during the Nazi era had
a moral duty to look out for the interests of, say, high-ranking Nazis—
i.e. fellow citizens of Germany—before considering the plight of the
non-German victims of Nazi oppression. I assume, on the contrary, that
the opposite is in fact the case: a morally upstanding German citizen
would have had a duty to concern himself with the safety and rights of
the victims, even when those victims were non-compatriots.

---

[25] We have already seen that this sort of requirement is not plausible as a general basis
for inclusion within the ambit of distributive justice itself. See Ch. 1, where 'subject-
centred justice' is favoured over its more tough-minded alternatives.
[26] This point has been emphasized by Samuel Scheffler in 'Families, Nations and
Strangers', Lindley Lecture 1994 (Lawrence, Kan.: University of Kansas, 1995), 9–12.
[27] Nathanson, *Patriotism, Morality, and Peace*, 118–19.

To summarize, we have noted the following features of compatriot favouritism:

1. *Special Concern*: CF supports special concern for compatriots as against non-compatriots.
2. *Consistency with Impartiality*: This special concern need not violate the impartialist demands of morality.
3. *Ground-Level Equality and Superstructural Inequality*: CF accepts the claim that each person is due equal moral consideration, regardless of citizenship. It urges, however, that this ground-level ethical equality does not rule out differential treatment of persons, treatment based, perhaps, on the actions people perform as members of collectivities (most importantly, the state of which they are citizens).
4. *Conditionality*: The acceptability of CF is *conditional* upon the characteristics of the state in question. There is no such thing as a compatriot favouritist attitude that is justified independently of any information about the ethical character of the state concerned.

Apart from noting these elements of CF, we have also rejected an argument in its favour. Our criticism of that argument brought out the problems for CF generated by the third point mentioned immediately above. That is, on the one hand, compatriots *and non-compatriots* contribute to the well-being of the citizens of, say, the United States, so where contribution counts there is no argument for limiting obligations to compatriots; and on the other hand, some compatriots do not contribute to the well-being of their fellows, yet we think it is right to show concern for them regardless of their inaction.[28]

Having thus clarified the main features of CF, we should further pursue the arguments on both sides.

5.5. COMPATRIOT FAVOURITISM:
FOR AND AGAINST

We have seen that compatriot favouritism can take some account of the interests of those outside one's borders, and that although there is no *general* impartialist reason against special relations, nevertheless this does not show that *all* special relations are justified. More needs to be said

---

[28] I am referring here, of course, to the handicapped to whom we correctly think we owe a duty of justice. I do not intend to defend the behaviour of free-riders who are able to contribute but choose not to do so.

about arguments for and against compatriot favouritism. That is the purpose of this section.[29]

One point merits repeating here. Patriotism is not a general duty of persons, since patriotic loyalty should not be directed towards one's country unless there are certain characteristics present in an accurate description of that country that give rise to legitimate loyalty. 'My-ness' is a necessary but not a sufficient condition for a justified patriotism. (It is a necessary condition because it is impossible for someone to have a patriotic attitude toward some country which is not her own.) Commitment to a non-aggressive foreign policy, or to protection of the natural environment, might be relevant loyalty-generating characteristics. I should add that there is no definite set of features the presence of which guarantees that patriotic loyalty will be legitimate. Rather, some qualities will count toward considering a country as a proper object of loyalty, and other qualities will count against doing so, but many features will simply call for particular actions (on the part of patriots) aimed either at reinforcing those features or at ending one's country's commitment to them. Hence the particularity of patriotic loyalty is conditioned by the need for any *virtuous* patriotism to include the citation of some admirable characteristics which add some credibility to the (always elliptical) claim that 'I should be loyal because it is *my* country.'

There is one central reason, then, why compatriot favouritism might be desirable from an ethical point of view: one's country could have admirable characteristics that call forth support from its members. If loyalty to one's country is, in part, dependent upon an appreciation of the features of the country that make it worthy of one's devotion, then the need for individuals to support valuable collectivities will go some way toward justifying love of one's own country over others. Note again, however, that patriotic loyalty is on this view *conditional* upon one's country possessing features that themselves either permit or require persons to take up the position of loyal supporter. And conditionality does not merely weaken the potential grip of patriotism, it also threatens to support *anti-patriotism*. If a citizen of country A should show special concern for country A because it exemplifies certain virtues in its everyday practice, then a citizen of country B—a country more vicious than virtuous, or a country whose virtues pale in comparison to those of country A—should not be a compatriot favouritist. On the contrary, citizens

---

[29] A related strategy is pursued in Ch. 8 below, where I consider some prominent attempts to show that significant implications follow from the view that states are valid associations.

of country B should show special concern for country A and therefore ought to be non-compatriot favouritists! Consequently, what appeared to be a strong reason for adhering to CF turns out on examination to provide a reason for pledging allegiance only to the country (or countries) that pass some more objective ethical test; so there can be no general defence of CF grounded on this argument.

Good reasons for acknowledging the ethical importance of close bonds with one's community are not hard to find, however. And these reasons could provide some defence of compatriot favouritism in a specific instance. Individuals gain a sense of themselves only in the context of their particular communities. Each of us probably needs to feel that we belong somewhere, and to participate to some degree in a culture. Being 'at home' in a culture and a society provides us with some of the elements necessary for living a meaningful human life, and it seems inevitable that persons who develop cognitively, socially, and emotionally in a certain social and cultural context will come to regard the distinctive aspects of that context—of their country—with special affection. To the extent that one's culture is enabled to thrive by state support, one would have good reason to show special concern for one's state.

Further insight into the grounds for compatriot favouritism can be gained by attempting to answer the following question: why should we care more for some people than we do for others? One plausible answer is that some people are especially vulnerable to us and our actions. It is this vulnerability which explains why special duties are properly assigned in one way rather than another by an adequate moral theory.[30] The problem for compatriot priority, as it relates to this argument, is that many foreigners are highly vulnerable to our actions, perhaps more vulnerable than our compatriots are. In that case, of course, the vulnerability argument recommends favouring non-compatriots over compatriots. This sort of argument is different from one in which co-membership *itself* justifies special obligations. Here, rather, it is the supposed *correlation* between citizenship and some other, morally relevant characteristic (i.e. vulnerability) that justifies compatriot priority. If that correlation fails—as, it is claimed, it does when non-citizens are more vulnerable to our actions than citizens are—the argument's conclusion is that (as long as the vulnerability relation remains as it is) non-compatriots take

---

[30] Robert E. Goodin, *Protecting the Vulnerable: A Reanalysis of Our Social Responsibilities* (Chicago: University of Chicago Press, 1985) develops the vulnerability model at some length. However, he thinks it provides support for compatriot favouritism only within certain limits.

priority. Therefore, even if we accept the vulnerability model of special obligations, that model provides no general rationale for compatriot favouritism. Where there is in fact a high correlation between vulnerability and co-citizenship, this model would support CF, but we would still have no reason for supposing that CF is, in general, a plausible account of our ethical responsibilities in this regard. All that would follow would be the wisdom of discovering degrees of vulnerability; and even where we find the aforementioned correlation, it is the vulnerability and not the shared citizenship that is doing the moral work of generating duties. Compatriot favouritism would be an alternative way to describe what we should call, more accurately, special concern for the vulnerable. And shared citizenship would be a decidedly secondary part of any satisfactory moral explanation, i.e. an explanation of why persons have the moral obligations they are properly said to have.

With regard to this discussion about vulnerability, there arises an interesting and important point about the proper focus of a citizen's concern: if one's own state can, by its actions, significantly affect the well-being of non-compatriots, then, as a citizen who accepts the vulnerability criterion, one should take the most effective means to ensuring that those persons are not made to suffer. In democratic states, it follows that citizens should especially concern themselves with the *policies* of their own government wherever those policies impinge upon foreigners, since one's goal (to protect those vulnerable to one) is best promoted by focusing one's energies in those places where they are likely to have the most significant effect. But this special concern for the policies of one's own country is not to be confused with partiality in favour of the *individuals* who are one's compatriots. Again, the ethical work here is being done by the vulnerability of persons to the actions of one's government, and if one accepts the moral importance of the vulnerability relation, uncontroversial considerations of rationality dictate that one should concern oneself with the policies of one's own state. This concern is, however, only a means to protecting the vulnerable.

Let us now turn to some other considerations relevant to judging the acceptability of compatriot favouritism. Foremost among these considerations is the claim that individuals maintain various degrees of allegiance and loyalty to numerous, often rival communities.[31] This simple point is potentially devastating to compatriot favouritism because it might

---

[31] This is pointed out by, among others, Shue, *Basic Rights*, 137–8, and George P. Fletcher, *Loyalty: An Essay on the Morality of Relationships* (Oxford: Oxford University Press, 1993), 58.

turn out on examination that some community or communities other than one's country take ethical precedence in many important contexts, thereby relegating compatriot favouritism to a secondary status. People are loyal to fellow members of religions, races, and ethnic groups, for instance, and nothing has yet been said to support compatriot priority in cases where it conflicts with allegiances to any of these groups. Why should moral significance be accorded to the borders of nation-states when doing so would override loyalties to one or more of these collectivities? We know why co-religionists feel attachments to one another: they share beliefs about fundamentally important aspects of human existence such as the origin and meaning of life; consequently, they naturally feel a bond with others who share such deep commitments (regardless of the truth of their shared beliefs or the ultimate rationality of those commitments). Since compatriots do not necessarily share beliefs and commitments in this way, it is unclear why anyone should favour compatriots over co-religionists when it is necessary to make a choice between one group and the other.

We can call this *the problem of conflicting loyalties*. It is the problem of determining the ethical implications of the fact that people have deep attachments to more than one group—for instance, someone could consider herself both a Jew and a Canadian. We can imagine circumstances in which loyalty to one of these groups requires action that would violate a requirement recognized by that same person in her capacity as a loyal member of the other group. The dilemma, then, concerns deciding which way to turn. This sort of problem shows—what many would take to be evident in any case—that nation-sates are not obviously the supreme objects of loyalty in the modern world. The upshot of this point for international justice is as follows. The restriction of duties of justice most often recommended in current discussions is a restriction of concern to compatriots, i.e. *fellow members of one's state*. But if state membership lacks sufficient ethical pull in many contexts to override attachments to a religious group or intra-state national community, then it is unclear why citizenship should be the proper feature for determining the obligations of justice. Even if there are grounds for limiting concern to some group, why should that group be the citizens of one's state? Since there are various individuals and groups toward which we can show legitimate devotion, prioritizing one's country becomes an unrealistic demand, especially in cases of conflicts of loyalty.

In the context of severe global deprivation and poverty, we need to understand what could provide a reason for thinking that one's

compatriots are the group toward which one should recognize the strongest
moral obligations. We have seen that family ties and the bonds of friendship, each of which are constituted by legitimate special responsibilities,
are grounded in the importance of intimacy or depth of participation in
close-knit relationships. Are compatriot relations analogous to these?
Another potential foundation for heightened concern for compatriots is
the presence of community-wide attachment to a set of values or principles. Sharing a commitment to principles with one's compatriots might
constitute a reason for caring more for other adherents to these principles than one does for non-adherents.[32]

These two possible grounds advanced for moral priority are, first, intimacy and deep personal involvement, and secondly, agreement about basic
principles or values. The first sort of ground may be priority-generating,
as in the case where we say that spouses can with justification show
deeper ethical concern for one another than they do for those with whom
they are unacquainted. But, as we have seen, this is not likely to provide
much support for *compatriot* priority, since people are not, nor could they
be, intimate with all of their fellow countrymen and countrywomen.
Even if intimacy and depth of involvement generate special obligations,
this is no help to the compatriot favouritist.

The second kind of reason for priority, i.e. co-membership in a 'community of principle', is similarly unlikely to correlate with co-membership
in a nation-state. The reason for this is—as is all too clear—compatriots
are often deeply divided on questions of devotion to basic principles,
values, and goals. This is, of course, one reason why liberals recommend that peaceful and stable political arrangements should not require
that everyone be committed to the same basic values or 'conceptions of
the good'. Public order itself perhaps demands that proposed solutions
to disputes about such large issues should not be made matters of government policy. But it is not only that there is disagreement between
compatriots about moral and political principles, there are also fundamental principles attachment to which people share with foreigners but
not with compatriots. Nation-states are certainly not, in general, communities of principle in any sense that would exclude outsiders from the
special duties owed to co-adherents to a given set of principles. It might
be objected that everyone in a liberal society must share a commitment
to the society's principles of *justice*, if not to some unified account of the

---

[32] These potential foundations for compatriot priority are discussed by Henry Shue in
Basic Rights, 135.

good life for human beings. The answer to this charge is that citizens need only *act* in conformity with those principles, they need not *believe* them to be true.

5.6. PATRIOTISM AND GLOBAL JUSTICE

We have failed to find any cogent arguments in support of compatriot favouritism. CF is not necessarily an immoral doctrine, for its particularism does not itself render it guilty of any violation of morality; however, CF is just as clearly lacking any general, defensible rationale. We should be open to other arguments, of course, but so far we are right to reject it. Having said this, I now want to suppose for the sake of argument that compatriot favouritism is justified. On this basis we can assess the relationship between patriotism thus conceived and the conclusions about global distributive justice reached in Part I of this book. Even if we are correct to remain sceptical about the strength of claims for patriotic loyalty, I will here suppose that patriotism can be a virtue and assess the implications of accepting this claim for the questions of international distributive justice. This strategy has the additional virtue of permitting us to evaluate the arguments of some prominent compatriot favouritists, so we will be able to continue to look for reasons to accept that widely held but weakly defended doctrine.

The main claim I want to emphasize is that no defensible form of patriotism justifies denying the basic human rights of persons. It can be morally permissible, even required, that one be patriotic and loyal to one's country, but such permissions and requirements can never override the demands of impartial justice. I propose in this section to assess attempts on the part of some compatriot favouritists to show that *justice* is not the sort of virtue that can properly extend beyond one's compatriots. These attempts, by Alasdair MacIntyre, George P. Fletcher, Daniel Bell, and Richard Rorty, constitute explicit denials of the central positive claims I have made.

Alasdair MacIntyre and Inter-Community Conflict
Over Scarce Resources

Alasdair MacIntyre offers an argument against the very possibility of maintaining both (i) commitment to one's country, and (ii) commitment to principles of impartiality. This is a radical criticism in so far as it says that even a limited compatriot favouritism is not possible so long as one acknowledges the impartial perspective. MacIntyre claims that so-called patriots who at the same time accept 'liberal impersonal morality' would show their lack of true patriotism when faced with certain kinds of difficult choices. Interestingly, for our purposes, MacIntyre gives an example of a dispute between two communities over the use of scarce and vital natural resources.

Imagine two communities, both requiring the same essential resources for their survival or flourishing as a community. According to MacIntyre, each community should strive to further its own interests in this matter, and in fact, 'patriotism entails a willingness to go to war on one's community's behalf'.[33] Someone who acknowledges the claims of impartial morality, on the other hand, will not be able simply to opt for his own community when faced with this sort of conflict. In violation of patriotic loyalty, he will choose 'an allocation of goods such that each individual person counts for one and no more than one'.[34] We can see, then, that MacIntyre's patriotism denies the basic moral idea that each person counts equally from a moral point of view. But it is implausible to hold, as MacIntyre does, that *no* account needs to be taken of the interests of persons in the community whose interests conflict with one's own. We have distinguished between compatriot favouritism and exclusionary patriotism, but MacIntyre's patriot seems to be of the exclusionary variety. Moreover, even if one adopts the compatriot favouritist standpoint, why should it follow that one's community is not required to settle this sort of dispute through an impartial negotiating process? MacIntyre seems to see no merit in arriving at a settlement that satisfies both communities, but he gives us no reason to agree with him on this point. This is especially troubling since compatriot favouritism, if it is at all defensible, permits special concern for compatriots only with respect to *some* of their interests; it does not necessitate total denial of the basic human rights claims of outsiders. Cosmopolitan arguments have been adduced in support of the importance of basic human rights, but MacIntyre's account offers no grounds for overturning the prima facie case we have made in Part I, apart from his claim that patriots cannot take up the impersonal perspective of morality. This last claim, however, is patently false.

MacIntyre commits the notorious fallacy of incomplete disjunction. He offers us only two alternatives, but he ignores a third option which

---

[33] MacIntyre, 'Is Patriotism a Virtue?', 6.   [34] Ibid.

is not only available but is in fact correct. He assumes that persons devoted to their country, that is, committed patriots, cannot take up a detached perspective from which the claims of conflicting parties can be adjudicated.[35] Hence MacIntyre's scenario presents us with a stark choice: *either* we can support our country in its struggle with another country over control of resources *or* we can detach ourselves from the perspective of a patriot, thereby exposing our true lack of commitment to our country. It follows, according to MacIntyre, that someone who opts for the second alternative—the alternative favoured by anyone who acknowledges the claims of compatriots *and* of non-compatriots—is not a true patriot. But there is a third alternative: patriots can be specially concerned with their fellow countrymen while at the same time recognizing that other communities have the very same need for the particular scarce resources in question. MacIntyre might object that his patriot can do this; it is simply that he attaches no moral weight to the needs of others. But nothing in MacIntyre's argument shows that recognizing the legitimacy of the claims of non-compatriots is impossible, nor that it is unjustified. Of course, this does not settle the difficult question of what to do when any distribution of resources will leave some people with their basic needs unsatisfied. But MacIntyre's position precludes our asking this hard question, since the dilemma it proposes does not arise for his patriots. An even greater worry here is that the general tenor of MacIntyre's position seems explicitly to deny that patriotic loyalty can itself be wrong in cases where one's country is committed to evidently immoral ends.

The upshot of this brief discussion is to re-emphasize what we have seen earlier. First, exclusionary patriotism is indefensible. Secondly, it is possible for patriots to assume an impartial perspective, especially when faced with conflicts of interest. If this were not possible, such conflicts would be settled by force alone.[36] But there is no need to equate concern for one's compatriots with support for muscle-flexing. Indeed, one benefit of compatriot favouritism (as identified by the third alternative above; and, of course, assuming it can be defended on other grounds) is that it holds out the hope of resolving conflicts by a process of discussion in which all interlocutors show consideration for one another.

---

[35] See Nathanson, *Patriotism, Morality, and Peace*, 82.

[36] Of course, self-interest may dictate peace, but only where the state with whom one's own state's interests conflict is strong enough to withstand attack and to inflict damage on one's own state.

George Fletcher, Patriotic Loyalty, and Justice

Is cosmopolitan justice in the end a credible doctrine? One good reason for trying to understand the pros and cons of compatriot favouritism is that some of its defenders have offered arguments to show that cosmopolitans are fundamentally mistaken in various ways. George P. Fletcher, for instance, cautions that '[i]t might be an ideal to extend our loyalty to everyone on the planet, but nourishing utopian visions about faraway places sometimes makes people indifferent to the real suffering next door'.[37] Cosmopolitans can make two responses to these claims. The first has to do with the possible objects of loyalty implicit in them. The second concerns the assertion about the neglect of local suffering that it is claimed will follow (sometimes) from the adoption of a more expansive view.

First, then, the point about loyalty itself: perhaps loyalty is the sort of commitment that loses its proper sense when faced with very large numbers of people.[38] So it might indeed be utopian to recommend that each of us should feel a sense of *loyalty* to everyone else, including those in 'faraway places'. But, then, the cosmopolitan is not claiming that we should be *loyal* to the group of all human beings. He is, rather, committed to acknowledging the equal claims of all persons on everyone else, *despite* the fact that we experience a sense of loyalty to less inclusive groups. The point the cosmopolitan is trying to emphasize here is that, even though the demands of loyalty cannot and should not be denied with respect to many of the claims we make on one another, there are some claims—most notably, claims to the protection of one's vital interests—the *content* of which renders them immune to the (partly countervailing) ethical pull created by group loyalty. What we might call 'Basic Interest Immunity' protects persons in other countries from the otherwise justifiable claims of patriotic loyalty that compatriots make on one another: the basic interests of badly off individuals in country A cannot be subject to dismissal by an argument from a relatively well-off citizen of country B that appeals only to the value of compatriot relations.

Fletcher suggests that we should think of the patriot-versus-impartialist dispute as one of conflicting loyalties, where we must choose between the undeniable attachments of the 'historical self' to his compatriots, on the one hand, and, on the other hand, the utopian ideal of 'loyalty

---

[37] Fletcher, *Loyalty*, 20.

[38] On the other hand, imagine how plausible a commitment of 'loyalty to everyone on the planet' might look as a response to an invasion of the earth by strange and violent extraterrestrials!

to everyone on the planet'. My point, in response to Fletcher, is that the issue is *not* one of deciding which of these two potential objects of loyalty has more compelling ethical credentials. Instead, the cosmopolitan impartialist should grant that loyalty is a virtue, when it is so, *only* for circumscribed groups, but refuse to conclude on that basis that the vital interests of some persons should count for less simply because they do not belong to the favoured group.

My second response is as follows. As a reason against extending ethical commitment to all persons, regardless of citizenship, Fletcher says that doing so 'sometimes makes people indifferent to the real suffering next door'. Is Fletcher claiming that my concern for the plight of people in East Timor and Lebanon somehow could lead to my failing to care about those forced to sleep on the streets of London (i.e. those close to home)? I suspect that whether this claim is true depends on what the *grounds* are for my caring about how people's lives are going; and if those grounds turn out to be a concern for the protection of persons' vital interests, then I ought to care about deprivation and suffering wherever it exists; and if some people, in their zeal for the struggle against faraway injustice, lose sight of the importance of nearby suffering, it should be clear that the theory outlined in Part I of this book provides no grounds for doing so.[39]

Fletcher's attack on cosmopolitan justice also includes a claim about the connection between justice and loyalty: 'Loyalty is a critical element in a theory of justice; for we invariably need some basis for group cohesion, for caring about others, for seeing them not as strangers who threaten our security but as partners in a common venture.'[40] This seems to me to set up a false dichotomy between: (*a*) thinking of others as 'partners' or fellow group members, and (*b*) thinking of these others as 'strangers who threaten our security'. According to this view, other people are either part of my group, and hence the proper objects of my concern and devotion, or they are potential threats to the satisfaction of my interests as a 'private self-seeking' member of a 'consumer society'.[41] Reality, however, is more complicated than Fletcher makes it out to be. My compatriots are, after all, mostly strangers to me, but I can regard them as partners in a common project none the less. Hence, in fact, most

---

[39] In Ch. 6, I address a related point made by David Miller, on the question of the relation between fulfilling duties at home and fulfilling similar duties to outsiders. As I point out there, the Scandinavian countries show more concern for fellow citizens *and* give far more international aid than other countries.

[40] Fletcher, *Loyalty*, 21.   [41] Ibid.

of my national 'partners' are strangers, in which case we have a third alternative not identified in (*a*) or (*b*) above, namely: (*c*) thinking of others as strangers with whom I am embarked on a joint venture in so far as we all register our allegiance to a set of institutions embodying reasonable principles of distributive justice.

Moreover, many other strangers are, of course, not participants in the common venture I share with my compatriots, and yet this other set of strangers can hardly be said to threaten my security, especially if 'me' in this context refers to a citizen of a relatively rich country. If anything, it is I—or at least my government—who constitutes a threat to the security of deprived persons in the poor nations. It is therefore incorrect to claim that, 'when we take people as they are', we need patriotic loyalty if we are to avoid being engulfed by self-centredness and mistrust. There is another alternative: we can combine a concern for one's own country with a commitment to helping those in need, regardless of citizenship.

But Fletcher continues to pursue his anti-cosmopolitan point. He adds: 'There is no easy response to the idealist who insists that all five billion people constitute one community, with one cause. The answer must begin with an understanding of how we as human beings are constituted and what our natural limits of sympathy may be.'[42] Three points in reply to Fletcher suggest themselves here. First, Fletcher sets up a straw man when he says that his opponents see all human beings as pursuing one cause. Secondly, once this first point is recognized, it is clear that we need not choose between (i) commitment to one cause for all persons, and (ii) acceptance of patriotic loyalty, with its consquently weakened moral ties to foreigners. Thirdly, if the implication of Fletcher's remarks about the natural limitations of our capacity to feel sympathy for others is supposed to be relevant to a theory of international justice, then the proper reply is that, as human beings, we cannot (nor should we) feel the same sort of sympathy for every other person that we feel for those with special ties to us. If we did, we could scarcely go through life without constantly experiencing depression due to our awareness of the massive suffering our fellow human beings constantly endure. But the limits of human sympathy are not as Fletcher describes them, nor is the capacity for sympathy as straightforwardly relevant to global justice as might be thought. Many of us *are* capable of showing sympathetic concern for the suffering of other human beings, say, when they lack adequate food and water and physical security. We have a natural capacity to recognize

---

[42] Ibid.

that, if things had been different in various ways, we might have been the ones who suffered, and the fact that none of us can feel sympathy in precisely the same way for every person whose plight is potentially sympathy-generating is entirely beside the point. What matters is only whether or not we can recognize that deprivation exists, and that we can understand arguments aimed at showing us that such deprivation calls for action designed to eradicate it.

Let me go over in more detail the three points mentioned in the last paragraph. It is indeed idealistic to maintain that the entire human population of the planet constitutes 'one community, with one cause'. It is an idealistic belief, but at any rate, there is nothing immediately mistaken about being idealistic. Some theorists would take the idealism of this view to be a point in its favour. More importantly, however, it is also pretty clearly false. In any case, cosmopolitans need not believe that there is one cause that all human beings pursue in common.

Does anyone seriously maintain that all persons constitute one community, *with one cause*? Certainly liberals do not need to maintain any such thing, for one of the most prominent problems motivating research in liberal political theory is the realization that people pursue different and conflicting causes, and a popular solution to this plurality of causes is to maintain that governments should be so constructed that such pursuits can remain live options for everyone, within the constraints of an institutional structure that protects against rights-violations. Perhaps there are those who believe that we are, all of us, pursuing 'one cause', but this is no part of the commitment of those who believe simply that every person's basic interests are sufficiently important to merit protection. The cosmopolitan can quite consistently say that everyone should be able to pursue a variety of conceptions of the good life, within the limits of justice.[43]

Now, as I mentioned above, the fact that Fletcher has set up a straw man here implies that our options are larger than he suggests, for we do not need to be compatriot favouritists simply because there is no single

---

[43] These points are related to Terry Nardin's defence of international society as a practical, non-purposive association in *Law, Morality, and the Relations of States* (Princeton: Princeton University Press, 1983). International society might be understood to be committed to a common cause, if by this we mean that the demands of justice must be met by every state. But if this is Nardin's view, it would seem to be a long way from an Oakeshottian account of international politics (i.e. Nardin's aim), according to which, one would have thought, meeting those demands would constitute a commitment to an illegitimate enterprise. For further discussion of Nardin's views, see Brown, *International Relations Theory*, 124 ff.

cause to which the entire human race is committed. This is my second point: we can admit that people pursue various and conflicting causes, while at the same time denying that, as a consequence, we are justified in saying that people should favour compatriots over others.

My third point is that the limits of human sympathy are relevant to the acceptability of impartialist accounts of international moral obligations, but not in the way Fletcher thinks they are. Fletcher suggests that loyalty is necessary because it provides the basis 'for caring about others', and that 'our natural limits of sympathy' are such that we are incapable of showing concern for 'all five billion people' in the world. Now if Fletcher's claim is that we cannot, in our daily lives, show equal concern for everyone else, then there is a sense in which this is true and a sense in which it is false. It is true that we cannot, as individuals, (nor should we) show the same concern for strangers' children that we show toward our own. But it is false to assert that we cannot *both* realize that each person is equally a proper object of concern and respect, *and* undertake to support *institutions* whose purpose is to ensure that everyone has their vital interests protected. Consider a domestic analogue of this point: redistributive welfare states do not require each citizen to have an identical attitude of sympathy toward each and every compatriot. The fact that we cannot extend similar sympathy to each person in a country populated by many millions of people does not entail that principles of justice cannot include this entire population within their scope.

More generally, I think that Fletcher's argument overlooks that fact that in serious ethical thinking there is a complicated 'interaction of sentiment and principle'. Henry Shue suggests, 'with apologies to Kant, that sentiments unconstrained by principles lack authority, principles unsupported by sentiments lack effect. Sentiments, both in others and in ourselves, can be judged critically. The expression in action of some sentiments is to be welcomed, the expression of others is to be discouraged. For assessing sentiments one needs principles.'[44] The point, in brief, is that we no doubt need sympathetic identification with others to support our conclusions about moral obligations, but criticism of our sentiments is necessary to judge whether such identification meets the criteria suggested by moral principles. Applying this type of move to the present point, we might ask whether someone's claim that he cannot sympathize with the suffering of the distant poor is based on (i) some fundamental feature of human nature (from which it might follow that he *cannot* extend

---

[44] Henry Shue in *Basic Rights*, 146.

his sympathy so far), or (ii) a convenient refusal to consider that the ethical principles he actually accepts might require that he extend his sympathy further. In the second case, if he *can* show equal concern for all other persons, then his stubborn refusal to do so amounts to nothing more than stubborn refusal. Of course, if there is some principled reason for limiting one's sympathy to compatriots, it can be introduced at this point in the argument; but Fletcher does not offer any such principled reason. In any case, if we recognize both that other people are due a certain respect as persons and that we are constitutionally incapable of uniform sympathy for everyone, then there is a rationale for developing the impartial perspective in order to make up for our incapacity in this regard.[45]

Another point that some compatriot favouritists are apt to make is that we must accept a trade-off between commitment to our country, on the one hand, and our adherence to independent critical thinking about the requirements of justice, on the other. Again, Fletcher puts the point succinctly: 'The moral challenge for every devotee of a cause is to find the proper balance of loyalty and independent moral judgment.'[46] This suggests that we must strike a balance between two competing ethical values, loyalty on the one hand and independence of judgement on the other. On the contrary, however, I think there is no head-to-head conflict of the sort Fletcher hints at here, for the 'independent moral judgment' to which he refers should always, I submit, take priority where possible. If appeals to such judgement fail to support the loyalist, then loyalty is not in that case justified; but if loyalty is shown, by independent judgement, to be justified, then the two standpoints coincide. In the latter sort of case, it is incorrect to say that a balance has been struck between loyalty and independent moral judgement, since both lead to the same conclusion, and Fletcher gives us no plausible examples where one should remain loyal to some country while eschewing critical assessment of the reasons one can muster for such commitment. Fletcher's problem of striking a balance between loyalty and independent moral judgement most clearly arises in cases where one has a sense that the object of one's loyalty (e.g. one's country) might not be worthy of one's devotion, but it is in precisely those cases that 'independent moral judgment' is called for. Moreover, the outcome of critical evaluation of one's country could well be that one is justified in *explicit denial* of the claim that one's country is a proper object of loyalty.

[45] Cf. Scarre, *Utilitarianism*, 36.   [46] Fletcher, *Loyalty*, 35.

Analysis of Fletcher's views has led to the following conclusions. First, loyalty is indeed a special attachment to some person or group, so that it is implausible in normal contexts to maintain that one should be loyal to all human beings. But this point does not refute the cosmopolitan assertion that some human interests are sufficiently important to generate protections which no appeal to the value of loyalty can override. Secondly, care and concern for faraway suffering need not result in blindness to deprivation close to home. Thirdly, we should be wary of attempts to portray compatriots on an analogy with co-members of more close-knit groups. Most of my compatriots are strangers to me, so it is inaccurate to say that we must make a choice between compatriots whose closeness generates mutual trust, and others who are threats to our well-being. The reality is that increased physical distance does not necessarily coincide with increased threats to our security. Fourthly, cosmopolitans are not wedded to the view that all human beings are pursuing one cause; they need only believe that no human being's interests should be excluded from equal consideration. Finally, there is no unbridgeable conflict between loyalty to compatriots and critical moral judgement, for this sort of loyalty (as any other) is not criterionless; accordingly, there is always room for evaluation of any object of loyalty.

Bell, Rorty, Communitarianism, and Bounded Justice

Daniel Bell's recent book, *Communitarianism and its Critics*, is in the form of a dialogue between a liberal, Philip Schwartzberg, and a communitarian (and compatriot favouritist), Anne de la Patrie.[47] Judging from the book's introduction, Bell himself sympathizes with the communitarians, especially on the question of the scope (national versus global) of distributive justice. At one point, Bell has Anne say the following:

Any effective scheme of distributive justice, as I see it, presupposes a bounded world of people deeply committed to each other's fate—most of us will not agree to enshrine generous actions in law, and to live by those laws, if we can't identify in some way with recipients of those generous actions—and it just so happens that the nation-state has emerged, for whatever concatenation of historical reasons, as the unit within which our sense of solidarity is strongest.[48]

Anne is mistaken. Three features of these claims call for comment. The first has to do with an apparent confusion between the descriptive and the

---

[47] Daniel Bell, *Communitarianism and its Critics* (Oxford: Clarendon Press, 1993).
[48] Ibid., 137–8.

normative, the second concerns Anne's point about solidarity, which I believe is correct but does not prove her larger point about 'bounded' justice, and the third concerns the notion of generosity and its relation to the virtue of justice.

First, then, the claim that the nation-state is the *de facto* centre of solidarity can help to explain why the nation-state is generally thought to be the proper site of distributive justice. However, no claim about the way things *are* is conclusive in the context of an argument whose concern is with the way things *ought to be*. The presumed fact that allegiances do not presently extend beyond national boundaries does not make it reasonable to deny appeals for the extension of those allegiances to all human beings.

The second, related point is that Anne proposes the reasonable idea that identification with the recipients of welfare assistance is necessary if people are to agree to give up some of their own wealth and resources. But then, if one can present plausible arguments for the view that each person should, at some level, identify with every other person, the ground is laid for implementing a global redistributive regime. The burden of the argument for basic human rights is to show that there are indeed reasons for identification across the entire class of persons. In this context it is important to remember the history of arguments for patriotic loyalty itself. Because justifications of patriotic loyalty have (historically) attempted to show the arbitrariness of devotion to local groups, those arguments have themselves made it possible to argue, in turn, that loyalty to one's country and loyalty to more local groupings are arbitrary in much the same way. If there was good reason to give up parochial attachments to clan and town in favour of nation-state allegiance, then it might be reasonable to give up patriotism in favour of global moral concern. What we might call the *expansionary momentum* of these arguments from moral arbitrariness could very well make it reasonable to believe that nation-state allegiance lacks a credible defence of its restricted special regard for one subset of persons.[49]

And finally, Bell's use of the word 'generous' in this context suggests, misleadingly, that the actions required by the demands of distributive justice exhibit a special sort of kindness, or a commitment to sharing that goes *beyond* that which might normally be required. But generosity comes into play only *after* the claims of justice have been met, and the meeting of rights-claims can be demanded without requiring 'generosity'

[49] Cf. Stephen Nathanson, 'In Defense of "Moderate Patriotism"', *Ethics*, 99 (1989), 549.

on the part of duty-bearers. People are generous when they give more than they are strictly obligated to give, but justice focuses on more strict obligations, therefore to be generous is to exemplify an attitude quite separate from any required for the demands of justice to be met.

Bell not only sympathizes with Anne's claim about the restricted character of distributive justice, he also cites Richard Rorty on 'the point that identification with "fellow human beings" seldom provides the motivational force for generous actions'.[50] Rorty offers an interesting piece of evidence against the possibility of global solidarity in the name of justice.

Consider . . . the attitude of contemporary American liberals to the unending hopelessness and misery of the lives of the young blacks in American cities. Do we say that these people must be helped because they are fellow human beings? We may, but it is much more persuasive, morally as well as politically, to describe them as fellow *Americans*—to insist that it is outrageous that an *American* should live without hope . . . [Our] sense of solidarity is strongest when those with whom solidarity is expressed are thought of as 'one of us', where 'us' means something smaller and more local than the human race. That is why 'because she is a human being' is a weak, unconvincing explanation of a generous action.[51]

Daniel Bell continues in the same vein:

That our sense of solidarity is strongest where 'us' means something smaller and more local than the human race provides a strong argument against the feasibility of a world-wide system of distributive justice (regulated by law), but of course it doesn't follow that the range of 'us' can't be extended in the direction of greater human solidarity for more narrow purposes, e.g. making people more sensitive to instances of cruelty in faraway lands (Rorty thinks that novels, with their detailed descriptions of particular varieties of pain and humiliation, are particularly suited for this purpose).[52]

By responding to several of the points made in these passages, we can gain a better grasp of the commitments of cosmopolitans on the question of international distributive justice.

On the last point, that novels are well-suited for the purpose of increasing global sensitivity to suffering, this is no doubt true, but it is also important to take note of the reports of Americas Watch, Africa Watch, Amnesty International, and similar human rights organizations, since these are vital organs of information about torture and suffering around the world.

---

[50] Bell, *Communitarianism*, 150.
[51] Richard Rorty, *Contingency, Irony, and Solidarity* (Cambridge: Cambridge University Press, 1989), 191, emphases in original.
[52] Bell, *Communitarianism*, 150–1.

Simple awareness of the facts of suffering is likely to generate widespread concern, even without literary devices of sentiment-building.

More importantly, why can the extension of solidarity towards all human beings embrace only sensitivity to cruelty? If we can sympathize with the plight of persons who are victims of torture in faraway lands, why can we not also sympathize with those far-off persons who lack access to basic nutritional requirements, adequate housing, education, and health care? That is, there is nothing in this argument that explains why expressions of concern should be limited to 'instances of cruelty'. But if no 'limitation argument' can be given, then a 'world-wide system of distributive justice' seems a plausible option.

Rorty's central claim, that it is best to point out that those who suffer are part of *our* community, seems to me to be a point about strategy rather than a point of any substance on the question of why it is that the destitute should be helped. If it is the case that this strategic move is *properly* recommended, this could signal at least two things.[53] First, it could signify moral shortcomings in the addressees of these calls for help, i.e. the (relatively) wealthy and powerful Americans, who according to Rorty lack the moral vision to see that *human* suffering calls for ameliorative measures.[54] Secondly, and somewhat less plausibly, Americans could be appealing to their sense, as Americans, that they should not neglect co-participants in their great national project. I say that this option is less plausible because, if we take a serious look at American history, it is evident that blacks in the United States were not considered co-participants in that project at all. Consider merely a small sample of evidence from the history of the treatment of blacks in the United States. John Locke's 'Fundamental Constitutions of Carolina' (1669), for instance, say that 'every freeman of Carolina shall have absolute power and authority over his negro slaves',[55] and in 1850 the morally indefensible Fugitive Slave Act was passed by Congress, signed by the President, and approved by the US Supreme Court.[56] The hopes of black Americans for equal

---

[53] There is, of course, good reason to doubt the effectiveness of pointing out that 'it is outrageous that an *American* should live without hope'. If it is maintained that this sort of claim is 'morally as well as politically' persuasive, one would have to point to instances where this strategy had any noticeable effect.

[54] One of the problems with Rorty's view is that he does not think that the need to put one's arguments in terms of 'us' rather than 'human beings' suggests anything morally amiss with the prevailing condition of moral debate.

[55] Cited in Howard Zinn, *Declarations of Independence: Cross-Examining American Ideology* (New York: HarperCollins, 1990), 234.

[56] Ibid. 237.

treatment remain, in many ways, unrealized, and it is no wonder that the black Supreme Court Justice Thurgood Marshall, speaking at the Bicentennial of the Constitution in 1987, said: 'Some may . . . quietly commemorate the suffering, struggle, and sacrifice that has triumphed over much of what was wrong with the original document, and observe the anniversary with hopes not realized and promises not fulfilled.'[57]

These elementary features of the American black experience threaten the credibility of Rorty's claims. Of course, black Americans once excluded are now, if only rhetorically, included in many contemporary conceptions of the American community. But, as Marshall's words make clear, and as the experiences of countless millions of black Americans bear witness, there are good grounds for suspicion of any appeal to a common project in which all Americans participate by virtue of their shared citizenship. There is, therefore, no *moral* argument we have yet seen which supports the restriction of arguments about justice to compatriots.

This discussion of Bell and Rorty has generated at least four positive conclusions. First, the fact that the prevailing view is that the nation-state is the proper focus of justice-related solidarity does nothing to show that this is the way things ought to be. Argument on this score is needed if the claim is to be maintained in the face of widespread global deprivation and suffering. Secondly, if solidaristic identification with others is a necessary condition for dependable commitment to a scheme of justice, *cosmopolitan* justice is precluded only if it can be shown that such identification is not possible with non-compatriots. That impossibility claim is deeply implausible. Thirdly, once it is admitted that it is both possible and desirable to show concern for the victims of cruelty in faraway countries, there is no obvious reason for limiting concern and opposition to acts of cruelty alone. It then becomes possible to recommend a world-wide scheme for the protection of basic human rights. And finally, despite claims to the contrary, it is not true than an argument from justice cannot appeal to the fact that it is wrong *for a human being to suffer needlessly*. If we phrase our arguments in terms of compatriots, as in the American appeal to the wrongness of 'American' suffering, this can only be for strategic reasons which themselves suggest something about the moral corruption of contemporary ethical and political debate.

In closing, I want to return to another prominent discussion of one of the main issues addressed in this chapter. Richard Rorty has recently

---

[57] Ibid. 232.

addressed what he takes to be the question most in need of answering by 'moral educators': 'Why should I care about a stranger, a person who is no kin to me, a person whose habits I find disgusting?'[58] The following answer Rorty finds unconvincing: 'Because kinship and custom are morally irrelevant, irrelevant to the obligations imposed by the recognition of membership in the same species.' The problem with this answer, according to Rorty, is that it is *question-begging*, it assumes that 'mere species membership is . . . a sufficient surrogate for closer kinship'.[59] If this is meant as an attack on a certain mode of cosmopolitan argument, it fails, for it misrepresents the *role* played in that argument by appeals to the fact of membership in the class of persons. The ties that we, as persons, have to other persons, do not function as 'surrogates' for the kinship ties we recognize (and value) towards those close to us. Rather, we neither can nor should renounce the close, deep relationships—and corresponding duties—we share with immediate family and trusted friends. But we do not have to choose between only two alternatives: (i) retaining kinship and friendship ties, or (ii) giving up those ties in favour of taking on obligations to all persons equally. Rorty's accusation of circularity works only if impartial justice demands that we renounce kinship ties, but we have seen that impartiality, properly understood, requires just the opposite.

5.7. CONCLUSION

This chapter has attempted to assess the case for special duties to compatriots and the related question of the link between patriotism and obligations of global justice. I have argued that compatriot favouritism is potentially compatible with a commitment to acting morally, but that there is no sound, general rationale for being a compatriot favouritist. When considering patriotism and global justice, I have defended cosmopolitanism against the central claims of MacIntyre, Fletcher, Bell, and Rorty on the ethical acceptability of favouring co-citizens over foreigners.

In conclusion, I should stress that the argument of this chapter is *not* that no forms of partiality are justified. Am I saying that one is never justified in favouring one's own child over other children? Certainly

[58] Richard Rorty, 'Human Rights, Rationality, and Sentimentality', in Stephen Shute and Susan Hurley (eds.), *On Human Rights: The Oxford Amnesty Lectures 1993* (New York: Basic Books, 1993), 111–34, at 133.
[59] Ibid.

not, but it is important to remember that even this legitimate version of favouritism itself is limited in its extent, because the reasons that justify such favouritism themselves suggest that impartial concern for others is a precondition for partiality. The problem of partiality is perhaps most starkly evident when we consider global poverty: the absence of impartial justice may make valuable forms of partiality impossible by denying some persons the material resources necessary for such partial conduct. Hence a proper concern for partiality requires that we focus on impartial justice. If impartial justice is not implemented globally, the partiality that is quite properly valued by many people—theorist and non-theorist alike —will lack the resource-base necessary to make it meaningful, since preferential treatment would not (in many cases) adequately answer to the needs of many of the vulnerable.[60]

In any case, it is vital to recognize that the type of partiality with which we have been concerned is *patriotism*, and our question has been to evaluate the case for preferring compatriots to non-compatriots when it comes to determining the appropriate distributions of benefits and burdens. While partiality is justified in the interactions of individuals with one another (though only where it is also consistent with impartiality), the concerns of justice are not addressed to this interactional level. Rather, appropriate principles of international justice will aim to provide the theoretical underpinning for an institutional framework that can be defended to each person affected by that framework. My claim is that there are no good grounds for setting up a distributive scheme in such a way that the strength of a person's legitimate claims depends on that person's citizenship.

---

[60] This point is well made in Marilyn Friedman, *What are Friends For? Feminist Perspectives on Personal Relationships and Moral Theory* (Ithaca, NY: Cornell University Press, 1993), 75: 'we live in a world in which many people do not have adequate resources for caring for their loved ones effectively. Under these circumstances the social practices by which we each favor only our respective "own," if untempered by any methods for redistributing caretaking resources, would result in gravely inadequate care for many of the world's people.'

6

Miller, Nationality, and Distributive Justice

6.1. INTRODUCTION

In this chapter my main objective is to consider the implications for questions of distributive justice of theories attaching fundamental ethical significance to nations, and an analysis of David Miller's contribution is, I believe, a useful tool in reaching that objective. In recent years, Miller has been developing some challenging ideas on the topic of nationalism.[1] National communities figure prominently in Miller's version of communitarianism, where special obligations to co-nationals are founded on the ethically valuable national community. His work demonstrates that there is a version of nationalism which can stand up to ethical criticism; however, as I hope to show, Miller's theory of *nationality*—his word for the position he defends—does not justify linking the duties of distributive justice so closely to membership in national communities.[2]

Miller cites an exchange between the Mole and the Rat in Kenneth Grahame's *The Wind in the Willows*,[3] in which the Mole is wondering what is to be found beyond the world of the river bank with which they are both familiar. 'Beyond the Wild Wood comes the Wide World,' [said the Rat]. 'And that's something that doesn't matter, either to you or me.

---

[1] This discussion is based mainly on Miller's recent book and five of his articles. The book is David Miller, *On Nationality* (Oxford: Clarendon Press, 1995); the articles, which often contain arguments and claims not made in the book, are 'The Ethical Significance of Nationality', *Ethics*, 98 (1988); 'In What Sense Must Socialism be Communitarian?', *Social Philosophy and Policy*, 6 (1988–9); 'In Defence of Nationality', *Journal of Applied Philosophy*, 10 (1993); 'The Nation-State: A Modest Defence', in Chris Brown (ed.), *Political Restructuring in Europe* (London: Routledge, 1994); and 'Nationality: Some Replies', *Journal of Applied Philosophy*, 14 (1997). See also, David Miller, *Market, State, and Community* (Oxford: Oxford University Press, 1989), ch. 9: 'Community and Citizenship'. Where a claim or argument in *On Nationality* is also found in an earlier article, I cite only the book, since this may be taken to be Miller's (conditionally) definitive statement of his position.

[2] See Miller, *On Nationality*, 7–12, for a statement of the distinguishing claims of a conception of nationality, along with some remarks about the uses of the terms 'nationality' and 'nationalism' in recent theorizing on the subject.

[3] Kenneth Grahame, *The Wind in the Willows* (London: Methuen, 1926).

I've never been there, and I'm never going, nor you either, if you've got any sense at all. Don't ever mention it again, please.[4] The Rat displays complete indifference to the world beyond the river bank, a view which is a source of some concern for most moral philosophers, versed as they are in the ideas of universality, impartiality and equal consideration of all agents, regardless of geographical location. Miller does not endorse the Rat's indifference, but he does defend the need for 'some kind of equilibrium between the everyday and the philosophical, between common belief and rational belief, between the river bank and the Wide World'.[5] By contrast, I believe there is more to be said for the 'philosophical Mole' (Miller's invention, since Grahame's Mole fails to jump at his opportunity). This Mole asks the Rat, 'What's so special about this river bank? . . . Why is this river bank a better place than other river banks beyond the Wood?'[6] Though I believe the truth lies somewhere between the two poles of *national allegiance allied to indifference to outsiders* on the one hand, and *outright denial of the ethical claims of nationality* on the other, I propose to show that Miller's arguments fail to take sufficiently seriously the claims of non-nationals.

My analysis has four parts. First I outline Miller's characterization of nationality. In the second part, I look at some arguments purporting to show the ethical relevance of national commitments. Thirdly, I discuss reasons for rejecting the ethically foundational character of nations, and finally, I ask what obligations go along with national allegiance, with special reference to the obligations of distributive justice. At each stage my aim is not simply to record Miller's ideas and arguments but also to subject them to criticism. The chapter as a whole may be seen as an attempt to clarify one version of nationalism and to show how the ethical importance of such a view does not fundamentally alter the duties persons owe to one another as human beings.

6.2. MILLER'S CHARACTERIZATION OF NATIONALITY

Before embarking on an outline of Miller's views, it will be helpful to state what I take to be the main jobs to be done by an account of the ethical significance of nationality. We must distinguish two central aspects of the nationality debate, corresponding to two tasks for political

[4] Ibid. 16–17.
[5] Miller, 'In Defence of Nationality', 15.   [6] Ibid. 3–4.

theorists. First, there is the problem of the proper characterization of the principle of nationality. Dealing with this problem requires the statement of an ethically defensible conception of nationalism. Let us call this the *nationalism characterization task*. Secondly, and of equal importance, there is the problem of delineating the form, content, and strength of the duties co-nationals owe to one another, as well as the relation between these duties and other, more general duties to other persons (i.e. 'outsiders').[7] Let us call this the *duties formulation task*. The theorist needs to formulate explicitly which duties are owed to whom and why. The strength of duties to fellow nationals will, of course, depend to a large extent upon the form of nationalism in question; similarly, justifications of special duties to co-nationals will appeal to the prior characterization of nationalism. For both of these reasons, then, the second task awaits completion of the first; the complete formulation of duties and the statement of their supporting grounds await a characterization of nationalism. Accordingly, my discussion of Miller's views will outline his conception of nationalism in general before discussing his position on the duties persons owe to one another.

Miller's characterization of nationalism can be succinctly stated: a nation is 'a community (1) constituted by shared belief and mutual commitment, (2) extended in history, (3) active in character, (4) connected to a particular territory, and (5) marked off from other communities by its distinct public culture'.[8] Perhaps the central distinguishing feature of a nation is that 'a nationality exists when its members believe that it does'.[9] Nations are communities of belief, and the particular features of any given nation will depend on the actual beliefs that members take as constitutive of membership. Since nations are belief-dependent entities, any proposed criteria of nationality which are *independent* of persons' beliefs will fail in at least some cases to distinguish nations from one another. For example, common language has been put forward as such a criterion,

---

[7] This way of putting the point is not strictly accurate, since a person's general duties will not be owed *only* to outsiders and not also to co-nationals. On the contrary, the set which makes up a person's duties will normally include as well duties to co-nationals which are owed to them simply because they are persons. That is, as a Canadian, I may have some nation-based duties to other Canadians, and as a human being I have some generally characterizable duties to other persons—*both Canadian and non-Canadian*—duties based on the interests persons have quite apart from their national attachments.

[8] Miller, *On Nationality*, 27. For a related, earlier statement, that a nation is 'a community constituted by mutual belief, extended in history, active in character, connected to a particular territory, and thought to be marked off from other communities by its members' distinct traits', see Miller, 'In Defence of Nationality', 8; 'The Nation-State', 141.

[9] 'In Defence of Nationality', 6; 'The Nation-State', 138.

and it does provide one mark of nationhood in some instances; however, its success as a distinguishing feature depends on the members' belief that their fellow nationals must speak a common language. As Charles Taylor puts it, 'nations exist not just where there is the objective fact of speaking the same language and sharing a common history, but where this is subjectively reflected in a people's identification'.[10]

One important nation-constituting belief is that the nation is an historical community whose forebears have toiled to make the nation what it now is. From this conception of an historical community there arise obligations of present-day members to carry on the national tradition: because the nation extends into the past, and into the future, the obligations arising from national membership are not ones that can be renounced as one might renounce obligations voluntarily undertaken. National communities ground duties not only to one's contemporaries but to previous and future generations—duties to the former, to carry on the national projects; and duties to the latter, to ensure that the national community is passed down to them in a healthy condition.

If Miller is correct about the impossibility of renouncing one's historic national community (or aspects of it), one might think that the ethical claims of that community could not be denied.[11] So it is worth pausing here to question Miller's assertion. I believe that his denial of the possibility of renunciation is either false or unproven. It is false if it is meant as an empirical claim about what can and cannot happen, for the fact of historical continuity does not rule out of account the present generation's refusal to identify itself with the national community as it has come down to them, even though it may make it improbable. It is unproven if it is understood as a normative claim about what the present generation can *justifiably* do. From the fact that the nation stretches across

---

[10] Charles Taylor, *Reconciling the Solitudes* (Kingston & Montreal: McGill-Queens, 1993), ch. 3, 'Why Do Nations Have to Become States?' (originally published in 1979), 56. The question of the relation of language to national identity is interestingly addressed by Taylor, who makes a strong case for taking common language to be a necessary feature (though in some cases only implicitly) of any national identity. Where the national identity involves reference to more than one language—say, in the most plausible version of the Canadian identity, where French and English are accorded equal respect—national identity still makes essential reference to language. The possibility of such national identities shows, however, that no *single* common language is necessary for a nation to exist.

[11] See *On Nationality*, 24, for the claim that the nation is 'a community that, because it stretches back and forward across the generations, is not one that the present generation can renounce'. And see ibid. 42, for the assertion that 'in a national community a case can be made out for unconditional obligations to other members that arise simply by virtue of the fact that one has been born and raised in that particular community'.

the generations it does not follow that one generation can have no good reason to repudiate various claims that 'the nation' makes upon it. Hence while nations may be ethical communities—one of Miller's central claims for nations—national ethical communities do not necessarily generate duties which must in all cases be upheld.

The next two features are straightforward: nations are active communities, they engage in various activities together; and nations are tied to particular territories, nations are linked with homelands. The activist element seems undeniably important, for it would be odd to say that a community exists where 'members' fail to engage in activities in common. The territorial claim is slightly more controversial, at least in contemporary circumstances, in which there is 'the real likelihood that, so to speak, the most powerful Croatian nationalists have no intention of living in Croatia, but carry Croatia around with them in North America'.[12] Still, if there were no Croatian homeland, and no appeal to one, either in the past or in the future, we would be hesitant to call the phenomenon in question nationalism at all.

The final characteristic, namely, the belief in the distinctiveness of one's nation's public culture as against other nations, emphasizes another element of a person's belief-set which must be present for the nation to exist. We should note, however, the relevance of the obvious point that *beliefs may be false*: if members of a nation have false beliefs about the national past or about the distinctiveness of their nation, the ethical claims of the nation will be weakened, at least to the extent that false beliefs are not an acceptable basis for contested obligations. Miller recognizes this problem and attempts to deal with it, and I will outline and assess his attempted move, a move designed to save nations from ethical oblivion, in the context of assessing the main criticisms of Miller's principle of nationality in section 6.4.

6.3. WHAT REASONS ARE THERE FOR PERSONS TO VALUE NATIONAL COMMUNITIES?

With this outline of Miller's conception of nationalism in hand, we can now search for reasons why nations should generate ethical obligations. We need an answer to the question, 'Why should national communities

---

[12] Benedict Anderson, 'The Psychology of Nationalism', unpublished paper delivered at the Conference on the Ethics of Nationalism, University of Illinois at Urbana-Champaign, Apr. 1994.

be valued?' There are at least two strategies to use in answering this question. The first, which I call the critical strategy, is to assess the value to individuals of belonging to nations. Here we might imagine persons without national allegiances and then consider how their lives might be less attractive than those of nationally affiliated individuals. The second strategy is more conservative, since it rejects attempts to justify national allegiances, and instead favours an approach which rationalizes national attachments on the grounds that they accord with the way people actually think of themselves. On this latter approach, the search for universally applicable reasons for national commitments is not necessary. Miller in fact favours this strategy, though he does discuss attempts to justify national allegiances on universal grounds.[13] I now propose to describe and criticize what I call the *conservative* strategy of rationalizing national commitments.

The defence of nationality can start from the undeniable fact that people do have national allegiances and attachments. The role of the political philosopher, according to Miller, is not to reject such commitments if they lack a rational grounding, but rather to retain those commitments unless they can be shown to be flawed in some way. He should take national allegiances as given and then 'try to build a political philosophy which incorporates them'.[14] Rejecting the universalist approach, Miller maintains that '[t]he particularist defence of nationality begins with the assumption that memberships and attachments in general have ethical significance'.[15] In this way, Miller attempts to shift the burden of proof in political argument on to one who would deny the acceptability of undefended national commitments.

Miller's claim, that *where we begin* the task of moral and political theorizing will have a marked effect on how we proceed, is highly misleading. As Joshua Cohen has said in criticism of a view similar to Miller's—namely, Michael Walzer's approach in *Spheres of Justice*—there is no real disagreement among theorists about where the theoretical enterprise should *begin*.[16] Kant, Mill, Sidgwick, and countless others start their theorizing from the commitments to be found in everyday moral and personal beliefs; they are led to philosophy by the problems and contradictions which arise when the attempt is made to understand and

---

[13] See *On Nationality*, ch. 3, and the earlier articles, 'In Defence of Nationality' and 'Ethical Significance'.

[14] Miller, 'In Defence of Nationality', 4.   [15] Miller, *On Nationality*, 65.

[16] Joshua Cohen, 'Review of Michael Walzer, *Spheres of Justice*', *Journal of Philosophy*, 83 (1986), 467.

defend those common-sense views. Thus, from a number of common
starting-points the views of theorists diverge. Where disagreement begins
is in the *attitude* one takes in one's theorizing toward the commitments
constituting that shared beginning. Two main attitudes present themselves: first, one can look for ways to incorporate people's allegiances
into one's political theory (on the grounds, perhaps, that since 'people
generally do exhibit such attachments and allegiances', those attachments
and allegiances must have some acceptable rationale); or secondly, one
can critically assess the ethical and other grounds for the commitments
in question, in order to judge whether, say, (*a*) national loyalties as they
are found in contemporary societies can meet objections purporting to
show that they contradict other ethical beliefs also held by the citizens
of contemporary nation-states, for example, sentiments of benevolence
or generalized concern for other human beings, or (*b*) national allegiances fail to stand up to moral criticism more generally—i.e. whether
or not that criticism can be shown to stem from the prevailing beliefs
of citizens. Joshua Cohen's criticism of Walzer's approach in *Spheres
of Justice*[17] is that Walzer seems to want his philosophical account to
end up by justifying the shared values of the community in question. Or,
to put the point another way, Walzer's view fails to question the community's shared values, and for this reason it fails as a philosophical
account of those values: the philosopher's job is not merely to accept
the norms he discovers in his own society; rather, he should subject them
to critical scrutiny, thereby assessing their reasonableness.[18] The same
criticism applies to Miller's preferred approach to political philosophy:
it is unacceptable to argue that nations should be valued simply because
people value them.

Let us return then to the first strategy of justifying national commitments, what I call the *critical* strategy. Taking this tack, we do not
accept that nations are ethically significant communities unless there
are reasons for supposing that national allegiances have ethical value.
Moral egalitarians might note that nationality is, to some degree, an ally

[17] Michael Walzer, *Spheres of Justice: A Defence of Pluralism and Equality* (Oxford:
Basil Blackwell, 1983). I discuss Walzer's views in more detail in Ch. 7.

[18] John Rawls, *Political Liberalism* (New York: Columbia University Press, 1993), 44
n. 47, expresses his own indebtedness to Joshua Cohen's review of Walzer and notes that
Cohen 'argues that Walzer's view about how political philosophy should begin does not
differ essentially from Plato, Kant and Sidgwick. The difference is where Walzer argues
it must end up, namely, with our shared understandings.' These points are relevant to what
Onora O'Neill calls the 'accessibility' of ethical reasoning; see her *Faces of Hunger*, 41.

in the struggle against unjust power differentials between groups. As J. Donald Moon has noted, 'the idea of the "nation" generates a certain pressure in the direction of moral equality, for it unites people horizontally and defines them as having a common identity, at least vis-à-vis outsiders'.[19] Moon stresses the egalitarian thrust of nationality, its power to identify every member of the group as the moral equal of every other member; this power should not be overlooked, especially where it has been instrumental in overcoming entrenched social hierarchies that stand in the way of bringing about justice. Nevertheless, as Moon notes, the horizontal unification of people that nations generate does come at some cost: outsiders are excluded, treated as morally unequal, removed from the primary ethical horizon and placed at some vertically lower level of consideration. From a moral point of view, then, the nation seems a decidedly ambivalent community, even in its most attractive variants.

Before assessing two of the most important arguments in favour of the nation, we should note that the critical strategy being pursued here need not emanate from a purely detached, external perspective. Even if we accept Miller's claim that we all have nationalist sentiments—though for the most part our co-national loyalties are 'subterranean' and exposed comparatively rarely[20]—we may still wonder whether those sentiments can withstand criticism, whether we should affirm or reject the loyalties we find as part of our received identities.

Of the various reasons which might be offered in defence of the nation, Miller focuses on the idea that national loyalty can provide the foundation for sentiments of *solidarity* which can in turn make possible mutually beneficial projects requiring substantial individual sacrifice. Without the communal feelings that national allegiance creates, it will be much more difficult—perhaps impossible—to put into practice any long-term plans for social improvement which require persons to give up something now for benefit in the future. This consideration highlights the importance of *trust* between people, especially whenever some difficult or risky enterprise best serves their long-term interests. I call this the *argument from the need for solidarity*. This argument has considerable plausibility, and is especially significant in light of the redistributive practices now characteristic of modern welfare states: if solidarity with

---

[19] J. Donald Moon, *Constructing Community: Moral Pluralism and Tragic Conflicts* (Princeton: Princeton University Press, 1993), 67. Moon refers us to Benedict Anderson, *Imagined Communities*, rev. edn. (London: Verso, 1991), ch. 4, for development of this point.
[20] Miller, *On Nationality*, 14–15.

fellow nationals can render consent to such practices more likely, then
the nation may be an important object of ethical commitment in contemporary circumstances.[21] If, as Miller claims, 'the nation is *de facto*
the main source'[22] of the solidarity needed to underpin duties of mutual
aid in contemporary, largely anonymous societies, nations would appear
to be indispensable. There is nothing in this argument, however, to rule
out the extension of solidaristic attachments to the entire human race,
regardless of national membership. But more worrying is the fact that
the argument itself seems to be question-begging, since it defends co-
national priority on the grounds that nationalist sentiments will solidify
redistributive regimes within nation-states. The problem is that, even if
this last claim is true, it does not address the question of why *intra-
national* redistribution is justified in the first place.

Another argument for the ethical value of nations points to the combined effect of (*a*) historical attachment and (*b*) commitment to worthwhile values. Together, it is claimed, these generate special ties amongst
co-nationals: members of a national group who have shared a common
historical past in which they or their forebears have engaged in ethically commendable activities have good reasons to recognize special duties
to one another. The Canadian philosopher, Thomas Hurka, has offered a
version of this argument, filling in the details by discussing the analogy
with personal relationships.[23] In the case of my relationship with my wife,
it cannot be only her possession of admirable qualities that grounds my
special ties to her, it is also certain facts about our historical connected-
ness, facts that single *her* out from anyone else with similar qualities. I
wouldn't simply give up my attachments to my wife if I discovered another
woman who possessed my wife's admirable and desirable qualities to
a higher degree, for that would constitute a denial of the value of the
common past we share with one another. It is important to remember,
however, that it is not *only* the 'particular relationship of association'[24]
that gives value to the relationship. If it were only that, then if my wife
changed such that she no longer possessed the qualities she once did—
say, she no longer showed her characteristic intelligence, imagination,
sense of humour, and care and concern for others—it would still make

[21] See *On Nationality*, 90–6, and 'The Nation-State', 141–4.
[22] Miller, 'In Defence of Nationality', 9.
[23] Thomas Hurka, 'The Justification of National Partiality', in Jeff McMahan and Robert
McKim (eds.), *The Morality of Nationalism* (Oxford: Oxford University Press, 1997).
[24] Alasdair MacIntyre, 'Is Patriotism a Virtue?', The Lindley Lecture (Lawrence, Kan.:
University of Kansas, 1984), 4.

perfect sense for me to retain my attachments to her to the same degree. But it wouldn't make sense, for my wife's becoming uncaring and humourless would rightly alter my special ties to her, at least to some extent.[25] Justified partiality, whether to loved ones or to fellow nationals, thus has a 'double basis' which includes shared history as well as favourable general qualities. Partiality to co-nationals depends not only on the fact that we can point to a common past, but also on the general features the nation displays. National commitment to racial discrimination is not partiality-generating, while allegiance to equal opportunity may be. This argument is plausible, but my present purpose is simply to note that it relies to some extent on the existence of a common national history. The objection I will now consider casts doubt on any argument that relies on the reality of a shared history.

6.4. OBJECTIONS TO CONCEIVING NATIONALITIES AS ETHICALLY FOUNDATIONAL

I will now look at two objections to the view that nations have basic ethical value; I call them the objection from historical myth and the objection from the inadequacy of partiality.

The *objection from historical myth* runs as follows. Nations are manufactured; they are imaginary communities whose histories are to a large extent false. Consequently national loyalties are in part loyalties to communities which do not exist—after all, the communities in question are supposed to include those not yet born and those already dead. Obligations to co-nationals thus lack a rational foundation.[26] Stated quite so baldly this objection is not especially troubling for the defender of nationality, since there is a clear sense in which nations do exist, so to claim that they do not exist is contrary to the facts in cases where a community believes itself to be a nation. But the 'historical myth' objection need not be quite so simplistic; it need not claim that, because their 'histories' are fabricated, nations do not exist. Rather, it can maintain that elements of national history appealed to *in defence of special obligations to*

---

[25] Although it depends on the reasons why she changed. For example, if she were suffering from Alzheimer's, my attachments would remain strong. This suggests that changes for which she bears no responsibility are not such as to alter our ethical ties to one another.
[26] Miller discusses this objection in *On Nationality*, 35–42, 'Ethical Significance of Nationality', 653 ff., and *Market, State, and Community*, 241–5.

co-nationals might lack the ethical power to support those obligations, because (1) a particular story is false or misleading, or (2) other, neglected historical events pull in the other direction, thereby weakening the alleged national solidarity. Hence, the special duties claim can fail *even though* nations as belief-communities do exist, and where their existence is proven by appeal to shared history.

One of Miller's replies to this objection appeals to 'a distinction between beliefs that are constitutive of social relationships and background beliefs which support those constitutive beliefs'.[27] For example, a constitutive belief in the case of friendship is 'that each is willing to put himself out for the other'. Constitutive beliefs, then, are necessary conditions of the relationship's existence, i.e. without those beliefs the relationship does not exist. Hence false constitutive beliefs imply the absence of the relationship. Background beliefs may be false in some cases, but a relationship can withstand false background beliefs provided that the constitutive beliefs are true. Thus a family's mistaken belief that one of its beloved, supported, and supportive members is biologically related to the rest (where the belief is mistaken because of a baby mix-up at the hospital) does not negate the worth of the familial relationships, since the belief in direct genetic proximity is merely a *background* belief. As long as the constitutive beliefs of family members remain true—for example, they actually are committed to mutual love and support—the relationship retains its ethical value.

This raises the following question: are beliefs about the historical continuity of the nation *constitutive* or *background* beliefs? Miller's position would seem to be that they are largely background beliefs,[28] although '(some version of) the common story' of historical origin and development must be true if the nation is to be an ethical community, so some very 'general story with many basic facts not in dispute' appears to count as part of a person's nationality-constituting belief-set: 'the constitutive belief is only that there should be some national past'.[29] The problem here is that Miller has saved nationality at the cost of reducing considerably the ethical attraction it might derive from an appeal to shared historical struggles. If the backward-looking searches of co-nationals turn up only repeated disputes between different elements *within* the national community—rather than a series of solidaristic joint projects carried out in the interests of all—then there may not be much left to ground national

[27] Miller, 'Ethical Significance', 655.
[28] Hence the falsity of *some* historical 'stories' does not nullify *all* historically based ties between co-nationals.
[29] Miller, 'Ethical Significance', 655–6.

allegiances ethically, at least where the appeal to the past is concerned.[30] The case of oppressed groups, those whose interests have been consistently ignored for generations, represents a clear case in which the appeal to a 'common national past' may fail to generate any sense of duty to co-nationals.[31] The objection from historical myth stands. In so far as nations as ethical communities are historical fictions or historically more ethically ambiguous than generally believed, they cannot legitimately generate significant obligations on the part of co-nationals for one another.

I now turn to the *objection from the inadequacy of partiality*. The idea here is that the appeal to nationality is ethically inadequate because it introduces an irreducible element of partiality into the deliberative process, and partiality is contrary to the widely accepted view that a moral perspective requires one to be impartial.[32] To explain Miller's response to this objection I need to say more about his characterization of the national point of view.

Miller points out that national loyalties do not fit easily into the now common picture of two competing ethical standpoints, the personal —where agent-relative reasons prevail—and the impersonal—where agent-neutral reasons dominate. It is now standard to say that practical reasoning should give some role to both sorts of reasons.[33] First, we have the agent-neutral viewpoint, from which each person counts equally; then, there is the agent-relative viewpoint, from which an individual's personal goals and integrity loom large, and where a moral space is created in which individuals can pursue their own personal projects and commitments. It might seem at first sight that national allegiances require the creation of a third category of moral reason, which we might call

[30] The American historian Howard Zinn has claimed that the solidaristic stories of national glories are indeed false: 'Nations are not communities and never have been. The history of any country, presented as the history of a family, conceals fierce conflicts of interest (sometimes exploding, most often repressed) between conquerors and conquered, masters and slaves, capitalists and workers, dominators and dominated in race and sex.' Zinn, *A People's History of the United States* (London: Longman, 1980), 9–10.

[31] Cf. Stephen Nathanson, *Patriotism, Morality, and Peace* (Lanham, Md.: Rowman and Littlefield, 1993), 208. On achieving community at the cost of excluding various groups from membership in that community, see Will Kymlicka, *Contemporary Political Philosophy: An Introduction* (Oxford: Clarendon Press, 1990), 225–9, and, more generally, Derek L. Phillips, *Looking Backward: A Critical Appraisal of Communitarian Thought* (Princeton: Princeton University Press, 1993).

[32] In this discussion I am assuming that the objector accepts the (to my mind incorrect) view that one's ethical theory cannot provide satisfactory justifications for both partiality and impartiality, within their proper domains. See Ch. 5 above.

[33] See Thomas Nagel, *Equality and Partiality* (Oxford: Oxford University Press, 1991).

'nation-relative' reasons. However, Miller denies that such reasons are *sui generis*, for 'they appear to represent, not a different segment of moral life, but a competing way of understanding the concepts and principles that make up the impartial or agent-neutral standpoint (consider, for example, the different conceptions of distributive justice that emerge depending on whether you begin from a national or a universal starting-point)'.[34] National allegiances do not fit well into the common picture of morally relevant perspectives, and Miller says that it is this feature of national loyalties—i.e. that they reorient the ideas constituting the agent-neutral or impartial standpoint—that explains why national allegiances directly challenge the dominant view of morality in our culture, namely, the universalist view of morality.

Let us be clear about what Miller is claiming. If we accept the distinction between agent-neutral and agent-relative reasons, Miller claims that the ethical perspective of nationality represents an alternative understanding of what is a relevant reason from the *agent-neutral* viewpoint. A national ethic, therefore, competes with universalist morality, the latter being the dominant ethical conception, at least among philosophers. Miller identifies the *impartial* standpoint with the *agent-neutral* standpoint, so we should understand him to be claiming that the *national* perspective is also an impartial one. This seems odd, since impartiality, as it is usually understood, rules out bias in favour of any person or group at the expense of any other, while the national view would seem to *require* such bias, at least in some cases. Of course, it may turn out that national favouritism can be justified—after all, some bias is unavoidable, and some may be required of us. But that possibility should not be confused with the claim that nationality is the proper heading under which we should understand *impartiality*. I believe Miller's view cannot withstand careful scrutiny, and that we would be better advised to follow Thomas Nagel, who claims, contrary to what Miller holds here, that the national perspective 'is just another basic aspect of the personal perspective, and it is not going to disappear'.[35] Thus, Nagel does not identify the impartial and national perspectives; he identifies the national and personal perspectives, or rather, he sees the national viewpoint as one aspect of the personal. He further thinks it will be around at least for the foreseeable future and we should, therefore, take its existence into account in our theorizing.

---

[34] Miller, 'In Defence of Nationality', 4–5.
[35] Nagel, *Equality and Partiality*, 177.

Is there any way to account for the strangeness of Miller's nationality/ impartiality identity claim? Perhaps Miller would respond to my criticism by claiming that I am begging the question, that his point is to challenge the dominant conception of impartiality and replace it with another which better corresponds with our common-sense notions about our obligations. In this context, my objection that Miller's conception contradicts the received view of impartiality merely restates what he is already, and admittedly, claiming. But is my objection question-begging? The issue here is one of the proper assignment of the burden of proof, and since it is Miller who is rejecting the received view of impartiality and substituting what appears to be a form of favouritism, it is up to him to show that the national perspective should be counted as a version of impartiality. In short, my criticism amounts to a request for an argument where none has been given.

We should accept Miller's claim that nationalism may be, but *need not* be, a reactionary doctrine; and if nationality can be philosophically respectable, perhaps its respectability can be found in its superior fulfilment of the requirements of impartiality. Nevertheless, this point goes no way toward *showing* how the national and impartial perspectives might coincide. The impartial standpoint may, in the end, suggest that the ethically preferred option is to accord priority to national allegiances and obligations. But even if this is the correct conclusion, it is distinct from the nationality-impartiality identity claim. There are two possibilities: (1) from an impartial perspective, we have good reasons to think that it is plausible to encourage national loyalty, and (2) the impartial and national perspectives are identical. While (1) may be correct, it is different from (2), and if Miller is asserting (2), we have yet to see his reasons for doing so.

Miller might respond to my criticism, however, by saying that I have misrepresented what it means to be impartial. He maintains that impartiality does not require identical treatment of every person but, on the contrary, it demands that rules and criteria for treatment of individuals within some context should be conscientiously followed. Impartiality applies to the observation of rules within some relevant group but not to decisions about who is to be included within the group in the first place.[36] Yet this conception of impartiality—according to which we need first to know whether national boundaries are significant before we can judge whether special obligations to insiders are partial—is potentially confusing.

---

[36] See Miller, *On Nationality*, 53 ff., and 'Nationality: Some Replies', 11.

It is better, in my view, to admit that what we have here is partiality, but to defend national partiality in the same manner in which other forms of partiality are defended. As was argued in Chapter 5, the argument would claim that, from an impartial, all-encompassing perspective, it is reasonable to recognize special duties to some subset of persons: in short, from an impartial perspective, partial concern may be justified.

The proper conclusion, then, is to admit that the national perspective is partial; but this admission does not rule out accepting this kind of partiality in one's ethical theory. For partiality is not ruled out by a proper understanding of morality; on the contrary, common-sense morality, which on this point can be vindicated, 'actually requires us to be especially attentive to the needs of people we love and have special attachments to'.[37] Some version of national partiality might be a plausible view (though I am not arguing that point here). What ultimately matters is that co-national priority does not negate consideration of outsiders, especially such consideration as is necessary to fulfil the demands of justice.

6.5. WHAT ETHICAL COMMITMENTS GO ALONG WITH ALLEGIANCE TO ONE'S NATION?

I will now consider the relation between the ethical obligations one owes to co-nationals and those owed to others. In keeping with my larger theme, the focus here is on one particular subset of moral duties, namely, the duties of distributive justice.

What are the implications for obligations of justice of the acceptance of the claim that nations are 'ethical communities'?[38] The potential importance of nations in this respect is linked to the undeniable fact that nationality is a central element in the self-identity of many people.[39] Seeing oneself as fundamentally a member of some national community can help to give one's life meaning and direction, so we should not be too quick to dismiss the nation as a candidate for the status of an 'ethically significant yet not-fully-inclusive human community'. Moreover, the nation may be an appropriate focus for the promotion of cultural goods which are themselves valuable instruments of individual self-development. However, the importance of the nation for these purposes does not entail

[37] Nathanson, *Patriotism, Morality, and Peace*, 27.
[38] Miller, *On Nationality*, 11, 49.
[39] Miller is not alone in making this point. J. Donald Moon, *Constructing Community*, 66, contains a statement of a similar view by an American liberal theorist.

that nationality constitutes the proper criterion for the inclusion of persons within the scope of *distributive justice*. We should bear in mind then, as we proceed, that accepting the moral significance of nationality does not in itself justify restricting the scope of justice to exclude non-nationals from primary concern.

It seems clear that any favouritism of co-nationals cannot, while remaining a moral appeal, make any claim about the *absolute* overridingness of obligations between co-nationals. Miller agrees. His defence of nationalism—of 'nationality'—is conditional: it 'includes the condition that in supporting my nation's interests, I should respect others' national identities (and the claims that follow from them) as well'.[40] This might be understood as the defence of only a particular conception of nationalism, rejecting those conceptions which allow nations to pursue any course of action as a means to upholding their national ideal.[41] Moreover, I would add that where priority is given, it remains a prima facie priority, and is subject to denial whenever the claims of outsiders are of a certain strength. This is a fairly vague claim, but it stresses the important idea that, contrary to what some defenders of nationality might hold, no national moral priority claim has anything like an absolute hold on persons. So co-nationals can make no *exclusive* claims of distributive justice on one another. That is, whatever increased ethical bonds exist as a result of common national status, they are not such as to rule out the distributive justice claims of those lacking that status. But why not?

In fact, Miller does believe that '[n]ational identities ground circumscribed obligations to fellow nationals'.[42] To assess the plausibility of this belief we need to look at his reasoning in some detail. Miller claims that 'our sense of national identity serves to mark out the universe of persons to whom special duties are owed; it may do this without at the same time determining the content of those duties'.[43] The way of life of a nation is

expressed in the public culture. Various interpretations of the public culture are possible, but some of these will be closer to getting it right than others, and this also shows to what extent debates about social justice are resolvable. It follows that what social justice consists in will vary from place to place, but not directly in line with sentiments or feelings. A Swede will acknowledge more extensive

---

[40] Miller, 'In Defence of Nationality', 15.
[41] Such rejection is the analogue of my rejection, in Ch. 5, of the view known as *exclusionary patriotism*.
[42] Miller, 'In Defence of Nationality', 3.   [43] Ibid. 14.

obligations to provide welfare for fellow-Swedes than an American will for fellow-Americans; but this is because the public culture of Sweden, defining in part what it means to be Swedish, is solidaristic, whereas the public culture of the U.S. is individualistic. . . . This may still sound an uncomfortably relativistic view to some. What I have argued is that nationalists are not committed to the kind of crude subjectivism which says that your communal obligations are whatever you feel them to be. Membership of a national community involves identifying with a public culture that is external to each of us taken individually; and although we may argue with one another about how the culture should be understood, and what practical obligations stem from it, this is still a question to which better or worse answers can be given.[44]

We need to ask how we are to judge which answers are better and which ones worse. Why is the public culture of either Sweden or the US justified at all? Miller has offered us no answer to this question apart from the claim that 'what social justice consists in will vary from place to place', but this is true only if it is taken as a descriptive rather than as a normative claim. No doubt, Miller believes that the public culture of a nation is subject to alteration—he thinks this is one of the positive features of nationality—but here he appears to be saying that the critic of the norms of justice embodied in the national public culture can get no foothold, for those norms are simply given. To be Swedish is to recognize that one has fairly extensive obligations for the welfare of fellow nationals; to be American is to see that one's obligations are less burdensome, and so on. It depends on the contingent fact that one's preferred answers to questions about distributive justice have been expressed at some earlier point in the nation's history! But why can social reformers not introduce new ideas about justice, ideas which have no prominent place in the nation's history?

Miller's answer to this question is as follows:

Philosophers may find it restricting that they have to conduct their arguments about justice with reference to national identities at all. My claim is that unless they do they will lose contact entirely with the beliefs of the people they seek to address; they must try to incorporate some of Hume's gross earthy mixture, the unreflective beliefs of everyday life.[45]

But how much of Hume's gross earthy mixture gets incorporated into a justifiable account of obligations of justice depends on the reasons that can be offered in support of the earthy mixture, and it is unnecessarily

---

[44] Miller, 'In Defence of Nationality', 14. See also, Miller, *On Nationality*, 68 ff.
[45] Ibid.

restricting to allow only certain sorts of reasons to be relevant in such discussions. Hence we return to Miller's idea that 'the unreflective beliefs of everyday life' must be given their due, even, it seems, if those beliefs lack a coherent rationale. To this claim I reply that philosophers —and non-philosophers too—can engage with everyday beliefs without accepting them. To realize that such views are the data from which political argument must begin is simply to acknowledge that argumentation must, if it is to convince, proceed from shared premises. But the *point* of such argumentation is very often to show the weaknesses in accepted opinions and to change those opinions for the better. We are thus returned to the earlier point about the proper conception of philosophical starting-points, and again I maintain that the place from which we begin is not sacrosanct, especially since those disadvantaged or treated unfairly by the institutions justified by commonly accepted views have a legitimate claim to a hearing for their dissenting opinions.

Elsewhere, Miller voices his opposition to 'a naive form of internationalism that is grounded on an inadequate view of ethics and that appears to offer a simple solution to the problem of international obligations but does so at the cost of losing touch with *the way we actually think about such issues*'.[46] This is question-begging, for the arguments against the ethical principle of nationality—at least in so far as that principle offers a justification for co-national favouritism—may, if they have sufficient strength, lead us to change 'the way we actually think about such issues'.

Miller maintains that we owe duties of distributive justice in the first instance to fellow nationals. As an example of a claim of distributive justice, Miller considers the principle of distribution according to need. He says:

We do not yet have a global community in the sense that is relevant to justice as distribution according to need. There is no consensus that the needs of other human beings considered merely as such make demands of justice on me, nor is there sufficient agreement about what is to count as a need. It is therefore unrealistic to suppose that the choice lies between distributive justice worldwide and distributive justice within national societies; the realistic choice is between distributive justice of the latter sort, and distributive justice within much smaller units—families, religious communities, and so forth.[47]

Miller's appeal to a lack of consensus is taken as evidence for denying cross-border duties of distributive justice. But, again, this begs the question against his opponents, since it is that very lack of consensus

[46] 'Ethical Significance', 648, emphasis added.   [47] Ibid. 661.

about whether every person's needs should make some demands on all persons that is the object of dispute. Miller apparently does not think he is begging any important question here, for he continues as follows:

We may still be tempted to reply: if distributive justice can only function within communities with predefined memberships, so much the worse for distributive justice. Our concern should be with the sick and the starving regardless of membership and regardless of how we conceptualize our obligations to them. The question this raises is whether we should think of ethical concern as a commodity in limited supply, such that if we intensify our concern for our fellow countrymen, we diminish our concern for those outside our borders. I have no space here to tackle this question properly, but it is worth saying that the picture of ethics implied in it is far from self-evident. Indeed a very different picture is intuitively more plausible: so long as different constituencies do not impose conflicting demands on our ethical capacities, a strengthening of commitment to a smaller group is likely to increase our commitment to wider constituencies. Empirically it does not seem that those most committed to distributive justice at home are in consequence less inclined to support foreign aid.[48]

Let us outline the dialectic of this passage. The imaginary objector accepts Miller's (contentious) view of the conditions necessary for the assignment of obligations of distributive justice, but claims that we should care for the most needy first, regardless of membership in any communities, national or otherwise. Miller replies that ethical concern is not a commodity in limited supply, since caring deeply for the plight of co-nationals can actually *strengthen* our concern for outsiders. Hence commitments to fellow members of one's nation can actually make it more likely that one will show concern for those beyond national borders.

I have a reply to Miller's reply. We may accept the empirical claim he makes about the relation between local and global concern for others. A comparison of the foreign aid records of Sweden and the United States provides some evidence for that claim. Moreover, if commitment to co-nationals disappeared, it is not obvious that felt obligations to humanity would result; rather, there will be the danger of 'a narrowing, rather than a broadening, of the scope of people's sympathies and moral concerns', where individuals focus only on themselves and their families or particular racial or ethnic groups.[49] But, as Miller admits, there will be a problem where 'different constituencies . . . impose conflicting demands on our ethical capacities'. We *will* in many instances have to choose between seeing to the needs of fellow nationals and of outsiders, and

[48] 'Ethical Significance', 661–2.
[49] Nathanson, *Patriotism, Morality, and Peace*, 21.

(since, as I have said, Miller's refusal to accept world-wide obligations of distributive justice is question-begging) if more pressing needs make stronger claims, then foreigners will rightly take priority in some instances. From his words we may infer that Miller sympathizes with the claim that the sick and the starving should be helped, for he responds to the criticism not by denying this claim but by denying that national favouritism —i.e. co-national priority—leaves the foreign sick and starving out in the cold. My point is that, where a choice must be made between meeting the needs of co-nationals or of outsiders, it will often be preferable to favour the outsiders. Miller might agree with this in some cases, but I see no reason for denying that the claims of outsiders are in these cases claims of distributive justice. The problem is that *if* faced with the prospect of bringing about 'distributive justice at home' when that can only be achieved by withholding foreign aid, is it then correct to maintain that there is a prima facie claim in favour of the domestic obligation?

In closing this section, one point needs emphasis: nationalist attachments need not contradict the claims of cosmopolitan morality. This is a claim made most clearly by Charles Beitz, who argues that cosmopolitanism

need not be indifferent to particularistic values such as the loyalties and affiliative sentiments characteristic of membership in cultural or national groups. If it is a fact (as normally it is) that membership in a distinct political community has value for the members of that community, then, on a cosmopolitan view, this fact should matter for practical reasoning. The important question is not whether it should matter, but how.... In fact, if membership in a flourishing community of a certain kind is a value for people, cosmopolitanism requires us to bring it into account.[50]

Hence national attachments can find a place in the cosmopolitan picture of the moral landscape; of course, bringing the importance of national values into account does not imply acceptance of all nationalist claims. The main point to make is that no nation-based ethical commitments can ever constitute the entire sphere of a person's legitimate obligations. Where the legitimate interests of outsiders are of sufficient strength, the duties fellow nationals owe to one another will be overridden by duties to outsiders. The basic claims of distributive justice—what I earlier called the basic rights to a moral minimum (security, subsistence, and liberty)— are the most important case of claims with the requisite strength.

[50] Charles Beitz, 'Cosmopolitan Liberalism and the States System', in Brown (ed.), *Political Restructuring in Europe*, 129–30.

Miller himself acknowledges the role of the cosmopolitan perspective:

Although I have been resisting cosmopolitan attempts to deal with the issues of sovereignty and state borders entirely in terms of universal principles such as individual rights, individual consent and distributive justice, I should be the first to concede that trade-offs have to be made. The case for the nation-state is not that it spontaneously satisfies all the political ideals we might want to espouse, but that it uniquely embodies a distinct value that has no less a claim on us than these others.[51]

My only disagreement with this passage is that it contends that the value of the nation-state is equal to the values embodied in the claims of distributive justice.[52]

The philosophical Mole asked the question, 'What's so special about this river bank?' We have seen the problems with the conservative strategy of answering this question, and we have noted the difficulties with Miller's arguments for the special claims of co-nationals. The topic of the justification of national partiality has hardly been addressed in this chapter, but I have shown that is it mistaken simply to *assume* the ethical relevance of nationality. We can therefore conclude that, even if the nation can in the end be the legitimate focus of some ethical claims, the philosophical Mole has been vindicated.

6.6. CONCLUSION

The defence of nationality discussed in this chapter is important, not least because Miller himself explicitly endorses a basic rights approach. Yet even here we can see the difficulties in the attempted combination of basic rights with a strong attachment to co-nationals. Miller maintains

---

[51] Miller, 'The Nation-State', 158–9.

[52] I agree with many of Michael Freeman's criticisms of Miller in his 'Nation-State and Cosmopolis: A Response to David Miller', *Journal of Applied Philosophy*, 11 (1994), 79–87. But I think his account suffers from one central confusion, namely, he identifies UN 'cosmopolitan liberalism' with the liberal universalist position to which Miller opposes his own view. But this identification is inaccurate because it places the debate at the wrong level. If Miller gives us an account that is intended to justify the *nation-state*, his arguments should be countered by alternative accounts which give us reasons to question the moral legitimacy of the nation-state. UN liberalism is perhaps justifiable by such an alternative account of our obligations, although it does have the added feature of accepting the sovereignty of nation-states, hardly a view opposed to Miller's. The proper alternative to Miller's ethical perspective is indeed a *cosmopolitan* view, but by that I mean a general moral position that requires impartiality and the inclusion of all local points of view. See Beitz, 'Cosmopolitan Liberalism and the States System', 124.

that, in addition to these rights, a commitment to nationality complicates the picture of ethical obligations by adding special responsibilities tied to national membership. He is led to deny that basic rights should come first in all cases; instead, he holds that the urgency of these rights counts in their favour, but that our obligations to co-nationals may in some cases override these urgent claims.[53] Since we have seen reason to deny the overarching priority of nationality as a ground for special duties, and have earlier defended the priority of basic rights for all persons, we should deny Miller's claim that unconditional support for basic rights is too simplistic.

We began this chapter by outlining Miller's helpful account of nationality, and then assessed the ethical status of co-national special responsibilities. After rejecting what was labelled the conservative strategy of defending such responsibilities, we rejected as (at the very least) unproven the so-called argument from the need for solidarity and the argument from the 'double-basis' of justified obligations. The latter argument's weakness depended on a nuanced understanding of what it is precisely that weakens the appeal to shared history: the objection from historical myth recognizes both that nations are communities of belief and that such communities do exist, but it denies that the objects of shared beliefs are in many cases of the proper character to provide reasons in favour of strong special obligations between co-nationals. On the vexed question of the proper understanding of impartiality, we have seen reason to retain our original protest that co-national special concern is indeed a species of partiality, and to note that this does not in any way require us to reject such concern. On the question of the relation between nationality and justice, we have denied that there are any sound general reasons for prioritizing co-nationals, and we have defended the claim that duties of justice attach to persons regardless of their national affiliation.

Much more could be said about the supposed defects of cosmopolitanism as against the strong communal ties generated by nationalist sentiments, but in conclusion we should be careful to distinguish moral cosmopolitanism, the position outlined and defended in Part I of this book, from allegedly related positions. Both Miller and Samuel Scheffler claim that there is a 'cosmopolitanism of the economic market and the multinational corporation, where states are increasingly powerless to prevent flows of capital, goods and services (including cultural goods and services) across their borders, or to alter the way the market distributes

---

[53] Miller, *On Nationality*, 74–5.

resources to individuals'.[54] If this is meant as a criticism of moral cosmopolitanism, it commits the fallacy of guilt by association. The advance
of international capitalism, with its elitism, destruction of traditional
cultures, and impoverishment for vast numbers of people, is in no way
a form of the cosmopolitan view that we should show equal moral concern for every human being. The proper response to this objection, then,
is to point out that the cosmopolitan perspective requires one to reject
both the nationalist or patriotic parochialism embodied in the restriction
of concern to co-nationals *and* the unregulated world market with its the
depressing prospect of a global 'McWorld' dominated by multinational
corporations.[55] If cosmopolitanism is best interpreted as a commitment
to the protection of basic human rights, then cosmopolitans will want
to halt 'the relentless march of the global economy' when that march
tramples on the basic rights of persons.

[54] Miller, 'Nationality: Some Replies', 2. Scheffler calls this a 'pathological' form of
cosmopolitanism in his review of Martha Nussbaum *et al.*, *For Love of Country*, in *The
Times Literary Supplement* (27 Dec. 1996), where he points to 'the relentless march of
the global economy, presided over by an ascendant high-tech international elite'.

[55] For a discussion of the negative impact of McWorld, see Benjamin R. Barber, *Jihad
vs. McWorld* (Toronto: Random House, 1995).

7

Relativism, Universalism, and Walzer

> Distributive justice is relative to social meanings.
>
> (Michael Walzer, *Thick and Thin*, 26)

> A given society is just if its substantive life is lived in a certain way—that is, in a way faithful to the shared understandings of the members.
>
> (Michael Walzer, *Spheres of Justice*, 313)

> . . . these citizens of Prague [during the revolution of 1989] were not marching in defense of utilitarian equality or John Rawls's difference principle or any philosophical theory of desert or merit or entitlement. . . . What they meant by the 'justice' inscribed on their signs, however, was simple enough: an end to arbitrary arrests, equal and impartial law enforcement, the abolition of the privileges and prerogatives of the party elite—common, garden variety justice.
>
> (Michael Walzer, *Thick and Thin*, 2)

The challenges to cosmopolitan justice that I will now consider come from relativist ethical views, and the ideas of Michael Walzer, who has recognized both the validity of universal norms and the importance of a more thickly articulated ethical culture. My aims in this chapter are, first, to identify certain salient features of ethical relativism and subject them to criticism, and secondly, to examine Michael Walzer's approach to international justice, bringing out its relativist as well as its universalist features and showing exactly how Walzer goes wrong in partially denying the implications of the sort of transcultural human rights principles I would defend.[1]

---

[1] The first two quotations at the head of this chapter exhibit Walzer's relativizing tendency, while the third appeals to some notion of justice that seems to apply across societies.

7.1. ETHICAL RELATIVISM

For the ethical relativist, moral rightness for a culture or society is determined by that society's accepted moral standards. To act rightly one must
conform to the standards of one's society, and it is a mistake to try to apply
one society's moral code as a tool for judging the ethical acceptability
of a different society's code. Clearly this type of relativism threatens any
universalist moral claims such as those put forward by defenders of
cosmopolitanism. In order to allay criticism from this quarter, I want to
make three claims in connection with ethical relativism in general. Each
assertion supports the need for the development of universal moral principles. The three claims are:

1. Diversity of moral codes between societies is not necessarily indic-
ative of the relativity of core ethical values.

2. The universalist appeal to reason does not require the imposition
of a single code of morals upon all societies. On the contrary, defenders
of human rights to liberty, subsistence, and security will encourage the
development of cultures through their various internal dynamic processes,
objecting only to those features of a culture which violate human rights.

3. Ethical relativism has certain prima facie unpalatable implications.
For instance, it seems to rule out completely any cross-community ethical
criticism, and it unnecessarily restricts the possibilities for moral progress.

Cross-Cultural Variation and Relativism

Ethical relativism is sometimes defended by appealing to the actual variation of moral beliefs across communities; and I think it is undeniable
that particular manifestations of certain basic values will vary across societies. This, however, does not amount to relativism, at least not at the
level of the basic values, which might still hold for every society. The
fact that specific moral rules differ in different societies does not, then,
prove that morality is 'relative' in any sense that challenges cosmopolitan morality. Diversity of moral opinion does not necessarily entail disagreement about moral values at any deep level.

The evidence for this claim is as follows. The supposed deep diversity
of moral views around the world is put into question if we distinguish
between the *specific rules* followed by particular societies and the *general
principles* of which those rules are the manifestations. There may be
different ways of protecting the very same values, depending on the
conditions specific to any given culture. Hence cultural differences at the

level of specific rules could be explained by differences of context or belief rather than differences in evaluative judgements. An undeniable relativity would then be no evidence of any deep value conflict, so we can dismiss any direct move from cross-community disagreement to ethical relativism. Cosmopolitan morality is not therefore threatened by the presence of global dissensus concerning specific moral rules.

Imposing Justice?

The world consists of countless cultures, each with its own characteristic outlook on the world and its own distinctive moral views. Is the cosmopolitan really justified in imposing his preferred moral views upon members of cultures whose ethical commitments conflict with cosmopolitan morality? What are human rights theorists to make of the fact that some cultures deny that such rights exist? Would human rights theorists run roughshod over cultures that deny the rights they recognize, imposing their rights on everyone regardless of the opinions of those subject to this imposition?

In response to this challenge, the defender of human rights says (or should say) that not only is the variety characteristic of human cultures acceptable to the human rights theorist, but this variety is actually *encouraged* by any defender of the various freedoms to which persons are taken to have rights.[2] This point is related to another, namely, that one can be a moral universalist without believing that there is a 'single moral code' with specific rules which every human society must follow. The point is that, within the constraints set by human rights protections, it is permissible and even laudable that different cultures carry on their social life in distinctive ways.[3] Moreover, consider the consequences of ensuring that for all persons the moral minimum is met: peoples who once suffered the effects of malnutrition and disease would now be freed from these evils to pursue their own distinctive ways of living.

Some Implications of Relativism

A third and final point to notice about relativism is its evidently unsavoury implications. If it were true that the only correct standards of

---

[2] Cf. Peter Jones, *Rights* (London: Macmillan, 1994), 214.

[3] The differences between relativism, a defensible universalism, and the 'single moral code' view, are discussed in Stephen Nathanson, *Patriotism, Morality, and Peace* (Lanham, Md.: Rowman and Littlefield, 1993), 98.

justice are those of one's own society, it would be *impossible* to judge the justice of arrangements in other societies. So, for example, racist or slave societies would be immune from criticism by those in other societies, or indeed by those *within* those racist or slave societies who disagree with the prevailing moral code. Of course, the main point of assessing relativism is to question this assumption, so I do not claim to have refuted it here. The present point is simply to note one important implication of relativist claims about morality and justice; this entire chapter may be understood as my response to this point. At any rate, it will hardly do to define morality or justice so that it follows from the definition that cross-cultural judgements are impossible, for that begs the very question at issue.

Moreover, accepting a relativist view about justice leaves us with an impoverished conception of moral progress.[4] On the relativist account, moral reformers cannot challenge the prevailing principles of justice; they may only point out inconsistencies between those principles and the practices current in their society. As we will see below, this criticism seems, if only at first blush, to apply to some statements of Michael Walzer's conception of morality and justice.[5]

7.2. SHARED UNDERSTANDINGS AND GLOBAL JUSTICE

Michael Walzer has defended the view that there is no account of distributive justice that applies to the world as a whole. As he puts it, '[e]very substantive account of distributive justice is a local account'.[6] My main purpose in this chapter is to question this claim. More generally, Walzer's views have attracted various objections, the most prominent of which are: his conception of justice contains two main ideas, an appeal to shared meanings and a requirement of spherical separation, and these ideas are inconsistent with one another; the shared meanings on which he would

---

[4] There is an excellent short statement of this point in James Rachels, *The Elements of Moral Philosophy*, 2nd edn. (New York: McGraw-Hill, 1993), 22.

[5] Brian Barry, 'Spherical Justice and Global Injustice', in David Miller and Michael Walzer (eds.), *Pluralism, Justice, and Equality* (Oxford: Oxford University Press, 1995), 75, points out that Walzer does want to say that we can criticize 5th-cent BC Athenian society, but only with regard to the ideals of 5th-cent Athens and not with regard to the ideals of 20th-cent. American society.

[6] Michael Walzer, *Spheres of Justice: A Defence of Pluralism and Equality* (Oxford: Basil Blackwell, 1983), 314.

base his theory of justice are indeterminate; Walzerian justice is too conservative in its implications. Each of these criticisms is important, but I consider them here only where they affect the credibility of Walzer's theory of *international* justice.[7]

Walzer claims that justice for any given society or community is determined by the shared understandings of that community about the social meanings of the goods whose distribution is potentially in dispute. The idea here is that a community's shared beliefs about justice tell us what is actually just for that community. However, an inconsistency is raised by the fact that, when we consider the Walzerian claim that justice is relative to shared social meanings, it seems that Walzer does not heed his own advice on this matter. I propose to focus solely on Walzer's claim that justice is relative to shared social meanings, independently of its relation to his equally central spherical separation thesis, for if the social meanings thesis can be maintained, international distributive justice would appear to be an impossibility.

The first thing to say about Walzer's shared meanings thesis is that Walzer himself, wisely in my view, does not seem to take it seriously when he engages in analyses of specific problems. That is, as Joseph Carens has pointed out, Walzer does not himself follow his own advice that conclusions about justice should be derived from the interpretation of a political community's shared meanings:

Walzer says that it is wrong for new states formed after the demise of colonialism to expel current inhabitants who do not share the race or ethnicity of the newly established dominant majority. The sort of case he has in mind presumably is the expulsion of Asians from Kenya and Uganda in the 1970s. But he makes no appeal to African or even Asian understandings of community and of responsibilities towards those seen in some way as outsiders. Instead, he cites Hobbes.[8]

This is an interesting and revealing point about Walzer's theorizing; it might even show that Walzer, in his discussion of specific problems, implicitly recognizes the difficulties of this aspect of his theoretical position.

---

[7] For the claim that there is, at least potentially, an internal conflict in Walzer's theory between the separation of spheres (or anti-'tyranny') on the one hand, and, on the other hand, the appeal to a community's shared understandings, see Susan Moller Okin, *Justice, Gender, and the Family* (New York: Basic Books, 1989), 62–8; James S. Fishkin, *The Dialogue of Justice: Toward a Self-Reflective Society* (New Haven and London: Yale University Press, 1992), 63–6; and Brian Barry, 'Spherical Justice and Global Injustice', in Miller and Walzer (eds.), *Pluralism, Justice, and Equality*, 74–5.

[8] Joseph Carens, 'Complex Justice, Cultural Difference, and Political Community', in Miller and Walzer (eds.), *Pluralism, Justice, and Equality*, 49–50.

Nevertheless, I will evaluate the theoretical view itself in what follows, and we will see that his position is not as simple as it has been made out to be.

The shared meanings on which Walzer would base his theory of justice are themselves indeterminate, and his privileging of the political as against the philosophical fails to take account of the fact of disagreement at the political level, and so underestimates the need for philosophical argument in disputes about justice. Let us for the moment assume that Walzer is correct in saying that justice is rooted in a community's shared understandings. What follows for those of us in the capitalist democracies of Europe and North America? Are we required to eschew criticism of other political communities on the grounds that '[t]he questions posed by the theory of distributive justice admit of a range of answers'?[9] And what is demanded of those in the developing countries of Asia, Africa, and Central and South America? May they not object to the distributive decisions we make? Even to ask these questions puts Walzer's wider theory in doubt, for we can and do readily understand the notion that 'the capitalist democracies of Europe and North America' constitute some kind of community within which it makes sense to ask questions about justice in distribution.[10] Consider the implausibility of the alternative, say, that British citizens can have *nothing* relevant to say about the acceptability of American 'shared meanings' about justice. In short, Walzer's idea that distinct political communities are the only legitimate arenas for meaningful moral debate is deeply implausible.

But there is a deeper problem with the idea of shared meanings itself: it is often unclear just what the shared understandings are on any given topic. Precisely how do we determine what a community's shared understandings about justice are? Do we come to know the shared understandings about the distribution of wealth in a society by determining what the accepted practices are and (historically) have been? Or is the shared understanding to be extracted from some underlying principle(s) that, in certain circumstances, justifies particular practices?[11] The proper way to understand to what the notion of a 'shared understanding' refers is, in any case, a secondary issue. Far more important, and more troubling, is that whichever option is taken, Walzer believes that the understandings

---

[9] Walzer, *Spheres of Justice*, 5.

[10] Many European countries already constitute a community in a more formal sense, for the European Union countries contribute money partly for the purposes of redistribution to the poorer member countries.

[11] See Joshua Cohen, 'Review of *Spheres of Justice*', *Journal of Philosophy*, 83 (1986).

shared by a society are *for that very reason* judged to be just. Of course, the attempt to condemn criticism of established understandings about justice and morality in general will not work in societies like ours in any case, for it is part of our tradition in liberal-democratic societies to question and criticize moral positions.[12] I return to this point below.

Perhaps Walzer's criterion of justice is derived from his opposition to philosophical arguments that do not resonate with a given population. Walzer emphasizes the political as against the philosophical, and this would rule out international justice, since political questions are defined by Walzer in such a way that they can be asked and answered only by members. Accepting the shared understandings thesis would lead one to believe that philosophical questions, such as 'What principles of justice would be fair for inter-society relations?', are misplaced, and that questions are always asked by those already *within* some political association or other. On this reading, members can properly ask about the purpose and structure of their government,[13] but there can be no single, general right answer to the question of which form of organization is better than any other, nor can there be any question about the ethics of inter-society relations. To his credit, however, Walzer does not restrict discussion in this way, since he has written a book, *Just and Unjust Wars*, whose aim is to assess principles governing the relations of states with one another.

Is it wrong to judge a particular community by criteria derived from philosophical argument which appeals to universal standards of justice? Is Walzer correct to dismiss such criteria in favour of standards which emerge from democratic political processes within particular communities? To see what is wrong with Walzer's claim here we need to point out that the attempt to present philosophical arguments for, say, a list of basic human rights, is in part motivated by a recognition of *dissensus* at the political level with respect to the content (or even the existence) of these rights. Therefore it is incorrect to believe, as Walzer does, that 'politics' can do what philosophy can never do—namely, settle questions of justice. Political deadlock will be broken only where it is possible to engage in some degree of abstraction from endless appeals to vested interests. This abstraction is therefore quite proper; indeed, it is a necessary condition of doing justice at all.[14]

---

[12] See Ronald Dworkin, *A Matter of Principle* (Oxford: Clarendon Press, 1985), 219.

[13] Michael Walzer, 'Philosophy and Democracy', *Political Theory*, 9 (1981), 379–99, at 393.

[14] A similar point, without the present emphasis on international justice, is made by Chandran Kukathas and Philip Pettit, *Rawls* (Cambridge: Polity Press, 1990), 115–16.

7.3. UNJUSTIFIED MORAL CONSERVATISM?

I have defended a conception of justice concerned with basic human rights, and this approach, if carried through consistently, will likely support significant changes in global institutional arrangements. While there is no single correct recommendation for institutional change, there can be no doubt that change of some sort will be demanded by the conclusions reached at the level of moral theorizing. Opposed to this view is Walzer's seemingly conservative approach to arguing about justice. I will now argue that those critical of their own society's institutions and practices would do well to reject the simple interpretation of the 'justice as shared understandings' thesis, for it limits the scope of social criticism and is, therefore, too conservative in its implications for political argument. This is relevant to the problem of international justice because Walzer's thesis, if not significantly qualified, would support the denial of the legitimate claims of the foreign poor to the wealth of those in the rich countries, on the grounds that the latter have reached a consensus to the effect that the former have no claims of justice against them.

Walzer recognizes the problem of conservatism represented by his shared meanings thesis, and he proposes to defend interpretation 'against the charge that it binds us irrevocably to the status quo—since we can only interpret what already exists—and so undercuts the very possibility of social criticism'.[15] We need to assess the claim that Walzerian interpretation is inherently conservative, but notice that it is *not true* that being limited to interpreting what already exists undermines 'the very possibility of social criticism'. The limits imposed by interpretation allow criticism of practices and institutions on the grounds that they contradict accepted understandings of what is morally permissible or required. The important objection is not that Walzer's interpretive method makes social criticism impossible; it is rather that his approach rules out criticism that cannot be tied in some way to moral views already accepted at some level in the society in question. It seems that Walzer's methods would allow for social criticism, but would restrict it considerably. Hence I will now examine the claim that Walzer's conception of social criticism is unduly conservative, despite his claims to the contrary.

Walzer believes that deep social criticism is possible, despite the fact that one's values are ultimately derived from one's community. The

---

[15] Michael Walzer, *Interpretation and Social Criticism* (London: Harvard University Press, 1987), 3.

problem with this view is that it leaves little room for innovative criticisms, since objections to the *status quo* must stem from principles and commitments that are either explicitly or implicitly already accepted within the community.[16] Moreover, as we have seen, where a distributive practice is disputed within a community, the best solution will require some rationale *beyond* simply showing that it can be derived from shared understandings, since *that* much is likely already true of competing solutions.

Walzer might be interpreted as saying that recommendations for action should avoid being utopian. They should, instead, take full account of current conditions and not require too great a deviation from the duties now recognized. Walzerian justice would then exemplify a pragmatic attitude to social criticism. If this were correct, then we would not recommend being too critical of widespread views, for instance, that rights-based duties should be accorded to compatriots while foreigners are to be seen merely as beneficiaries of charitable actions.

Moral duties might be restricted in this way because moral understanding is itself tied to particular cultures. From this it follows that abstraction from the culture in which recognized duties are embedded is simply not possible, that Platonic escape from the cave in which we live cannot provide the basis for effective criticism of a community. Such criticism must remain true to the shared understandings of the community in which it is made.

From this perspective, basic human rights claims look like irrelevant and wildly idealistic notions that will have no impact on current debates. On these grounds, then, internationally recognized and enforced rights (of avoidance, protection, and aid) are beside the point. But, again, the danger of taking this Walzerian tack is that it limits moral and political debate to considering questions that do not stray too far from prevailing opinions. Hence, if (in a given society) the view that women and men should have the same civil, political, and economic rights is widely regarded as beyond the pale, then offering that view as the most reasonable position on the rights of women is doomed from the start. Walzer therefore seems to limit moral criticism in ways that make his position virtually indistinguishable from more openly conservative perspectives.

In general, Walzer appears to be too concerned with political success, to the detriment of any focus on moral legitimacy. Against this, Will Kymlicka has rightly urged that 'the efficacy of a justice claim and its

---

[16] Cf. the point made earlier in this chapter concerning the limited notion of moral progress implied by relativist accounts of moral values.

legitimacy are two separate questions'.[17] And Brian Barry adds the following set of claims to his general attack on Walzer's approach:

[T]he search for influence is at best distracting and at worst corrupting. Political philosophers should say what they think is right, whether what they have to say is popular or unpopular. Perhaps they will with luck eventually extend the boundaries of what is politically thinkable. But even this is not likely to be achieved if we start by flattering our audience by telling them that if enough of them believe the same thing it makes no sense to say they are all wrong.[18]

We are therefore faced with an incongruity. On the one hand, Walzer claims for his conception of justice a significant degree of critical potential, but on the other hand his appeal to politics and to social meanings renders his claims unpersuasive to many who would take a critical stance towards the shared understandings of their own community.[19] While Walzer's radicalism in certain respects is beyond question, there is room for dispute as to whether there is critical potential in his conception strong enough to address the many injustices we still face.

But maybe the charge of conservatism is too strong. After all, considering Walzer's own recommendations, it might be open to him to argue, in the way he does in his defence of industrial democracy, that the implicit commitments of people in the rich countries entail a significant redistribution of wealth and power across state boundaries.[20] And in another sense, there may be, within any community, the moral resources to challenge any practice whatsoever, in which case the practical difference between Walzer's position and more overtly wide-ranging views would come close to disappearing.

7.4. A PARADOXICAL DEFENCE OF HUMAN RIGHTS

Walzer's particularism, on one interpretation, rules out moral judgements about non-members of specific political communities, but Walzer

---

[17] Will Kymlicka, 'Some Questions about Justice and Community', Appendix I, in Daniel Bell, *Communitarianism and its Critics* (Oxford: Clarendon Press, 1993), 215. And see, for the opposing view, Daniel Bell's defence of Walzer at ibid. 65–6.

[18] Barry, 'Spherical Justice and Global Injustice', 80.

[19] My discussion, in Ch. 6, of the conservative and critical strategies of political argument is part of my attempt to clarify and defend a more plausible approach to these issues.

[20] See David Miller, 'Introduction' to *Pluralism, Justice, and Equality*, 9, where the radicalism of Walzer's method of interpretation is noted.

himself wants to make such judgements. One way to interpret Walzer's theory is to see it as making a particularist claim about the impossibility of universal moral judgements. The argument would say that, given that moral principles originate within particular cultures, and that those principles are addressed only to members of those cultures and not to others, it is impossible to adopt a perspective from which all cultures, or the individuals who make up those cultures, can be viewed as objects of equal moral concern. Moral judgements, including judgements about justice, are judgements about the moral relations between members of a particular community; there is no scope for judgements about non-members.

This argument has a problematic consequence. It does rule out (i) impartial consideration of all persons regardless of their community attachments, but at the same time it rules out the claim that (ii) every community ought to be especially concerned with its own members. The second claim is ruled out because it is itself a universal claim, to the effect that intra-community special concern is justified.[21] As we will see, there is good reason for denying that Walzer holds this particularist view of moral argument, for he does want to make the universalist claim identified by (ii).

The shared understandings of justice in contemporary Western societies are themselves disputed, but to the extent that universal human rights are accepted by the members of these societies, Walzer's methodology must, paradoxically, generate a defence of human rights. Consider Walzer's claim that '[i]ndividual rights (to life and liberty) . . . are somehow entailed by our sense of what it means to be a human being. . . . [They] are a palpable feature of our moral world.'[22] This is nothing less than a universalist view of human rights, but how does this position relate to the more localist notions also to be found in Walzer's work? In the present context, the relevant point is that the reference to 'our moral world' seems to be, for Walzer, a nod in the direction of his favoured 'community-consulting' method for defending principles of justice. If it is the case that a commitment to universal human rights constitutes a central feature of the shared understanding of a contemporary Western society like the United States, then it follows that, from the Walzerian particularist perpective, we have a reason to accept that commitment to universal human rights. This is because the particularist character of

---

[21] Cf. Thomas Hurka, 'The Justification of National Partiality', in Jeff McMahan and Robert McKim (eds.), *The Morality of Nationalism* (Oxford: Oxford University Press, 1997).
[22] Michael Walzer, *Just and Unjust Wars* (New York: Basic Books, 1977), 54.

arguments about justice does not allow for external assessment of a community's moral consensus. Showing that this is in fact the social consensus of the society would then provide an argument in favour of universal human rights. I think, however, that this endeavour would be a waste of the theorist's time, for it turns out that this form of argument— the argument from community consensus—is inherently faulty, because it allows for the justification of any practice whatsoever if that practice is supported by the community's consensus.

The same sort of point can be made by noting the irrelevance of communal *dissensus* to substantive conclusions about justice. Suppose that some cultures or societies are committed to the denial of universal human rights. What is the proper response to this state of affairs? If before we were claiming that there is more agreement about values than it appears, we should now say that the existence of value *dis*agreement hardly constitutes a good reason for giving up one's assertion that the values expressed in human rights claims hold universally, quite apart from that disagreement. It is no refutation of a moral claim to say that there is no consensus in its favour in every culture in the world, nor is a moral claim plausibly defended by citing *only* its widespread appeal (though its popularity might, depending on other factors, count in favour of it). Moral views are properly judged not by determining how many people (or cultures) subscribe to them, but by the plausibility of the reasons adduced in their favour. Cross-cultural value disagreement does not refute the claim that human rights are universally valid, especially when we can (and have) presented arguments to show why it is plausible to accept that all human beings have basic rights. But those arguments are not best framed in terms of a given community's shared understandings, for human rights are properly understood as linked to particular contents (e.g. basic human interests), whereas a community's understandings need not make any essential reference to these contents.

7.5. JUSTICE AND AGREEMENT

I now want to assess the claim that one implication of Walzer's shared understandings thesis is that its grounds for denying international justice constitute equally plausible grounds for dismissing intra-community justice as well. If it is the absence of consensus about distributive questions at the *international* level that leads Walzer to dismiss the notion of international distributive justice, then is he committed to denying (on pain of inconsistency) what he cannot and does not want to deny—that there is anything properly called domestic or intra-community justice? Brian Barry has argued that 'the most obvious objection to Walzer's conventionalism' is that there are no shared understandings about justice within any given society.[23] I note this as a serious problem for Walzer, but its implications for international justice seem at least as worrying for his theory.

Consider the following point. At times Walzer seems to want to claim—and, note here that I'm not sure this *is* what he wants to claim (see below)—that international justice is impossible because there are no shared understandings within international society (or across national communities) about what justice requires. As he puts it, 'The only plausible alternative to the political community is humanity itself, the society of nations, the entire globe. But were we to take the globe as our setting, we would have to imagine what does not yet exist: a community that included all men and women everywhere. We would have to invent a common set of meanings for these people. . . .'[24] If that is indeed his view about international society, then—if he is correct about international society—he is required to reach similar conclusions about justice within any given nation-state. For shared understandings are missing in both cases, so consistency demands that Walzer give the same answer to the question of justice in both sorts of case. If, for Walzer's reasons, there is no international distributive justice, then it follows—if we employ Walzer's argument—that there is no 'national' or nation-state distributive justice either. But, of course, Walzer does not want to maintain the latter claim, and he is correct not to want that. My point, however, is that this line of reasoning simply reveals that Walzer has *not* shown that, by accepting his premises, it follows that international distributive justice is impossible. If it did show that, it would also have shown that domestic justice is similarly out of the question.

But perhaps this criticism oversimplifies the picture Walzer is trying to draw. It is not that we have two alternatives: agreement about distributive justice on the one hand, and disagreement about it on the other. Rather, what *is* true is that within certain (usually national) communities there is a significant degree of agreement, so that it makes sense to inquire about which interpretation of justice is best. Of course, nowhere

---

[23] Barry, 'Spherical Justice and Global Injustice', 78.

[24] Walzer, *Spheres of Justice*, 29–30. Again, it is unclear how this view coheres with the perspective underlying the discussion of the ethics of intersociety relations in *Just and Unjust Wars*.

is there complete consensus, but outside of communities that largely produce and distribute goods among themselves there is a much lower coincidence of views; consequently, international justice must rely on 'thinner' principles, such as those expressed in terms of human rights. This view is plausible; however, we will see that Walzer's particular version of universalism is not without its own problems. In any case, it is unclear to what extent the overall theory is still committed to the shared understandings claim, whose validity has already been put in question.

7.6. UNIVERSALIST CONSTRAINTS ON COMMUNITY CONSENSUS

Let us now consider the following claims:

(1) Walzer's defence of universalism conflicts with the relativist strand of his theory.

(2) The universal elements of Walzer's view are given an unnecessarily weak defence while being too limited in their implications.

(3) The entire Walzerian universalist edifice rests on a questionable basis.

In their strong forms, these claims would seriously weaken Walzer's project, so it necessary to consider them in turn. The second and third propositions more or less hit their mark. With respect to the first claim, however, I will now argue that, properly understood, Walzer's view is ultimately universalist rather than relativist, since the relativizing of justice to community is itself susceptible to constraints that apply to all societies. In addition to certain relativist tendencies—embodied most notably in the shared meanings thesis—Walzer has also claimed that there is a kind of justice that applies universally. Relativists are always in danger of defending a universalism which prioritizes social conformity on the one hand or, on the other hand, tolerance of other cultures. Walzer appears to fall into both traps, since he seems to believe (i) that justice must always be consonant with social meanings, and (ii) that toleration for other communities' ideas about justice is itself an ethical obligation.

In some places Walzer claims that, if there is widespread agreement within a society about what is just, then criticism of the *content* of that agreement is impermissible. As he puts it, 'A given society is just if its substantive life is lived in a certain way—that is, in a way faithful to the shared understandings of the members. . . . To override those understandings is (always) to act unjustly.'[25] Quite clearly, this is not a consistently relativist view, since it holds to an absolute principle, namely, that it is always unjust to challenge a conception of justice that constitutes the shared understanding of a society.

If one holds, as Walzer seems to hold, that *the moral approval of the community* is the criterion of justice, then such approval is the ground for justice within any given community. But imagine that community approves of some practice that we (Western universalists) take to be morally disgusting, such as the slavery of the indigenous female population. What can Walzer say to those who engage in this practice? The answer seems to be: nothing at all, at least so long as it really is the overwhelming consensus of that community that enslavement of their female population is a just practice.[26] To override that consensus is always to act unjustly, according to Walzer. One might be led to believe that part of the problem with Walzer's view, at least as stated here, is that it appears to divorce the *justifiability* of principles of justice from their *content*, with the consequence that principles with any content whatsoever may be justifiable, if only they form part of the community's shared understandings about justice. But this appearance is misleading, since it fails to acknowledge that Walzer's appeal is ultimately to the (implicit) *consensus* of the community, and this implies that the common understandings not be the product of manipulation or coercion: hence the shared meanings thesis must be significantly qualified in order to rule out communal beliefs generated in illegitimate ways. If the creation of consensus is itself subject to what we might call certain 'legitimacy constraints', then the link between the justifiability and content of principles of justice is tightened, because certain practices (say, slavery) are exceedingly unlikely to be accepted freely by those truly in a position to withhold their consent. Walzer is committed in a fundamental way to the notion of *equal citizenship*, so he unconditionally rejects any form of slavery or caste system.[27] In light of the concerns of cosmopolitans, however, the worry is that this egalitarianism applies only to members, that is, only to those already internal to a given community.

---

[25] Walzer, *Spheres of Justice*, 313–14.

[26] As we shall see, however, Walzer *does* want to say that slavery is wrong because it violates minimalist moral constraints. My point here is that there are no grounds for such a judgement in Walzer's shared meanings thesis.

[27] David Miller, 'Introduction', in Miller and Walzer (eds.), *Pluralism, Justice, and Equality*, 4.

What is the universal worth of compliance with shared norms? If conformity with the overwhelming social consensus is taken to be a value of *non-relative* importance, then anyone sceptical of this view is entitled to question it by pointing out other candidate non-relative values which he deems morally more important than conformity. For instance, an opponent of Walzer's position could say that the value of protecting innocent life should prevail over conformity when conformity dictates that foreign innocents should be killed. When following accepted standards conflicts with values such as protecting innocent life, it is reasonable to hold that it is right *not* to follow those standards.

Walzer's claim that it is wrong to override local understandings about justice suggests that he puts significant value upon *tolerance* of other communities. We should therefore evaluate the appeal to tolerance as a moral and political value. There is an uneasy relationship between ethical relativism on the one hand and, on the other hand, a tolerant attitude toward the norms accepted by outsiders. Relativists believe that the validity of ethical claims is community-relative, that validity depends upon whatever is customary within a particular community. Despite the frequent links made between relativism and tolerance for other communities or cultures, it is important to note that nothing about the value of toleration of other cultures and ways of living is implied by this type of relativism, nor by relativism in any of its other forms. The acceptability of toleration must depend, for the relativist, upon prevailing attitudes to toleration: cultures which are tolerant would demand toleration of other cultures, but intolerant cultures would require members to be *intolerant* toward other cultures. If relativists attempt to deny this, they run into the further difficulty of adopting a claim that purports to apply universally, i.e. the claim that toleration of alternative cultures and forms of life is an ethical requirement. But this claim is itself incompatible with relativism because the main point of the doctrine was supposed to be that there is no transcultural vantage point from which anyone can make any such claim about universal applicability.

We can see this potential tension between relativism and tolerance in the work of Walzer, brought out by statements such as the following: 'Justice is rooted in the distinct understandings of places, honors, jobs, things of all sorts, that constitute a shared way of life. To override those understandings is (always) to act unjustly.'[28] If Walzer wants to argue

---

[28] Walzer, *Spheres of Justice*, 314.

that the 'shared way of life' of a community should be respected by outsiders, then he needs to say why toleration is in order where that way of life includes what many would view as morally abhorrent behaviour. Defending toleration as a value in itself, while in many ways attractive, is not a relativist position; and once we have given up relativism we can concentrate on the issue of precisely when toleration of another society's (or one's own society's) practices might be wrong. Walzer's view does not embody any simple inconsistency between relativism and tolerance because, as we have seen, his position appeals to freely created consensus about justice within a community, and is therefore not relativist in any very deep sense, since the universal value of uncoerced opinion formation implicitly underlies the worth of communal agreement. Presumably, what motivates the proposal for tolerance of other societies is the assumption that those societies base their views about justice on a proper consensus; but where this is not so, Walzer's theory would, or should, recommend intolerance where those views violate practices whose universal validity is central to our own considered judgements. Of special interest to the defender of basic human rights would be a case in which a society does not recognize the claims of persons to have their security protected. Are we, in our society, then required to judge that this other society does not engage in an unjust practice?

Reasons for doubt on this matter stem from a point made by Joseph Carens, who notes that toleration of other cultures is a feature of *our own* societies, not of all societies, and that tolerance is not the *only* value embraced by our societies: 'the fundamental question is not really what do *they* think is right, but rather what do *we* think is right or what *should* we think is right? *Our* conception of justice includes respect for cultural difference as one of its components, but one that is balanced against concern for human rights . . . among other things.'[29] Toleration is *our* value and, moreover, it is not always of overriding importance.

I have argued that the shared understandings thesis, qualified by legitimacy constraints upon the consensus-creating process, is a universalist position. If this is so, then we do best to focus on the type of universalism in question—namely, the supposed attractions of conformity to shared values—rather than the merits or demerits of relativism. Many (theoretical) relativist positions seem in reality to be contestable forms

---

[29] Joseph Carens, 'Complex Justice, Cultural Difference, and Political Community', in Miller and Walzer (eds.), *Pluralism, Justice, and Equality*, 65, emphases in original.

of universalism.[30] If the relativist claim is that the most important ethical values for any community are determined by the culture of that community, then the position is no longer a version of normative relativism.[31] Defenders of universal human rights would then be opposed to a universal claim to the effect that anti-human-rights cultural attitudes which prevail in particular societies are, to the extent that they actually do prevail, ethically worthier than attitudes supportive of human rights. If the foremost ethical norm is that any given culture should be able to follow its traditional values and standards, then human rights will rightly be overridden whenever a particular culture embraces racist or sexist values, or when a culture permits or requires cruelty toward specific individuals. It is difficult to see any appeal in this sort of moral conformism.

As I have mentioned before, there is an explicitly universalist aspect of Walzer's view of justice, in which a minimum moral code is valid for everyone regardless of the particular society in which they live.[32] Strictly speaking, this conception is not compatible with the emphasis on local justice in Walzer's work.[33] We have noted that Okin, Fishkin, and Barry argue that the two central elements of Walzer's project threaten to conflict with each other: separation of the spheres of justice will collapse when a community's social meanings about various goods dictate the pursuit of boundary-crossing. My present claim is the different one that Walzer offers conflicting accounts of what justice demands, *even if* we ignore his claim about the need for spherical separation. He claims that shared meanings about goods within a particular community determine just distributions for that community. But he also believes

---

[30] We saw one instance of this with the alliance of an explicit relativism with an equally explicit call for inter-community tolerance. The latter is a universalist claim and so conflicts with the relativist element of the position. Below I consider a different internal conflict between relativism and universalism, one that is to be found in Walzer's theory of justice, namely, the incompatibility of local justice with 'minimalist universalism'.

[31] Rhoda E. Howard, 'Cultural Absolutism and the Nostalgia for Community', *Human Rights Quarterly*, 15 (1993), 315, calls this view 'cultural absolutism'. See also, Rhoda E. Howard, *Human Rights and the Search for Community* (Oxford: Westview Press, 1995), ch. 3.

[32] See for instance, *Interpretation and Social Criticism*, 24. This type of universalism is to be distinguished from universalist appeals to tolerance or to consistency with locally shared understandings.

[33] One might object that there is no incompatibility here. On the one hand, there is a universal moral minimum on which all cultures converge, and on the other hand there are 'thicker' conceptions of local distributive justice in different communities. The problem, however, is that both views address the question of *justice*, and it is therefore prima facie inconsistent to say both that justice applies equally to everyone and that it applies only to members of the local community.

that justice, at some level, is truly universal, and hence, it seems, not completely relative to shared meanings after all.

We therefore could ask a question requiring a yes/no answer: does Walzer hold that there are any universally valid principles of justice? In *Spheres of Justice*, the answer was 'No', since Walzer says there that justice is always local, never universal. But, as David Miller points out,[34] by the time Walzer gave the Tanner lectures in 1985,[35] he was saying that killing, deception, and torture are ruled out by principles which hold universally. So there are *some* universally valid moral principles. Miller maintains that this is a *qualification* of Walzer's earlier view, but it is more than that, for it amounts to a denial of the claim that no principles of justice are universally valid. Minimalist justice is, after all, still a species of justice.[36]

If Walzer believes that this minimal moral code derives its universal validity from the fact that, as Miller puts it, its requirements 'run across all cultures', then his universalism depends on an empirical assessment of cross-cultural systems of moral belief. This might be a risky position to hold, however, for two reasons. First, the fact that everyone believes that some practice is morally wrong is certainly evidence for thinking it actually *is* wrong, but widespread belief does not *make* it so. On the contrary, if the beliefs are true, one might be tempted to believe that it is the wrongness of the practice that makes them so. Similar reasons apply to agreement about moral rightness: universal agreement about the moral rightness of slavery would not be a good reason for taking slavery to be a morally acceptable practice. The notion of a social consensus is itself in need of critical scrutiny, and a brief consideration of its possible underpinnings suggests that it should not be accorded special respect even when it can be identified.

Consensus about a particular distributive question is not an appropriate basis for the legitimacy of views about justice when that consensus has been achieved by questionable means, most importantly, by unequal media access. Brian Barry makes the point that the existence of consensus in itself tells us next to nothing about the defensibility of the views

---

[34] David Miller, 'Introduction', in Miller and Walzer (eds.), *Pluralism, Justice, and Equality*, 2.

[35] Reprinted as the first two chapters of *Interpretation and Social Criticism*.

[36] The universal validity of 'moral minimalism' is a prominent feature of Walzer's recent work. See e.g. Michael Walzer, *Thick and Thin* (Notre Dame and London: University of Notre Dame Press, 1994), esp. chs. 1 and 2. Walzer's discussion makes it clear that he considers murder to be not only morally wrong but also unjust. See ibid. 26.

about which there is consensus, since (apart from much else) 'unequal access to the means of persuasion' will ensure that those who control the mass media will have an overwhelming impact on community opinion.[37] Not surprisingly, the interests of groups (i.e. corporations) whose economic resources dominate media operating on market principles— where money buys influence—will be very well-represented, not to say all-encompassing.

More generally, any theory such as Walzer's that emphasizes the normative relevance of prevailing beliefs must take seriously the possibility that the belief-generating process is skewed by power inequalities. As Jon Elster points out, Walzer identifies common understandings about justice and offers normative recommendations about distributive practices, but he fails to give any explanatory account of why people generally believe what they do about distributive justice. This is an important omission, for it permits us to overlook potentially objectionable means of generating consensus.[38] And this is true even if we admit, with Walzer, that 'the path of interpretation' does not consist merely in the description of prevailing opinions, that there is often a complex interpretive exercise required to render in a clear way the moral beliefs of a given community.[39] This objection is, then, that Walzer's own position requires that he stress more clearly the potential obstacles to the generation of noncoercive community consensus.

The second reason why Walzer's opinion-based universalism is risky is that it is open to refutation by the discovery of some society in which, say, murder is thought to be morally right.[40] Should such a discovery really dissuade us of the claim that murder is wrong, regardless of the cultural beliefs of those in the society in which it is committed? Perhaps, however, this is not such a serious problem for Walzer's view, since

---

[37] Barry, 'Spherical Justice and Global Injustice', 77. For evidence of the influence of the sphere of money in the sphere of communications, see Edward S. Herman and Noam Chomsky, *Manufacturing Consent: The Political Economy of the Mass Media* (New York: Pantheon Books, 1988).

[38] Jon Elster, 'The Empirical Study of Justice', in Miller and Walzer (eds.), *Pluralism, Justice, and Equality*, 81. In a similar vein, Simon Caney, in 'Liberalism and Communitarianism: A Misconceived Debate', *Political Studies*, 40 (1992), 287–8, rejects Walzer's appeal to the consent of the community because he rightly recognizes that Walzer 'relies on a naive social theory'.

[39] Walzer, *Interpretation and Social Criticism*, 3, 29–30.

[40] Walzer accepts that his view is susceptible to refutation in this way: he says that the prohibitions that constitute the universal moral code are 'almost universal', since 'the odd anthropological example' would overturn any view lacking the qualifier 'almost'. *Interpretation and Social Criticism*, 24.

there is reason to question whether there could ever be a *society* which did not recognize some prohibition on murder. In sum, moral opinions are relevant to moral theory, but they do not in themselves constitute evidence sufficient to justify any assertions about the status of moral claims and arguments. Walzer's appeal to a constraint-qualified community consensus might then be seen as recognizing the relevance of moral opinions but offering a criterion for excluding some of those opinions from consideration.

7.7. THE IMPORTANCE OF THINNESS

I now want to emphasize the importance of minimal or so-called 'thin' morality as against the thicker ethical conceptions favoured by Walzer. I maintain that what I will call Walzer's 'hotel room argument' fails in its attempt to privilege thick cultural systems of belief and action over the minimal requirements of universalism.

Walzer tells a story about the difference between the thick morality of a particular culture and the (thinner) 'principles of cooperation' adopted by those seeking agreement from behind a Rawlsian veil of ignorance.[41] According to Walzer, the latter principles will not be part of the morality of 'people who already share a moral culture'.[42] Implementing such principles in ongoing, real-life cultures would be like taking a hotel room 'as the ideal model of a human home'.[43] Walzer says that '[a]way from home, we are grateful for the shelter and convenience of a hotel room'. Refugees, of course, appreciate the importance of hotel rooms:

They need the protection of the rooms, decent (if bare) human accommodation. They need a universal (if minimal) morality, or at least a morality worked out among strangers. What they commonly *want*, however, is not to be permanently registered in a hotel but to be established in a new home, a dense moral culture within which they can feel some sense of belonging.[44]

There is here some acknowledgement of the claims of universal moral principle, but the 'hotel room argument' seems to constitute a denial of full-bodied universalist justice by way of an appeal to a metaphor. When we ask what the metaphor could mean in this case, I think we

---

[41] Walzer, *Interpretation and Social Criticism*, 14–16. The words 'thick morality' do not figure in this particular telling of the story, though I think the idea is best conveyed by the 'thick and thin' metaphor on which Walzer relies in his more recent work.
[42] Ibid. 14.   [43] Ibid. 15.   [44] Ibid. 15–16.

will see that the cosmopolitan need not be dissuaded from his position by this argument. To see why this is so, consider what hotel rooms and proper homes have in common. In both cases, individuals have some assurance that the basics of existence are protected: food and shelter are goods common to the two arrangements. Now the universalist does not have to deny that 'some sense of belonging' is necessary for a fulfilled human life; his only point here would be to emphasize that *no accommodation* is adequate if it does not provide the basics. A hotel room that does so is superior to a 'home' that (for whatever reason) does not. Walzer's metaphor carries weight only by *assuming* that the moral minimum is taken care of in any thick moral culture, but this is not necessarily true. To use Walzer's metaphor to explain my own view, the morality of basic human rights maintains that no home is satisfactory unless it protects the vital interests catered to by hotels; homes are preferable to hotels, but only where both meet the minimal criteria.[45]

Related to the argument we have been considering is Walzer's conception of minimalist morality itself, which I take to be something of a misdescription because it gives the false impression that the universal minimum moral code is merely a framework or set of background conditions, lacking in substance. On the contrary, I claim that the substance of that code is its very point and purpose. In a similar vein, Walzer now argues that human rights impose limits upon any scheme of distributive justice. The problem with this claim is that it fails to recognize that a commitment to rights-protections itself generates wide-ranging distributive (and, in contemporary circumstances, redistributive) responses. Human rights are a *part of* the theory of distributive justice. Moreover, once this is acknowledged, it upsets the view that justice cannot cross boundaries, for *human* rights attach to persons regardless of their citizenship status.

According to Walzer, minimalist morality is concerned with basic prohibitions—of murder, deception, betrayal, gross cruelty.[46] Moreover,

---

[45] Walzer uses the architectural metaphor again in *Thick and Thin*, 52. He there concludes that 'rightness is relative to architectural occasion. . . . Perhaps a minimalist universalism also develops, an international style—in hotel design, say—though this is unlikely to reflect the best architectural work.' Returning to the disputed case—the analogue in some respects confuses the issues—my view is that universalist moral minima do not necessarily represent 'the best work' on justice; rather, I maintain only that no work is up to standard if it fails to ensure that these minimal requirements are met. We might sum up by reverting to the metaphor: any building that does not meet minimal safety standards ought to be condemned!

[46] Walzer, *Interpretation and Social Criticism*, 23–4.

he claims that '[b]y themselves, though, these universal prohibitions barely begin to determine the shape of a fully developed or livable morality. They provide a framework for any possible (moral) life, but only a framework, with all the substantive details still to be filled in before anyone could actually live in one way rather than another'.[47] But Walzer's conception of the role of moral minimalism is inaccurate. Adherents of universal moral principles do not have to believe that the content of basic human rights provides all that is required for a thriving moral culture. A pluralism of moral beliefs and traditions can be accepted and even encouraged; the point is that human rights provide the background conditions for the development of thicker moral systems. Walzer misleads when he says that *all* the substantive details of morality remain to be filled in after the minimalist universal framework is put in place. Protections against killing and (on my theory) against lack of food and shelter provide much detail and substance, and it undermines the credibility of the cosmopolitan project to suggest that they do not. Walzer's claim can seem persuasive only if its misdescription of cosmopolitanism is taken to be accurate.

More recently Walzer has said that '[m]urder, torture, and enslavement are wrongful features of any distributive process—and they are wrong for reasons that have little to do with the meaning of social goods. We need a theory of human rights (or its functional equivalent in other cultures) to set the basic parameters within which distributions take place.'[48] This looks like a simple concession to the view that any set of distributive arrangements is unjust if it does not protect the basic rights of everyone, i.e. it appears to concede that the view I have defended is correct. But to say that human rights are 'basic parameters within which distributions take place' suggests that protecting those rights does not itself have distributive implications. The truth of the matter, of course, is that if people are going to have their rights protected and promoted, there must be a public commitment to distributing goods and services in a way that will ensure the protection and promotion of those rights. In short, it is worth repeating that human rights are a part of the theory of distributive justice, and they accordingly set limits on what any society may decide to do in the way of allocative arrangements. This point upsets any view that justice cannot cross boundaries.

---

[47] Walzer, *Interpretation and Social Criticism*, 25.
[48] Walzer, 'Response', in Miller and Walzer (eds.), *Pluralism, Justice, and Equality*, 293.

7.8. IS JUSTICE MERELY NEGATIVE?

Walzer has now retracted, at least in part, the basic idea of *Spheres of Justice*, but his emphasis on the *negativity* of universal justice leaves that conception incomplete while giving no reason for restricting it in the way he does. We have seen that, in his recent work, Walzer qualifies his relativism, but he continues to limit universal morality to certain *prohibitions*, leaving positive requirements to hold sway only within communities. These points are brought out by the following passage, in which Walzer expands on the main idea of *Spheres of Justice*.

I came to the basic idea of *Spheres of Justice* by reflecting on examples . . . in which the governing principles did not seem to have the universal reach that philosophers commonly look for. The basic idea is that distributive justice must stand in some relation to the goods that are being distributed. And since these goods have no essential nature, this means that it must stand in some relation to the place that these goods hold in the (mental and material) lives of the people among whom they are distributed. Hence my own maxim: distributive justice is relative to social meanings. I now hasten to add, given the storm of criticism this maxim has provoked, not relative simply, for justice in distributions is a maximalist morality, and it takes shape along with, constrained by, a reiterated minimalism —the very idea of 'justice,' which provides a critical perspective and a negative doctrine. Murder as a way of distributing life and death, for example, whether it is the work of a neighbourhood thug or the secret police, is everywhere ruled out.[49]

Walzer thus admits that there is a type of justice that applies universally. He says that 'the very idea of "justice" . . . provides a critical perspective and a negative doctrine'. Hence, murder 'is everywhere ruled out'.[50] Walzer therefore seems to acknowledge that justice—or, at least, justice in its 'minimalist' sense—provides the grounds for criticism of prevailing practices, even when those practices are widely accepted. He would agree, then, with the cosmopolitan claim that there *are* universally valid moral principles. However, Walzer's addition of the claim that justice, in its minimalist incarnation, is 'a negative doctrine', is puzzling. Is this meant to restrict the application of universal principles to some relatively short list of 'Thou Shalt Nots'? If so, some argument is needed to exclude from consideration various *positive* requirements, such as a duty to ensure that no one, anywhere, goes hungry when there

---

[49] Walzer, *Thick and Thin*, 26.   [50] Ibid.

is more than enough food available to feed everyone. It will hardly be convincing to respond to appeals based on human subsistence rights to be told that food has 'no essential nature', and therefore that universalist claims about the basic human interest in obtaining food for subsistence purposes are invalid.[51]

7.9. INJUSTICE AND PAST INTERVENTION

Walzer's most recent statement on the question of international distributive justice reveals his belief that prior engagement of outsiders in the internal affairs of a community is a necessary condition of that community's deprivation constituting an *injustice*. While the practical implications of his current view might not stray too far from those I recommended earlier in this work, I will now raise some doubts about Walzer's entitlement to say what he now says, given his other published positions on this question.[52]

In a recent response to his critics, Walzer addresses the question of 'the injustice of current international distributions'.[53] He claims that global inequalities in wealth, resources, and living standards are *unjust* only if those inequalities have been brought about by external intervention in the internal affairs of some otherwise properly self-determining group, nation, or country. Injustice arises from 'imperial wars; conquests, occupations, and interventions; the political control of trade, and so on'.[54] For Walzer, the only factor relevant to a positive judgement that a given inequality is unjust, in such a way that demands an international response, is that the country on the losing end has not been the determiner of its own law and policy. Internally manufactured injustice demands only domestic response. But when *external* determination of policy has 'deleterious social and economic consequences, then remedial measures are required. And these may well extend to far-reaching redistributions of wealth and resources.'[55]

---

[51] I should note here that, while Walzer correctly points out that food 'carries different meanings in different places' (*Spheres of Justice*, 8), no assertion about the variable social meanings of food in different communities entails that some human beings lack a vital interest in obtaining a certain minimum nutritional intake.

[52] Of course, I do not object to anyone changing his mind after reconsidering the arguments. My point is that Walzer seems now to deny his former stress on localism.

[53] Walzer, 'Response', in Miller and Walzer (eds.), *Pluralism, Justice, and Equality*, 292–3.

[54] Ibid. 292.   [55] Ibid. 293.

Like David Miller, Walzer believes that 'similar measures' are required as a response to serious inequality and suffering, but he denies that the problem is one of *injustice*. Presumably international aid (or international action of some kind) is, for Walzer, an expression of charity, for 'justice is not the whole of morality'. Again, unjust inequalities stem only from cases in which 'we can tell a story of engagement and responsibility'. In conclusion, Walzer thinks that 'for now at least, ordinary moral principles regarding humane treatment and mutual aid do more work than any specific account of distributive justice'.[56]

There are two separate questions raised by Walzer's argument. The first is the semantic question of the preferred use of the word 'justice'. In that dispute, Walzer disagrees with my position. Where I think it is unjust that millions suffer needlessly when so many others have more than they could ever use, Walzer thinks it is not unjust. On his view, this state of affairs is morally wrong but not unjust. This issue does not, perhaps, require settlement at the theoretical level, since we appear to agree about the practical upshot. But it is worth pointing out that if we consider the notions of rights and justice to be conceptually linked, so that we think of the latter in terms of the former, then Walzer's view would constitute a denial that people have *rights* not to suffer or be severely deprived. Others, including foreigners, would have duties to help them, but they would have no rights to be helped.

Secondly, there is the substantive question of what is to be done about the global problems of severe deprivation and large-scale inequality. On the evidence of the passage under discussion, Walzer believes that 'far-reaching redistributions of wealth and resources' are required in order to respond properly to this problem. I of course agree with this conclusion, but I have trouble determining whether Walzer's claim in this instance is consistent with his overall position about the strictly local character of principles of justice. We can make sense of Walzer's position if we take him to be saying that it is only *justice* that is restricted to specific communities, whereas other aspects of morality travel relatively easily.[57] But then it follows that fewer areas of social life are covered by the concept of justice than might have been supposed. For instance, the claim that people have rights to subsistence, security, and liberty could be accepted by Walzer, but in each case the claim in question would not

---

[56] *Pluralism, Justice, and Equality*, 292–3.

[57] Even this claim, however, is contradicted by the third quotation at the head of this chapter.

be a matter of justice but only a matter of the larger picture of morality
—which, it seems, is properly universalist in character. (This position,
however, does appear to be inconsistent with his recent emphasis on
'reiterative universalism', i.e. the idea that universal moral principles
derive their universality from their having been independently adopted
by successive groups across historical time and geographical space.)[58]

7.10. SHOULD WE DEFER TO THICK MORALITY?

Walzer's universalism about minimal morality is combined with an
emphasis on the priority of thick, local understandings about justice. The
universalism he defends is decidedly uneasy, for he still maintains that
justice requires deference to thick moral cultures, if only those whose
moral development has not been distorted by coercive methods of opinion formation.

In his latest work, Walzer refers again to his earlier discussion of 'the
cure of souls and the cure of bodies in the medieval and modern West',
and argues that 'the fact that [in medieval Christian societies] wealthy
and powerful men and women had access to medical treatment unavail-
able to anyone else' does not constitute an injustice.[59] As he puts it,

none of this seems unjust to me—and this is not because I am bound by my
'relativist' maxim to defer to the conventions of the age (any age). For if these
conventions were imposed by force, the mere ideology of the ruling class, the
idea of social meaning might usefully be deployed in criticism of them. But
what we have here is a maximalist morality, a thick understanding of life and
death, a human culture. To this we ought certainly to defer, for it makes no
moral sense to wag our finger at medieval Christians, insisting that they *should
have had* our understanding of life and death.[60]

Walzer thinks he is not bound to say that justice depends on deference
to the conventions of the age; he therefore takes himself to be denying
that his position is straightforwardly relativist. But why does he deny
that justice is simply a matter of convention? The answer is that 'if these
conventions were imposed by force, the mere ideology of the ruling class,

---

[58] See Walzer, 'Nation and Universe' (including 'Two Kinds of Universalism' and 'The
National Question Revisited'), Tanner Lectures 1989, in G. B. Petersen (ed.), *The Tanner
Lectures on Human Values, xi* (Salt Lake City: University of Utah Press, 1990), 509–56.
[59] Walzer, *Thick and Thin*, 28–9. Walzer says that this is his favourite example from
Spheres of Justice, and 'one that I would like, someday, to develop at length'.
[60] Ibid. 29–30, emphasis in original.

the idea of social meaning might usefully be deployed in criticism of them'. So Walzer is claiming *not* that we ought not to defer to conventions, but that we ought not to defer to conventions which have been *imposed by force*. His view, then, is that forced acceptance of conventions does not guarantee that the corresponding social meanings will be legitimate. This is a restatement of the point we made earlier, namely, that constraints of legitimacy demand the rejection of conventions created by immoral means.

Yet Walzer still thinks that 'we ought certainly to defer' to any freely accepted 'maximalist morality', with its 'thick understanding' of ethical requirements. We therefore should not (it would 'make no moral sense to') criticize medievals for their views on the justice of restricting health care to the private sphere, for they had different beliefs about life and death from our own. This conclusion might seem plausible when applied to the case of the medieval Christian view of the world—though even in that case we might doubt Walzer's claim—but when we consider the implications of Walzer's position for contemporaneous cross-community criticism of views on the justice of the distribution of basic goods (food, physical security, and so on), he seems to be on very shaky ground. For Walzer would have to say, for instance, that *if* a community really does assign to food a social meaning according to which its distribution is in part determined by race membership, then 'we'—who from our perspective find such a view morally abhorrent—should not 'wag our finger' at that community. This is tantamount to denying that outsiders have any role to play in debates about justice. This position is not defensible, and it is moreover inconsistent with the minimalist universalism Walzer also defends.

In closing, we should register agreement with Walzer's assertion that philosophical arguments appear to be unending, but we should reject the implications for theory which he wants to draw from this assertion. Potential interminability provides no reason for giving up the attempt to develop general arguments for conclusions about justice. Walzer offers further reason to deny that the appeal to general theoretical issues is helpful in deciding disputes about justice:

> The leap from inside to outside, from the particular to the general, from immanence to transcendence, changes the terrain of the argument, but I know of no evidence that the argument marches more readily toward closure on its new terrain. Even people who read the same books (of moral philosophy, say) are likely to disagree about which abstract and general theory is really the best.[61]

---

[61] Walzer, *Thick and Thin*, 48.

But social critics whose focus is not limited to a community's shared meanings are not as Walzer characterizes them. Consider the critic who appeals to values whose defence is *not* confined to searching for links to shared understandings. She does not have to (nor should she) hold that her arguments ought to bring an end to the debate—i.e. achieve what Walzer calls 'closure'—once and for all. Walzer glosses over an important distinction between

(i) the idea that social criticism should not be limited to the shared social meanings of a particular community, and should therefore be open to arguments framed in more general terms, and

(ii) the belief that appealing to general theoretical considerations will *settle* questions of justice by pointing to the 'one true theory' which any reasonable person must accept.

I affirm (i) but deny (ii). Accordingly, it must be possible to adopt a more general approach without thereby believing that one's own preferred conception of justice must be imposed upon everyone, but retaining an appropriately humble attitude toward one's own favoured conclusions, though this need not deter one from developing arguments.

Having considered the pros and cons of ethical relativism, as well as Walzer's complex account in which the values of both the local and the global are recognized, we have been given no reason to give up our commitment to basic human rights. The appeal to supposed local understandings—if they can be uncontroversially identified—clearly has some role to play in determining the appropriate moral relations between human beings. And we should always remain humble concerning suggestions about the ethical status of practices in cultures with which we are unfamiliar. But where local understandings allow or bring about severe deprivation such as the denial of the food and shelter without which life itself ceases, then the local views should be condemned.

7.11. CONCLUSION

This chapter began by laying out some of the most serious problems with ethical relativism, a view whose truth would irreparably damage any cosmopolitan conception of international justice. It then assessed Walzer's shared understandings thesis, rejecting any simplistic conception of that thesis and withholding judgement on the question of the conservatism entailed by Walzer's own more complex view. While endorsing the notion that there are legitimacy constraints on any consensus-creating procedure, and therefore acknowledging that Walzer's fundamental idea is limited by universalist considerations, I none the less criticized Walzer for under-emphasizing the value of the thin universalist morality that applies globally, for failing fully to note the demanding positive requirements of a commitment to basic human rights, and for linking global injustice to previous cross-border activities. It is by no means obvious that Walzer's general approach is inconsistent with cosmopolitan conclusions, for one could plausibly maintain that *the content of a suitably achieved consensus amongst individuals of equal status and power* would be universal in scope, entailing obligations of justice on everyone regardless of previous intervention, and recommending institutional enforcement at the global level.

8

Neo-Hegelianism, Sovereignty, and Rights

> [V]irtually all of the more concrete normative problems in inter-
> national political theory implicate relatively abstract issues about
> the significance of sovereignty. No argument about human rights
> in other countries, humanitarian intervention or international dis-
> tributive justice, for instance, can proceed much beyond its starting-
> point without encountering the question of the foundations and
> significance of sovereignty as a norm of international conduct.
>
> (Charles Beitz, in David Held, *Political Theory Today*, 237)

My aim in this chapter is to consider the prospects for a reconciliation
between cosmopolitanism and communitarianism in international political ethics. A promising means to this end is the neo-Hegelian or 'constitutive' theory defended by Mervyn Frost and Chris Brown.[1] The promise
of this approach lies in its ability to defend the ethical value of the state
while retaining a commitment to the moral importance of the individual.
Several questions suggest themselves. First, how important is the *state*,
from an ethical point of view, and what is entailed for international
justice by the requirement to take states and state membership seriously?
Secondly, what is the distinctive contribution of the constitutivists in
answering these questions? And thirdly, is their proposed reconciliation
of cosmopolitanism and communitarianism successful?[2]

I concur with the judgement of Chris Brown that 'the most central
of all issues addressed by normative international relations theory [is]
the question of the moral value to be assigned to state autonomy'.[3] The
purpose of assessing neo-Hegelian international theory is to judge the

---

[1] In this chapter I will use the terms 'neo-Hegelian' and 'constitutive' interchangeably.

[2] In asking this third question, I do not mean to suggest that the constitutivists view
their own work in this way. It is my own idea that this approach is, at least potentially, capable of reconciling the two sides, although we shall see that this idea is suggested by
Mervyn Frost's attempted reconciliation of the norms of sovereignty and human rights.
See section 8.4 below.

[3] Chris Brown, *International Relations Theory: New Normative Approaches* (Hemel
Hempstead: Harvester-Wheatsheaf, 1992), 15.

worth of a promising approach to this issue. Once we have seen what sort of defence of state sovereignty can be derived from this account, we can ask about its implications for international distributive justice. Two of my aims in this chapter are to outline the neo-Hegelian or constitutive theory of politics and then to show that, so understood, it is either compatible with cosmopolitanism or, if it is incompatible with cosmopolitanism, it is unacceptable.

8.1. WHAT IS NEO-HEGELIAN INTERNATIONAL THEORY?

How should we judge the ethical importance of sovereign states? Should state boundaries be accorded basic moral importance, or should we rather treat them as 'historically determined but morally arbitrary features of the earth's political geography'?[4] One approach to answering these questions is to set out a demythologized Hegelian political theory—i.e. a Hegelianism lacking Hegel's metaphysical commitment to *Geist* and its necessary historical development.

The development of individuality, according to neo-Hegelianism, depends upon the individual's participation in three social institutions: the family, civil society, and the state. In ethically valuable families, children are recognized as valued members and thereby gain a sense of themselves as worthy individuals. This sense of self-worth, however, depends merely upon family membership and is, moreover, dependent upon feeling, and is therefore lacking the requirements for a more robust self-conception that only participation in the society as a whole—i.e. beyond the micro-society that is the family—can provide.

Civil society 'includes not only the modern market system but also the legal and judicial system, a public authority responsible for social and economic regulation and the provision of welfare, and a system of voluntary associations'.[5] It enables persons to develop their individuality by, for instance, choosing their own way of life and entering into reciprocally voluntary relations with others. But the rules of civil society are held by its participants to be restrictions on individual freedom; it

⁴ Charles Beitz, 'International Justice: Conflict', in Lawrence C. Becker and Charlotte Becker (eds.), *Encyclopedia of Ethics* (London: Garland, 1992), 623.
⁵ Michael O. Hardimon, *Hegel's Social Philosophy: The Project of Reconciliation* (Cambridge: Cambridge University Press, 1994), 191.

is the role of the *state* to overcome the subjective experience of the rules necessary for social life as constraints to be grudgingly accepted as the price for individual welfare-seeking. 'The state provides the element of unity necessary if the individual is to overcome the separateness inherent in civil society.'[6] The Hegelian claim seems to be that the state does not undermine individuality because, as Brown puts it, 'for Hegel the ethical state is a constitutional state'.[7]

Further insight into the Hegelian view is to be gained by mentioning the distinction between *Moralitat* (morality) and *Sittlichkeit* (ethical life). Brown notes that 'some such distinction is commonplace in moral philosophy; the distinctiveness of the Hegelian position is that because individuals are constituted by the community, the demands of social ethics override—and should override—the imperatives of conscience'.[8] It is important to emphasize that the claim that the requirements of the community should override 'the imperatives of conscience' is more plausible than the claim that community demands should trump individual rights. If Hegelians are making the first assertion, their view could in some cases be granted, since that involves nothing more than denying the argumentative force of appeals to conscience. This denial is plausible because an individual's conscience can be mistaken and so lacks any strong justificatory power. It does not follow, however, that *all* conscience-based moral assertions are properly overridden by the community, since it is the *content* of those claims that determines their ethical force. But even if we grant that some appeals to conscience are rightly taken to be weaker than conflicting claims made by, or on behalf of, the community, the strength of *that* Hegelian argument goes no way towards supporting the state when doing so requires the denial of individual rights, for the role of the state on Hegel's theory is precisely to provide the preconditions for the full development of individuality.

One question to which we will return in the course of this chapter is this: does the modern state really make possible an ethical life that accords freedom to every citizen? Hegelians either answer this question in the affirmative or maintain that it is only if an affirmative answer can be given that the modern state is truly ethical. I will suggest that the

---

[6] Brown, *International Relations Theory*, 63.

[7] Ibid. 64. 'The ethical family, civil society and the corporation, and the institutions of a constitutional state provide, according to Hegel, a context in which the freedom of the individual is fully achievable without that loss of affective community thought unavoidable on the Enlightenment account of the conditions for human autonomy.' (Ibid. 65.)

[8] Ibid. 62.

latter option is more plausible and that the ethical importance of the state is, in fact, weakened by certain features of contemporary international political life.

8.2. ON THE VALUE OF THE STATE

We now turn to the question of the accurate representation of communitarian accounts of the state: are states intrinsically valuable or only instrumentally so? Are states the sort of things that can be, in certain circumstances, objects of unconditional loyalty?[9] Cosmopolitans and communitarians approach political life from different perspectives. As Brown puts it: 'From a cosmopolitan perspective, the role of the state is essentially instrumental and it is as such an inappropriate object for more than a conditional loyalty.'[10] Implicit in this claim is, I take it, a further assertion that communitarians—who, we may suppose, take issue with the fundamental beliefs of cosmopolitans—view the state as (i) potentially of intrinsic value (assuming it is a state that is organized in a particular way), and (ii) a proper object of unquestioning attachment or unconditional loyalty.[11] I think this contrast is instructive, but it is inaccurate in one important respect. Neo-Hegelian communitarians, as participants in debates about international ethics, see the state as itself an object of intrinsic value, but only potentially so; the emphasis is on the *potential* significance of states. Not just any state organization will be judged intrinsically valuable, and this is especially so in the modern period, when the claims of individuals quite properly populate public spaces. States must protect those claims; a state that does not do so is certainly not a proper object of patriotism. Hence modern-day communitarianism, in its neo-Hegelian or constitutivist guise, does not consider the state to be an object of unconditional loyalty. In taking what is to some extent a critical stance toward the state, constitutive theory therefore rejects direct appeals to tradition, local practice, or relativism

---

[9] These two questions are distinct, since someone could value some X intrinsically (i.e. not as a means to anything else), yet such valuing could at the same time be conditional.

[10] Brown, *International Relations Theory*, 53.

[11] I do not claim that Brown intended to characterize communitarianism in this way. I maintain only that, if cosmopolitanism and communitarianism conflict in respect of their fundamental commitments, then it seems to follow from this characterization of cosmopolitanism that, *for communitarians*, the state is intrinsically valuable and that individuals should be unconditionally loyal to it.

as justificatory strategies in support of citizen loyalty. These moves are also rejected by cosmopolitans, however, so it is not here that we will find the appropriate contrast between cosmopolitanism and neo-Hegelian communitarianism.

How, then, do constitutivists understand the value of states? Brown notes that '[t]he root notion of communitarian thought is that value stems from the community, that the individual finds meaning in life by virtue of his or her membership of a political community'.[12] But if value originates in the community, it is none the less value *for individuals* that matters for communitarianism so understood. Political membership is meaningful in so far as it provides a context and structure for the lives of individual persons who are members of states, i.e. for the lives of citizens. There is no suggestion here that communities are valuable in themselves, apart from what they contribute to the lives of individuals. And this is true even if we admit that political communities are indispensable for the living of a meaningful life by any person in modern circumstances. Political communities, then, are never intrinsically valuable.[13] Rather, they are often thought to be instrumentally valuable, but in a very strong way. Specifically, these communities are sometimes taken to be necessary conditions for the achievement of meaningful lives for the individuals who live in the contemporary world. On this understanding, states are necessary conditions for properly human lives; this makes states extremely important—in fact, indispensable—but it does not entail that they are intrinsically valuable.

Cosmopolitans and neo-Hegelian communitarians, therefore, do not disagree on the importance of individuals for political morality. Where they might in some cases diverge is on the question of the necessity of separate sovereign states for the living of individual worthwhile lives. (I say 'might' here because it is possible for moral cosmopolitans to agree that separate states are necessary for the living of meaningful individual lives. Their answer will depend on their assessment of the capacity of a system of sovereign states to meet the demands of cosmopolitan justice.)

---

[12] Brown, *International Relations Theory*, 55.

[13] This contradicts my characterization in the previous paragraph, but I think the notion of strong instrumentalism might amount to an assignment of importance to the state that some communitarians would rather characterize as equivalent to holding the state to be intrinsically valuable. However we describe it, the idea—that (a certain form of) the state is a necessary condition of the development of individuality—remains the same.

8.3. ON THE COMMUNITY–INDIVIDUAL RELATION

Brown points out that neo-Hegelian or constitutive approaches to inter-national ethics 'see the state as a manifestation of community, and see community as possessing moral value, distinct from the value to be assigned to the individuals who constitute this community'.[14] Brown's statement is insufficiently precise, and might therefore give a misleading impression of the ethical status of the individual–community relation according to constitutive theory (or, at least, according to a rationally defensible constitutive theory).

In the interests of clarity, we should distinguish between three con-ceptions of the ethical status of community, only the second of which is acceptable. They are:

1. *Pure instrumentalism*: Communities should be ethically assessed purely instrumentally, according to their capacity to protect the pre-existing interests of individuals.

2. *Constitutivism*: Communities are integral parts of individual interest-protection. While communities should be ethically assessed according to their capacity to protect individual interests—since communities do not themselves have interests in any but a derivative sense—the pure instrumentalist view found in (1) overlooks the fact that communities are constitutive of individuality itself, since some individual interests are both generated *and* provided for only in communities.

3. *Non-derivative communitarianism*: Communities have interests in their own right, i.e. interests not derived from the interests of individuals, and therefore there might be instances in which community interests rightly override the interests of individuals, in the sense that the community should be favoured despite some opposing set of individual interests.

Pure instrumentalism is indefensible since it fails to take full account of the ineliminable importance of certain communities in the creation and maintenance of individual interests. This perspective is a type of crude atomism according to which individuals are thought to be capable of developing asocially. Social development is, on this view, simply an option that we should assess by weighing its benefits against its costs. Non-derivative communitarianism is wrong because it appears to rest on an implausible metaphysical commitment to 'communities' as entities

----

[14] Brown, *International Relations Theory*, 117.

whose existence merits ethical consideration independently of the individuals who constitute them. The second, constitutive view is closest to the truth here, since it acknowledges the role of communities in constituting individuals. It will be acceptable, however, only if it also recognizes that the constitutive relation goes in the other direction as well, i.e. just as communities (in some sense) constitute individuals, so individuals (in a more straightforward sense) constitute communities: they are its elements, without which there would be no community at all. It is the failure of position (3) to accept this second constitutivity claim that renders it incredible as an account of individual–community ethical relations. There is a further point to be made here in connection with our continuing focus on basic rights. There can be no question of 'the community' overriding the vital interests persons have in avoiding starvation or torture. The very possibility of a common attachment to social life presupposes that the individuals who commit themselves to their community are guaranteed certain protections without which that commitment cannot honestly be given or expected.[15]

It is worth emphasizing what, on reflection, should be obvious: that human individuals are social creatures. We can, and should, grant the claim that individuals are (at least partly) who they are in virtue of their membership and participation in societies, and that some of their interests are therefore properly understood as being necessarily tied to that membership and participation. In other words, individuals are not social atoms; some of their interests will be overlooked if one considers them as naturally pre-social creatures who have joined societies only from a desire to protect a set of interests which does not expand upon their entering society. Such 'entering' never took place. Individuals can develop a sense of themselves and an ability to follow reasons only in the context of some community.

Having granted this much, we should note, further, that a certain kind of state—one based on the rule of law and the recognition of each member as a citizen of equal status to all the others—fosters an individuality in persons of a greater complexity and depth than is possible

[15] Cf., on this last point, Jeremy Waldron, *Nonsense upon Stilts: Bentham, Burke and Marx on the Rights of Man* (London: Methuen, 1987), 207. I should add that my defence of human rights does not commit me to the view that presocial individuals have rights, since I—along with Hegel—do not believe in presocial individuals; but I appeal to no such beings in my arguments for human rights. On the contrary, my defence depends in large part on the recognition by every person of their duties to everyone else, and these duties are dependent on the interests we all share as vulnerable, needy, social beings.

under less differentiated social arrangements (for instance, those in which family, civil society, and state are not clearly distinguished). Hegelian political theory does not oppose the interests of individuals to the state's interests; rather, it recommends a reconciliation between these two sets of interests. As Allen Wood puts it, 'it is a serious distortion of Hegel's meaning to think that the good of individuals is supposed to be swallowed up in, or sacrificed to, some quite different end. Hegel maintains that the modern state works only because the universal life of the state provides for the subjective freedom and particular happiness of its members.'[16] But if this interpretation of Hegel's conception of the modern state is accepted, we may still ask whether contemporary states *do* provide for their members as Hegel's theory rightly thinks they should (if, that is, they are to be *ethical* states). If, on examination, we discover that they do not, then we have good reason—and good *Hegelian* reason—to ask after the source of the state's inadequacy on this score and to attempt to remedy this inadequacy.

8.4. FROST AND THE CONFLICT OF SETTLED NORMS

Mervyn Frost's constitutivist account of international relations focuses on the 'settled norms' of international relations.[17] Frost identifies a list of eighteen norms, and this of course raises the possibility of a *conflict* of norms. This is what we in fact find: for example, the norm supporting *state sovereignty* is likely to conflict with the norm supporting *human rights* (for example, when a state's claim to sovereign immunity from external interference precludes outside help for citizens of that state whose human rights are being infringed by that very state).[18] If Frost is to carry out his project of showing how these settled norms cohere with one another, he therefore owes us some method for settling conflicts of norms; but if he opts for assigning priority to the norm of protection for

---

[16] Allen W. Wood, *Hegel's Ethical Thought* (Cambridge: Cambridge University Press, 1990), 28.

[17] Mervyn Frost, *Towards a Normative Theory of International Relations* (Cambridge: Cambridge University Press, 1986), esp. chs. 4 and 5, and Mervyn Frost, *Ethics in International Relations: A Constitutive Theory* (Cambridge: Cambridge University Press, 1996), ch. 4.

[18] I am here understanding by 'sovereignty' what F. H. Hinsley calls 'the idea that there is a final and absolute political authority in the political community . . . *and no final and absolute authority exists elsewhere*'. F. H. Hinsley, *Sovereignty*, 2nd edn. (Cambridge: Cambridge University Press, 1986), 26, emphases in original.

a society of sovereign states, he asserts the ethical primacy of sovereignty over human rights. This is a problem for Frost's account, unless he can defend this primacy on other grounds. Frost's (Hegelian) position is that he can do this, while at the same time fully reconciling rights and sovereignty within his overall theory of international relations.[19]

Again, one could reply to Frost by arguing that, since there is no available means of reconciling sovereignty and human rights given the standard background justificatory theories, reconciliation is not possible. But this conclusion is too quick, for we need to assess the capacity of constitutive theory to overcome this conflict. Frost holds that, since people do take sovereignty to be valuable, we should not reject it on the grounds that it does not satisfy our theoretically derived criteria for ethical acceptability. But I believe that the assignment of value to sovereignty, while not properly dismissed outright, is susceptible to critical examination. And it might turn out, after the arguments have been assessed, that the value people assign to sovereignty is misplaced.[20] The demands of distributive justice, understood here to involve protection for the rights of individuals, will play a central role in assessing the moral importance of state sovereignty.

Hegel's project was to reconcile modern individuals with their social and political lives. The reconciliation that Frost attempts is different. It amounts to a solution to the problem of sovereignty and justice, i.e. it is an attempt to show that continued commitment to sovereignty is consistent with the modern attachment to human rights.

The sophistication of Hegelian political theory can be seen in its *indirect* endorsement of state sovereignty. As Brown notes,

Hegelian thought does not simply endorse the right of all states to autonomy. Hegel's account of the necessity for state sovereignty is based on the role of the state in the constitution of individuality, and it is only the modern, rational, ethical state that can perform this constitutive role. A key issue is the extent to which actual states conform to the structures of the rational state, and whether the degree of conformity of actual and real is such as to pass on to existing states the moral immunity from external interference that only the truly ethical state can claim as of right.[21]

[19] There is a helpful account of Frost's view, an account of which Frost himself approves, in Brown, *International Relations Theory*, 118–21.
[20] I do not doubt that *states*—or rather, state representatives—assign value to sovereignty, but that is hardly probative of any claim in support of sovereignty. It is precisely this claim that states make which we are trying to assess.
[21] Brown, *International Relations Theory*, 111.

If state sovereignty is in some cases sufficient for the constitution of individuality, there remains none the less a crucial Hegelian challenge to sovereignty in cases where the state does *not* meet the standards of rationality proposed by the theory, i.e. cases in which sovereignty is not sufficient for individuality. In addition, if it turns out that state sovereignty is not even *necessary* for the development of individuality, then the ethical case for sovereignty will have failed.[22] Our focus should therefore shift to the degree to which modern states do in fact live up to the standards of ethical life imposed by Hegelian political theory, and the degree to which *alternative* political arrangements might also meet those standards.

Part of Frost's strategy is to show that alternative (i.e. non-constitutivist) background theories fail to reconcile the settled norms of international society. For example, utilitarianism as a background theory (i.e. a utilitarian justification for the settled norms of international society) fails because (in Brown's words) 'even if maximising aggregate utility is a coherent goal (and Frost thinks it is not), there is no reason to believe that the norms of the current international system promote this goal'.[23] I think the reply to Frost's dismissal of utilitarianism is as follows. Let us accept that Frost is correct in claiming that the *status quo* does not maximize utility. (I argued for this conclusion myself in Chapter 2 above.) But if one is using utilitarianism as a 'background theory', why should one not conclude that sovereignty cannot be reconciled with one's favoured deep moral view? Frost's argument could just as easily lead to the conclusion that the state sovereignty norm is ethically unjustified. Of course, if we understand 'background theory' to mean 'theory capable of effecting a reconciliation between sovereignty and the claims of individuals', then utilitarianism is unacceptable as a background theory. But why not reject this understanding of a background theory, on the grounds that it legitimates an undue attitude of respect for the settled norm of sovereign statehood? If one objects to this question by saying that it exemplifies an overly detached and external approach to the normative character of the society of states, that it *begins* with individuals and their interests rather than with the states system itself, the reply is that no matter where one begins the process of questioning and assessment, there is no good ethical reason to hold the norm of sovereignty

---

[22] At least, it will have failed to show that we need sovereign states if the international ethical order is to be defensible on moral grounds.

[23] Brown, *International Relations Theory*, 119. And see Mervyn Frost, *Ethics in International Relations: A Constitutive Theory*, 120–5.

in such high regard.[24] This reply immediately suggests that constitutivists owe us an account of *why* state sovereignty is so valuable; accordingly, we now turn to this question.

8.5. THE ETHICAL RELEVANCE OF SOVEREIGNTY

There seems little doubt that the focus on sovereignty—the need to block external intervention in the internal affairs of the state—can mask oppression caused by sovereign states themselves.[25] We should add that, if justice requires a concern with the plight of individuals, the restriction of emphasis to *externally* imposed mistreatment (i.e. by other states, foreign capital, etc.) is never justified, for it would enable domestically manufactured oppression to go uncriticized. (This, by the way, is a good reason to resist approaches to international justice which concentrate only on inter-country inequalities and neglect the equally serious domestic statistics.) Nevertheless, and keeping in mind this caveat, it is open to the neo-Hegelian to argue that state sovereignty is a crucial element of an ethically defensible international ethical order.

The neo-Hegelian view seems to be that the 'modern state' is already —albeit only potentially—capable of ensuring justice and freedom for all, hence there is no need to posit a global community whose purpose is to meet the demands of justice. Brown emphasizes that this neo-Hegelian position does not amount to 'a conservative acceptance of the status quo', since it rather enables us to see the extent to which present arrangements fall short of the requirements of a truly ethical community.[26] But if we accept this claim, as in charity we should, what practical implications follow? What do the central constitutivist claims imply about the ethical status of sovereignty? Here is a list of options:

1. *Sovereigntism*: State sovereignty should be protected at least as strongly as is suggested by the present norms of international society.

2. *Anti-sovereigntism*: The idea of state sovereignty should be given up altogether.

---

[24] See Ch. 6 (on nationality) for a discussion of the question of the relevance of where one begins one's theorizing.

[25] Brown, *International Relations Theory*, 130–1.

[26] Chris Brown, 'International Political Theory and the Idea of World Community', in Ken Booth and Steve Smith (eds.), *International Political Theory Today* (Oxford: Polity Press, 1995), 90–109, at 104.

3. *Qualified sovereigntism*: The importance of state sovereignty should be maintained, but it should be qualified where that seems necessary for the creation of the conditions required to provide justice and freedom for everyone in the world.

We now need to consider the merits of each of these views.

What can be said for and against sovereigntism? As Frost emphasizes, sovereignty is one of the central accepted norms of contemporary international society, so presumably it has something to be said in its favour. In reply to this claim, I think it is plausible to maintain that what sovereignty has going for it is precisely that it has allowed states to develop ethically defensible institutions, i.e. institutions which ensure that justice is done (at least within the scope of those institutions). But then, where this has *not* been achieved, where a state's institutional framework has not shown itself to be capable of providing justice for all of its citizens, what is left of the claim that state sovereignty deserves protection?

Against sovereigntism as here conceived, we should note that to protect state sovereignty by maintaining that each state is absolutely entitled to be recognized as independent, risks the interests, and in some cases the very lives, of the citizens of states. The same reason that justifies sovereignty in the first place also generates a motivation for *restricting* that sovereignty when it stands in the way of interest-protection.

What can be said for and against anti-sovereigntism? It seems clear that, if we were to give up our commitment to sovereignty, a major obstacle standing in the way of rights-protection would be removed. But such a drastic solution to the current problem might be too quick, since (i) states to some degree have made it possible to provide for justice in the modern world (at least within their particular jurisdictions), and (ii) this recommendation to override sovereignty claims might simply be unworkable.

This last point is indeed the main consideration against anti-sovereigntism: as a practical solution to the violation of human rights, it seems altogether unrealistic, 'utopian' in the bad sense of the word— i.e. a recommendation that neither is nor could be realized in any place in the foreseeable future. It follows from its utopian character that the desired end to human rights violations will not be achieved, thus adding to the unattractiveness of this solution.

What can be said for and against qualified sovereigntism? This compromise solution has all the attractions of any such answer: it is potentially acceptable to all parties to the dispute, thus promising the possibility of genuine reconciliation and progress; it avoids the main weaknesses of the more extreme alternatives (i.e. violation of individual interests, utopianism). Moreover, qualified sovereigntism ensures that the benefits of sovereignty are protected, but the qualifications are added when the same reason for *having state institutions*—i.e. to bring about and maintain justice—also constitutes a reason for *limiting sovereignty* whenever those institutions are not maintaining justice.

Against qualified sovereigntism we might also introduce the utopianism charge, but it will be less susceptible to that objection than antisovereigntism was. Furthermore, since restrictions on state sovereignty are *already accepted* in international law and practice, the accusation of utopianism against *qualified* sovereigntism loses much of its force.

I provisionally conclude that qualified sovereigntism is the best of the available alternatives, and that it supports a recommendation for changes to the current emphasis on state sovereignty. Constitutive theory can support qualified sovereigntism because 'the fact that a rational, ethical community is possible yet nowhere exists signposts the imperative need for a change in the way we live'.[27]

It should be emphasized that Hegel is himself not entirely antagonistic toward the ideals embodied in liberal individualist conceptions of the rights of persons, nor does he long for a return to a traditional society in which individual moral reflection is absent.[28] On this basis, we can rightly object to Hegel's exclusion of women from public affairs, giving as our grounds another of Hegel's own positions, namely, that each person is to be accorded equal rights as a moral subject.[29] Likewise, we should reject his view that states should be sovereign in the sense that they are 'independent units which make mutual stipulations but at the same time stand above these stipulations'.[30] If a state commits itself to violating basic rights, either directly or by allowing private concentrations of power to engage in such violations, that state cannot be legitimate; hence, the independence of states is weakened by some requirements that stand above any stipulations they might make. Hegel's (quite proper) sympathy with rights therefore has implications for a defensible Hegelian view of the ethical importance of state sovereignty.

We must now confront a problem with the neo-Hegelian resolution of the conflict between sovereignty and rights. Neo-Hegelian constitutive

[27] Brown, 'International Political Theory', 104.
[28] See G. W. F. Hegel, *Elements of the Philosophy of Right*, tr. H. B. Nisbet, ed. Allen W. Wood (Cambridge: Cambridge University Press, 1991), § 66, for mention of our 'inalienable' and 'imprescriptible' rights.
[29] Wood, *Hegel's Ethical Thought*, 245.
[30] Hegel, *Elements of the Philosophy of Right*, § 330A.

theory resolves the contradiction between sovereignty and human rights by arguing that individuality itself is not possible without the institutions of the modern state and, moreover, that such a state can provide the requirements of individuality only if it is recognized as sovereign by other states which are, in turn, accorded the same recognition. But several questions need to be asked of this account of the importance of sovereignty. Why is it that states cannot play their constitutive role in the absence of autonomy (or strong autonomy) in their relations with other states? What is so special about recognition by *other states*? Would a federation of states that allowed some autonomy, but restricted that autonomy whenever rights-violations were at issue, result in each state in the federation being incapable of constituting individuality in the required sense? And if restrictions to autonomous statehood are resisted while each individual sovereign state is required to meet strict standards of rights-protections—as a precondition of earning the honorific title of 'rational, ethical state' or 'state proper'—then would this not be simply another way of saying that individual rights will be everywhere protected by a justified system of states? In fact, the federation view looks like an improvement upon this latter approach, since federations presumably would have some formalized means of ensuring that rights protections are guaranteed, while traditional Hegelianism (i.e. Hegel's own position)— according to which states (properly so-called) are absolutely sovereign, but only states that meet strict criteria will qualify as states proper—need not require such formalization. The problem with the latter approach would be that, while it suggests similar constraints and positive duties of states, it (unlike the former view) provides no reliable means of ensuring that states live up to their ethical obligations.

Again, we need to raise the question of *why* rights can exist only in the context of sovereign states which are recognized by other sovereign states.[31] Moreover, we have seen that, since not just any society of sovereign states protects rights, we need to know what to do when an international society—for example, the present one—fails to protect the rights that states are supposed to be necessary to protect. In section 8.8, we will look at an argument for the necessity of a system of sovereign states which incorporates the kind of analogy of persons with states that seems to be assumed in neo-Hegelian reasoning about sovereignty.

[31] That this is the constitutivist position is confirmed by a reading of Frost, *Towards a Normative Theory of International Relations*, 177–83, and *Ethics in International Relations*, 150–5.

8.6. SOVEREIGNTY AND PROTECTION-FAILURE

It seems plausible to assert that 'a *state's authority over territory is based at least in part in its providing protection to all its citizens*—and that its retaining that authority is conditional on its continuing to do so'.[32] From this idea, an argument can be mounted in support of the claim that what we might call *protection-failure* (at the very least) weakens a state's claim to both internal sovereignty, i.e. final authority over all matters within its borders, and external sovereignty, i.e. 'supremacy with respect to its relations with other political units beyond its borders'.[33] What one means by 'protection' here is, of course, crucial to the acceptability of any argument for the weakening of the claims of sovereignty. The protection I consider here is the protection of the lives and vital interests of citizens—the most important protections in which a state can engage—and, accordingly, failure on this score will be the most momentous type of protection-failure, and will constitute the strongest reason for limiting sovereignty claims. We should perhaps point out that a weakening of the claim to sovereignty need not entail any good reason for the introduction of external or transnational jurisdiction over some formerly sovereign territory. In an example offered by Allen Buchanan, Jews in Second World War Poland would have been justified in seceding from the Polish state, and setting up a new state in a part of Poland, because the Polish state was not protecting them from Nazi extermination plans.[34] Thus a *new claim to sovereignty* is sometimes thought to be necessary in order to protect some group whose victimization is not being prevented by the existing state. The decision to accept the new state is presumably based in part on its potential for achieving the more important aim, namely, the protection of the victims, in this case the Jewish people. Note that no claim about the general admissibility (or inadmissibility) of external intervention is made here: that, again, depends on the prospects of intervention for bringing about the necessary security arrangements. I concur with this judgement, but the point is that the injustice must be overcome, and it is advisable to overcome the injustice without secession if this is possible, as it will be in many cases by introducing internationally binding duties on states. The main idea I note

---

[32] Allen Buchanan, 'Secession and Nationalism', in Robert E. Goodin and Philip Pettit (eds.), *A Companion to Contemporary Political Philosophy* (London: Blackwell, 1993), 586–96, at 591, emphasis in original.
[33] Ibid. 586.   [34] Ibid. 591.

here is that sovereignty should be taken seriously in the majority of cases, since denying its legitimacy could lead to international chaos.

The fact of 'interconnectedness' of states, i.e. their mutual penetration in the lives of citizens and non-citizens alike, represents a serious problem for the defender of sovereignty who would emphasize the strictly *national* scope of political decision-making and of principles of political and economic organization. Of the many difficulties this interconnectedness introduces, perhaps the most important is a questioning of 'the relevance of the nation-state, faced with unsettling patterns of national and international relations and processes, as the guarantor of the rights and duties of subjects'.[35] The question is whether nation-states are *capable* of achieving independently the rights-protections on which 'sovereigntism'— the robust defence of state sovereignty—would seem to depend. This point is a particular application of the 'ought implies can' principle: it is no good asserting that the development of individuality requires the maintenance of a society of sovereign states if it turns out that those states are not able to protect the preconditions for that development. And, faced with the facts of global interpenetration—where, for instance, environmentally momentous policy decisions made in one country directly affect the vital interests of individuals in another country who played no part in making those decisions—it seems hard to deny that sovereign authority, traditionally understood, is not sufficient to ensure the means to individual security-protection (to say nothing about the means to protect broader interests in individual self-development). If the defence of sovereignty depends on the state's being *sufficient* for such protection, then that defence is fatally flawed, given contemporary global realities.[36] Nominally sovereign states cannot guarantee the rights of their citizens independently of the actions of other states and of regional and international organizations.[37]

[35] David Held, 'Democracy, the Nation-State and the Global System', in David Held (ed.), *Political Theory Today* (Cambridge: Polity Press, 1991), 204.

[36] See ibid. 202. And see Henry Shue, 'Exporting Hazards', in Peter G. Brown and Henry Shue (eds.), *Boundaries: National Autonomy and Its Limits* (Totowa, NJ: Rowman and Littlefield, 1981), 107–45, and Andrew Hurrell, 'International Political Theory and the Global Environment', in Ken Booth and Steve Smith (eds.), *International Political Theory Today* (Oxford: Polity Press, 1995), 129–53. See the reference to Hedley Bull in Held, 'Democracy', 205, for the admission that this interconnectedness is not new.

[37] One might object here that sovereignty is a legal term, and so is not concerned with political power. Hence sovereignty is preserved if the bindingness of international agreements derives from the will of states. The problem with this argument is that it ignores the facts to which I have drawn attention. No state can bind itself to do something which it cannot in fact do.

The links between constitutivism, sovereignty, and environmental degradation call for further comment. In addition to the benefits provided
by an individual's citizenship in a state, we should assess the *damage*
created by constitutive attachments to see if that damage is not worse
than that which would be caused by giving up those attachments. This
will be one aspect of the project of assessing the reasons for and against
the available options. In this context, it is relevant to mention the point
that continued dependence upon the system of sovereign states means that
serious collective action problems will remain, most importantly the
problems associated with large-scale environmental degradation. When
there are many actors, it will be hard to reach an international agreement
on such matters. In this sort of case, the notion that the state is constitutive of an individual's identity does not look like such a strong point
in favour of the state, for a person's constitutive attachments might end
up contributing to a pattern of activity that does much more harm than
good, both for the individuals concerned and for future generations of
people.

On the other hand, the need for environmental cooperation and for
sustainable development can be seen as *deriving from* a concern for the
basic human rights to subsistence and security. If ozone-depletion, rain-
forest destruction, and similarly serious trends are allowed to continue,
ultimately it will be individual human beings who will suffer their effects.
Hence, it follows from the commitment to protect rights to security and
subsistence that one should be directly concerned with large-scale environmental degradation whose likely long-term consequences threaten the
interests those rights are designed to protect. Again, it seems that a commitment to one's state might make it *less* likely that these large-scale
global problems will be satisfactorily solved, so the ethical attraction of
sovereignty appears to be weakened, even for neo-Hegelians who hold
citizenship in such high regard.[38]

Let us return now to the relation between constitutive theory and
rights-protection. Mervyn Frost says that 'states ought to be recognised
and protected because it is only within states that individuals come to
have the rights of citizens and this set of rights is constitutive of free
individuality'.[39] The success of this rationale for the recognition of the
legitimacy of states clearly depends on the plausibility of the claim that

---

[38] On the problems for sovereignty presented by global environmental problems, see
Andrew Hurrell, 'International Political Theory', 129–53, esp. 147–51.
[39] Mervyn Frost, 'Constituting a New World Order', *Paradigms*, 8/1 (Summer 1994),
13–22, at 17.

states do provide the conditions necessary to protect the rights of citizens. But then, if this claim is false in any particular case, the legitimacy of the state in question is likewise compromised, and constitutive theory is then unable to provide the rationale for attaching primary importance to *actual* sovereign states.

Frost believes that a

significant strength of constitutive theory is the way in which it links the settled norm that accords value to human rights with the norm that accords value to sovereign statehood. . . . [Constitutive theory] demonstrates that sovereignty is not to be conceived of as an absolute value seen in isolation from other values. Those states claiming it for themselves are forced by constitutive theory to see that their sovereignty claims must be seen as bundled together with other norms. Where the states claiming sovereignty are not providing the other dimensions needed for freedom within their states, their claims are to that extent diminished.[40]

Hence Frost is explicit about the role of the sovereignty norm in his theory: sovereignty is legitimately claimed by states only when those states also meet other criteria (the rule of law, constitutional government, etc.), the most important of which for our purposes is the criterion that *the human rights norm is recognized and honoured*. According to constitutive theory, 'to make a sovereign claim is . . . to declare yourself open to inspection across a whole range of social values such as human rights, democracy, the rule of law, constitutional government, international law, and so on through the whole list of settled norms'.[41] This statement raises the following problems: what is to be done when some of the norms are honoured but others are not? I suggest that we then must attach priority to some norms as against others, and that the human rights norm is a good candidate for the most important norm of all. This is true not only for my own cosmopolitan theory but also for neo-Hegelian theory, since both approaches withhold approbation of states that do not provide the conditions for individual development. Consequently, we should deny the claim to sovereignty in cases where basic rights are not being protected. It follows that sovereignty cannot provide a free-standing reason for denying cross-border ethical concern with human rights because *that concern with rights is one of the tools we use to judge the plausibility of any given claim to sovereignty.*

---

[40] Frost, 'Constituting a New World Order', 17–18.
[41] Ibid. 19.

Chris Brown notices a vital inconsistency in Frost's approach which, I think, explains the problems we have identified. It is the attempt to combine (i) a starting-point in contemporary practice, with (ii) the need to distinguish states from one another from an ethical standpoint.

Part of the problem with Frost's formulation of these issues is a product of his desire to produce normative theory from the starting point of the ways in which normative issues are actually framed in the modern system of states. The first principle of prescriptive international relations, as promulgated by such bodies as the United Nations, is state sovereignty, and this notion is coupled with a refusal to distinguish between different kinds of states.[42]

Of course, this sort of refusal is entirely un-Hegelian, so if Frost indeed proceeds in this way then to an important extent he gives up an essential element of traditional constitutive theory, i.e. that only certain kinds of political arrangements count as ethically acceptable. But if, on the other hand, Frost wants to provide a theoretical framework from which present arrangements can be questioned, then he must deny any strong ethical appeal to contemporary practice. This latter approach is preferable, but it rules out Frost's central methodological move, i.e. to begin with the settled norms of current international political practice, for that would put sovereignty and human rights (to take the objects of the two most relevant norms) on an equal ethical footing.

Constitutive theory presents a fundamental objection to cosmopolitan political ethics. It is that the state is the largest independent ethical institution we have, whereas the cosmopolitan belief in the basic importance of 'humanity as a class' represents a utopian dream. Against this Hegelian celebration of the state, it should be noted that state sovereignty *itself* appears increasingly utopian in the light of the growing power of multinational corporations and other non-state influences (such as international religious movements).[43] Accordingly, we might view Hegel—in true Hegelian fashion—as a creature of his time, in that he thought the sovereign state would (eventually) be able to provide for the actualization of human freedom, when in fact we can now see that developments since the 1820s have rendered his own view itself merely an instance of wishful thinking. Protecting the rights of everyone, and ensuring for them the means to self-development, are not purposes that states in the contemporary world can achieve. We are therefore led to search for alternative means to actualizing these worthy goals, and a continued

---

[42] Brown, *International Relations Theory*, 121.
[43] Wood, *Hegel's Ethical Thought*, 30.

attachment to sovereignty as a necessary condition of justice in the world is, on this account, an obstacle to be overcome rather than a desirable feature of current arrangements.

8.7. POVERTY, HUMAN RIGHTS, AND STATE SOVEREIGNTY

Of direct relevance to the neo-Hegelian project of reconciling the norm of human rights with the norm of state sovereignty is the existence of *poverty* on a large scale. Interestingly, Hegel himself addresses this problem, though only in a domestic context, realizing that poverty—the condition of destitution and need which means that the poor person cannot properly participate in social life—represents a threat to the idea that the modern state is rational and therefore ethical.[44] At a very basic and important level, poverty constitutes a social evil. 'The enjoyment of the administration of justice is often made very difficult for [the poor]. Their medical care is usually very bad. Even if they receive treatment for actual illnesses, they lack the means necessary for the preservation and care of their health . . .'.[45]

In his discussion of poverty, Hegel notes that private charity is not sufficient to deal with this problem: not only is it unreliable and hence ineffective, but it is also 'unjustly humiliating' for the recipient.[46] What is needed is public action to eradicate poverty, but for Hegel the two different forms of this solution are both unsatisfactory. First, the poor can be helped with the proceeds of taxation of the wealthy. But this violates the principle of civil society according to which each person must earn his own keep by engaging in productive labour. Alternatively, the state might itself employ the poor in large public works projects, thereby honouring the aforementioned principle of civil society. The problem with this second proposal is that it would result in overproduction, one of the causes that generated a poor underclass in the first place. Hegel can therefore see no way to solve the problem of poverty.[47]

---

[44] Hegel, *Elements of the Philosophy of Right*, §§ 241–5.

[45] From an anonymous transcription of Hegel's 1819–20 lectures on the Philosophy of Right, quoted in Wood (ed.), *Elements of the Philosophy of Right*, 453.

[46] Hegel, *Elements of the Philosophy of Right*, § 253R.

[47] Cf. Shlomo Avineri, *Hegel's Theory of the Modern State* (Cambridge: Cambridge University Press, 1972), 154.

If we take seriously the idea that each person is a rights-bearer who should be accorded equal consideration, the existence of a large class of desperately poor people is cause for concern. And if there is no way out of this situation, it is unclear precisely why Hegel held to his view that the modern state is fundamentally rational and ethical. We might propose instead that a state—or a society of states—lacks ethical credentials at a very deep level in so far as it permits or even requires widespread poverty.

A modern solution might reject the Hegelian requirement of full employment and substitute the notion that individuals should engage in some productive work some of the time, thereby averting the difficulties associated with overproduction. Weakening one's commitment to the full employment condition in this way might still violate Hegel's principle of civil society, but the fact that this violation can also be described as *a necessary condition of the eradication of poverty* might be thought to add to its plausibility as an instrument of policy. In any case, *even if* one acts upon Hegel's preferred solution, to leave the poor to beg from the public,[48] one is still left with the problem of poverty *as well as* the violation of the principle of civil society directing everyone to work for their livelihood (unless one understands begging to be a form of productive labour). Moreover, the idea that individuals are constituted by their community—the fundamental premiss of Hegelian political theory— is surely strengthened by the realization that destitution is avoidable for some individuals only when the productive surplus of their community is utilized to ensure that each of them is guaranteed a certain social minimum.

The upshot of this short discussion of poverty is that redistributive taxation is an ethically acceptable way of dealing with large-scale impoverishment. In addition, if each human being has a right to be exempt from the hardships to which poverty gives rise, it is unacceptable to contain redistribution within nation-state boundaries, for such a limitation threatens to leave many individuals in poverty.

8.8. REJECTION OF AN ARGUMENT FOR THE NECESSITY OF A SOCIETY OF STATES

I promised earlier in this chapter to discuss an argument in support of the claim that a society of sovereign states is a requirement of a global

---

[48] Hegel, *Elements of the Philosophy of Right*, § 245R.

institutional arrangement that satisfies the demand to develop individuality. I will now consider such an argument, first setting it out in outline and then discussing its plausibility.

Premiss 1: The modern state, in its constitutional, ethical form, is a necessary condition of the full development of the individuality of citizens.
[Premiss A (support for premiss 2): Individuals are what they are only when they are recognized *as individuals* by other individuals. It is a precondition of the development of individuality that there are individuals who recognize each other.]
Premiss 2: Similarly [see Premiss A], states are what they are only when they are recognized *as states* by other states. Sovereign statehood requires states who recognize each other. (And there cannot be citizens if there are no states.)
Therefore,
Conclusion: The development of individuality requires a world of independent, sovereign states.

Our first task is to determine whether this argument is valid. First, notice that premiss A is not part of the main argument: it is rather a defence of premiss 2; thus *within* the main argument we have an argument by analogy with premiss 2 as its conclusion. I will return to this internal argument shortly. Secondly, if a certain type of state structure is necessary for individuality, and if states cannot exist without recognition from *other states*, then it follows that individuality cannot develop in the absence of a plurality of states. The main argument is, therefore, a valid argument, since—if its premisses are true—a single, global state structure would not be a state in the proper sense of the word, for it would lack the necessary other-recognition.

We should now consider the acceptability of the premisses. Is premiss 1 acceptable? Let us assume its truth for the sake of argument. Eventually I will reject the argument without rejecting this premiss. I should note, however, that opponents of Hegelianism might maintain that individuality can develop in the context of a society of states whose sovereignty is strictly limited by overarching principles whose application overrides individuality-threatening measures.

Is premiss 2 acceptable? I think it is not. My rejection of the argument hinges on my dismissal of this premiss. That is, I think that there could be, in principle, a state which was not recognized by any other state. A world-state would be such a state. Now the Hegelian denial of this claim works by introducing premiss A, i.e. an analogy between states and individuals. So we need to consider whether the analogical argument succeeds.[49]

First, it should be pointed out that the reasoning is plausible with respect to the claims about human individuality. At any rate, I will grant that an individual needs *other individuals* if his or her own individuality is to be recognized: proper recognition of one's individuality can come only from others who stand on a roughly equal footing with oneself.[50] Hence I will not question premiss A. Secondly, the two cases (individual and state) are relevantly dissimilar and, consequently, one can accept premiss A and deny premiss 2. The argument is formally invalid, and it is also weak when considered as a plausibilistic (non-deductive) argument. This is because the reasons that function to support the claim that individuality requires otherness do not apply in the case of states. States are not individuals in the same sense that human beings are individuals, nor is their 'individuality' a matter of ethical concern in the same way that human individuality is evidently important.

I take the main argument to be weak because its second premiss is implausible and unsupported. But let us consider what would be entailed by our acceptance of the argument's conclusion, that the development of individuality requires a world of independent, sovereign states. If this conclusion is accepted, must we deny that internal injustice is to be condemned (except in extreme cases)? I take it that this would depend on how we understand 'sovereign' in this context, and if sovereignty implies absolute and final authority—and rules out external standard-setting or external enforcement—then (for reasons given earlier in this chapter), since justice would be an internal matter, we would be committed to an unpalatable view about international ethics: internal injustice would be a strictly internal matter. Finally, even if we were to accept that sovereign statehood does require recognition of one's state by other states, this will not answer the fundamental question at issue, namely, that sovereignty itself requires some defence against the objection that some global legal structure (i.e. a structure that imposes some limits on sovereignty) would protect individuality in cases where sovereign states would threaten it.

---

[49] 'Without relations with other states, the state can no more be an actual individual than an individual can be an actual person without a relationship with other persons.' Hegel, *Elements of the Philosophy of Right*, § 331.

[50] Hegel's own discussion of the need for recognition by equally regarded others takes up a significant part of the *Phenomenology of Spirit*, tr. A. V. Miller (Oxford: Oxford University Press, 1977), especially the sections on 'Master and Slave', Stoicism and Scepticism, and the Unhappy Consciousness.

8.9. CONCLUSION

This chapter began with an outline of the neo-Hegelian or constitutivist theory of politics, understood as an attempt to reconcile cosmopolitan and communitarian conceptions of international ethics. Constitutive theory focuses on the importance of individuality while maintaining that a society of sovereign states is a necessary condition for the development of individuality. I accepted the claim that individuals are inherently social beings, but I noted that this belief in conjunction with a concern for individuals so conceived should motivate an evaluation of the condition of persons within the current system of states. Frost attempts to reconcile the received norms of international relations, including most significantly the norms of state sovereignty and human rights. I argued, on the contrary, that the neo-Hegelian attempt to discover a 'background theory' which achieves such a reconciliation is misconceived, since it assigns undue ethical weight to the sovereignty norm. Frost's strategy seems to beg the question, because it concerns itself with the norms shared by states within the present arrangement without questioning in sufficient measure the value of sovereign states themselves. I then inquired into the moral status of sovereignty itself, defending a 'qualified sovereigntism' and concluding that sovereign authority is empty where individual rights are violated by states claiming such authority. Relevant empirical considerations (especially those relating to environmental degradation) were adduced to challenge sovereignty, since the importance of this norm is in turn dependent upon the actual autonomous power of states to protect the basic interests of their citizens, and in many spheres of human concern this autonomy simply does not exist in contemporary circumstances. On the other hand, the effects of global environmental decline and the eradication of poverty, it was argued, should be among the primary concerns of defenders of basic human rights. Section 8.8 dealt with an argument for the necessity of a society of states which appeals to an unconvincing analogy between real human individuals on the one hand and individual states on the other. I argued that, while human beings need recognition from one another on a footing of equality, states have no analogous need, and so we should not in principle reject the call for restrictions on state sovereignty where those restrictions might better protect the basic interests of individual human beings.

Conclusion

In this conclusion I briefly lay out the practical implications of my argument for basic human rights, clarify the relationship between cosmopolitanism and world government, and defend my approach against the objection that it constitutes merely an exercise in utopianism.

In Part I of this book, I defended the view that every human being has certain basic rights and, in Part II, I rejected the claim that the obligations to which those rights give rise should be confined to fellow citizens or co-nationals. So my position is that we should recognize universal basic human rights and that there are no reasons of principle for believing that the corresponding duties attach in the first instance to some human beings and not others. Having said that, there clearly are good pragmatic reasons for recommending a division of labour in the fulfilment of what we might call the 'basic duties' of human beings. This view goes hand in hand with the belief that the universality of human rights nevertheless allows for significant scope for differences in specific ways of protecting those rights.[1] In many cases, local communities are best suited to provide for the subsistence needs of vulnerable children, and in many countries governments already have in place welfare schemes that address the basic rights of their citizens. Of course, local groups can lack the resources to meet the needs of their members, and some sovereign states *actively violate* the basic rights of their own citizens. In other words, while there is much to be said in favour of local meeting of needs, the protection of basic rights in the real world cannot and should not be left merely to the regional or national levels of government. When the traditional division of labour fails to achieve its objectives, other agencies must step in. These would include organizations like the European Union, the Organization of American States, and the United Nations, as well as non-governmental groups designed to provide protection on a multilateral basis. In Chapter 3, I argued that considerations of prudential rationality

---

[1] See David Held, *Democracy and the Global Order* (Cambridge: Polity Press, 1995), 200–1 and 211.

suggest that, if basic rights protection is our goal, we should reject solutions that depend upon the uncoordinated actions of individuals acting in isolation, and that we should instead commit ourselves to the development of *institutional* means of protecting those rights. But once we accept this need for institutions, we must ask whether current institutional arrangements are acceptable. It seems, clearly, that they are not.

Accordingly, if we place high value upon rights-protection, we should ensure that the institutions aiming at such protection are effective; otherwise, there remains an element of prudential irrationality, for we would have a clear goal with a means that is incapable of achieving that goal. It seems that the defence of basic human rights requires institutions of global rather than national scope and, in addition, that such institutions must be granted the power to enforce decisions made within them designed to defend those rights. Specific suggestions for institutional reform are beyond the scope of this book, but I believe that some of the recent literature contains proposals worth exploring. David Held, for instance, has called for a reform of the UN system to enshrine 'cosmopolitan democratic law', including the entrenchment of civil, political, social, and economic rights, the empowerment of international courts, and a reformed UN General Assembly.[2] The goal of such reform, again, is to implement the fundamental ethical requirement defended throughout the preceding chapters, namely, effective protection for the basic rights of persons.

These practical recommendations are still rather vague, and the critic might well wonder about the relationship between the view I defend and a commitment to world government. So I should say something on this point. This work has defended a moral cosmopolitan approach to international justice.[3] But *moral* cosmopolitanism does not necessarily entail *institutional* cosmopolitanism, where the latter signifies 'world government' or a global political structure in which supranational institutions would have significantly more power than they now have.[4] Nevertheless, I have argued that there are good reasons for moral cosmopolitans to take seriously the idea that governmental powers above the level of the state might produce greater benefits for the class of persons in whom they take

---

[2] David Held, *Democracy and the Global Order*, ch. 12. See also, Richard Falk, *On Humane Governance: Toward a New Global Politics* (Cambridge: Polity Press, 1995).

[3] See Ch. 1 for a discussion of the distinction between cosmopolitanism and communitarianism as alternative moral perspectives.

[4] For the distinction between moral cosmopolitanism and institutional cosmopolitanism, see Charles Beitz, 'Cosmopolitan Liberalism and the States System', in Chris Brown (ed.), *Political Restructuring in Europe: Ethical Perspectives* (London: Routledge, 1994), 124.

an interest (i.e. the class of *all* persons, regardless of race, class, sex, nationality, or citizenship). I do not intend to defend world government in any detail; however, I will mention a common complaint against it and attempt to weaken the force of that complaint. Institutional cosmopolitanism must face at least one major ethical objection. World government, it is argued, would entail an extreme concentration of power and consequent danger of tyranny, thereby putting in jeopardy the very rights that governments exist to protect.[5] The attempt to achieve justice through global institutional mechanisms is, according to this criticism, almost inevitably self-defeating.

The dangers of concentration of power are difficult to deny, but the objection does not show that the *status quo* is preferable to some alternative arrangement. The problem is that there is more than one way to avert the dangers of an absolutist global state. One way is to divide the world into territorially distinct sovereign states in which the functions of government and the rights of persons are confined within specific borders. Another way is to distinguish the tasks of government *functionally* rather than territorially, i.e. to ensure that there is a separation of government functions, with appropriate checks and balances.[6] This functional approach is in fact the way we deal with the potential for tyranny at the nation-state level: we do not protect against government tyranny by requiring states to split up into smaller units.

Moreover, if the case against global state structures (at least for some purposes) implicitly relies on the claim that the present arrangement successfully counteracts tyranny, then it is worth pointing out—as we did in Chapter 8—that sovereign states are themselves often the *cause* of the rights-violations of their citizens. Accordingly, rejecting a world state is no guarantee that tyranny will be overcome. Quite the contrary: refusal to set up and maintain global structures can in some cases endanger the very preconditions of a just society (for example, by failing to ensure that environmental standards are maintained both at home and abroad). When institutional structures actively deny individuals access to the means to satisfy their subsistence needs, basic rights are violated directly, but,

---

[5] A statement of this objection, from a theorist whose sympathies lie with the moral cosmopolitans, can be found in John Rawls, 'The Law of Peoples', in Stephen Shute and Susan Hurley (eds.), *On Human Rights: The Oxford Amnesty Lectures 1993* (New York: Basic Books, 1993), 54–5.

[6] This suggestion, along with several others, is offered by Onora O'Neill in her illuminating essay, 'Justice and Boundaries', in Brown (ed.), *Political Restructuring in Europe*, 69–88, at 71–2.

as Onora O'Neill has pointed out, people can be indirectly harmed when the social fabric or the natural world on which they depend is damaged.[7] Consequently, protecting individual rights demands some provision of care for the social and natural environments in which individuals live. In order to counteract both direct and indirect harm, therefore, recognition of a state's sovereign authority should depend on the existence of rights-protecting measures.

Still, the creation of a world government is not a realistic option in the short run, and the moves toward global stewardship of the planet— in the interests of every inhabitant—should be informed by a healthy scepticism of power structures with significant cross-boundary scope. Having said that, the central practical aim for now is to limit state sovereignty to ensure that the basic rights of everyone are met, regardless of citizenship, location, sex, class, and so on. Coinciding with this goal is the demand to provide states with the powers to protect basic rights for themselves, thereby removing the need for the second-best option of external rights-protection at some later time. In addition, those not catered for within current arrangements—stateless persons, for instance —are the responsibility of all of us, despite the absence of any direct, formal links between the world's eighteen million refugees and specific states recognized by the United Nations. In short, we should aim for what I have called 'qualified sovereigntism' (see Chapter 8 above), in which states and organizations of states retain elements of sovereign authority, with legitimate scope for higher-level overriding of that authority when it fails to meet the minimal cosmopolitan requirements.

I would like to address just one final objection, namely, that the principled approach to international justice outlined in these pages is an exercise in utopianism. Are the arguments put forward here irrelevant to any 'real world' concern with improving the global situation? Will people simply reject the claim that they have rather extensive obligations to help those in far-off lands whose lives are blighted by hunger, disease, and misery? While it is widely believed that people in the rich countries are not willing to recognize any very substantial duties to people in poor countries, there is some evidence to suggest otherwise. Let's take the United States as an example. In 1995, the Program on International Policy Attitudes at the University of Maryland conducted a study on American public attitudes about obligations to share wealth with poor nations. Some of the results might be surprising: 67 per cent agreed that

---

[7] O'Neill, *Towards Justice and Virtue*, 174.

the United States has a moral responsibility to poor countries 'to help them develop economically and improve their people's lives' and 77 per cent rejected the notion that the US should give aid only when it serves the national interest to do so. If these figures are accurate, then the population—as opposed to the leadership—of the United States is significantly in favour, on moral grounds, of giving aid to poor countries, quite apart from considerations of 'national interest'.[8]

The demand for the universal protection of basic human rights might be thought utopian because its specific requirements cannot be met. This returns us to the problem of overdemandingness mentioned in Chapters 2 and 3. And again, it is important to ask, 'too demanding for whom?' David Held has noted that 'North/South patterns of indebtedness have produced a net outflow of capital of an estimated annual $50 billion; that is to say, the cost of servicing the debts of the South exceeds direct development assistance by that amount each year.'[9] So the developing countries continue to fall behind the rich countries, placing increased demands upon impoverished populations. The other side of this story would suggest that it might not be so difficult for the world's wealthy people to ensure basic rights protections for the world's needy. Relatively small cuts in world military expenditure (10 per cent in the developing world and 1 per cent in the industrialized world) would go a long way towards eradicating malnutrition, illiteracy, and preventable disease. The ease with which such improvements could be made stands in stark contrast to the rejection of their importance by the world's most powerful governments. Just to take the most prominent example, the United States government spends $42 billion annually on arms purchases, and the Clinton Administration promised (in early 1997) to increase that amount to $60 billion by 2002.[10] None the less, the point remains that relatively minor changes could have monumental consequences: comparatively small amounts of targeted aid, along with a restructuring of Third World debt and interest payments, would probably have the desired effect.

---

[8] Steven Kull, 'Americans and Foreign Aid: A Study of American Public Attitudes', Program on International Policy Attitudes, Center for the Study of Policy Attitudes and Center for International and Security Studies, School of Public Affairs, University of Maryland, 1 Mar. 1995, 3, 16, 21, cited in David A. Crocker, 'Hunger, Capability, and Development', in William Aiken and Hugh LaFollette (eds.), *World Hunger and Morality*, 2nd edn. (Upper Saddle River, NJ: Prentice-Hall, 1996), 211–30, at 226.

[9] Held, *Democracy and the Global Order*, 256.

[10] Bruce Clark, 'Defence: Cohen set to call for large staff cuts', *Financial Times* (London, 19 May 1997).

Perhaps some progress can be made by showing that recognizing ethical demands can also be in one's own self-interest more narrowly conceived.[11] The creation of a global system of insurance against extreme need might be a reasonable requirement for populations in the industrialized countries, who are now becoming increasingly aware of the precariousness of their own position in the world economy. In this way, sympathy for the world's worst off can be generated by the experience of the world's better off. Moreover, even where destitution does not threaten the wealthy peoples, they may still worry about retaliatory actions by those in the impoverished countries, actions designed to reorient the global distribution of life prospects through extra-institutional means.

One tempting response to the utopianism objection is simply to say that, if a commitment to defensible ethical principles does in fact commit us to providing the means to protect all persons in their basic human rights, then no accusations of utopianism should deter us from recognizing the obligations to which rights give rise. Powerful people, of course, will deny these conclusions, for they find it difficult to accept measures that run contrary to what they perceive to be their interests. As Thomas Hobbes put it, 'Potent men, digest hardly anything that setteth up a power to bridle their affections.'[12] But an argument for a particular conclusion about moral obligations is not refuted by pointing out that those who refuse to follow the argument will not act in accordance with what it requires of us.

There are enormous difficulties standing in the way of implementing the kind of redistribution required by the commitment to basic human rights. However, this sort of worry should be distinguished from the moral arguments themselves. No doubt, there were massive obstacles standing in the way of the abolition of slavery in early nineteenth-century America. An analogous objection to the one we are now considering could have been put by someone who objected to morally based calls for abolition. To call for the complete abolition of slavery, it could plausibly have been said, is utopian, for too many powerful people have a vested interest in its continuation. With this sort of idea in mind, people did, in fact, recommend more 'realistic' measures, for instance, introducing regulations that would ensure better treatment for slaves. I assume that, even if we recognize that such proposals were well-meant, we none the less

[11] David Beetham, 'What Future for Economic and Social Rights?', *Political Studies*, 43 (1995), 58–9.
[12] Thomas Hobbes, *Leviathan*, ed. C. B. Macpherson (Harmondsworth: Penguin, 1968), ch. 30, 379 (1st publ. in 1651).

must judge that they were seriously inadequate to address the root problem. Similarly, present-day attempts to appease powerful states and other influential agencies merely provide support for the claim that their power entitles them to ignore the full force of ethical arguments suggesting that the interests of the weak should be better protected. Furthermore, as in the case of slavery, recognition of the injustice of a set of social arrangements can motivate opposition to those arrangements. So justice-based arguments that gain some currency in debates about the global order might very well play a role in changing that order in the direction suggested by those arguments. My claim is that reasonable persons can be convinced that the requirements defended in this work are feasible. I do not say there are any easy solutions, only that no fundamental re-structuring of human nature is necessary to bring about the obligatory changes. If the demands of the theory are not *too* demanding on persons, then we can avoid the objection that our conclusions are 'excessively high-minded'.[13] I have suggested on more than one occasion that the demands of a defensible cosmopolitan approach to international distributive justice need not be too great for human beings to bear.

[13] Thomas Nagel, *Equality and Partiality* (Oxford: Oxford University Press, 1991), 21.

BIBLIOGRAPHY

Anderson, Benedict, *Imagined Communities*, revised ed. (London: Verso, 1991).
—— 'The Psychology of Nationalism', unpublished paper delivered at the Conference on the Ethics of Nationalism, University of Illinois at Urbana-Champaign, April 1994.
Arneson, Richard J., 'Equality', in Robert E. Goodin and Philip Pettit (eds.), *A Companion to Contemporary Political Philosophy* (London: Blackwell, 1993), 489–507.
Avineri, Shlomo, *Hegel's Theory of the Modern State* (Cambridge: Cambridge University Press, 1972).
Barber, Benjamin R., *Jihad vs. McWorld* (Toronto: Random House, 1995).
Baron, Marcia, 'Patriotism and "Liberal" Morality', in D. Weissbord (ed.), *Mind, Value and Culture* (Northridge, Calif.: Ridgeview, 1989), 269–300.
Barry, Brian, *The Liberal Theory of Justice* (Oxford: Clarendon Press, 1973).
—— *Theories of Justice* (Hemel Hempstead: Harvester-Wheatsheaf, 1989).
—— *Political Argument: A Reissue with a New Introduction* (Berkeley and Los Angeles: University of California Press, 1990; 1st publ. in 1965).
—— 'Can States be Moral? International Morality and the Compliance Problem', in *Liberty and Justice: Essays in Political Theory*, ii (Oxford: Clarendon Press, 1991), 159–81 (1st publ. in 1986).
—— 'Humanity and Justice in Global Perspective', in *Liberty and Justice: Essays in Political Theory*, ii (Oxford: Clarendon Press, 1991), 182–210 (1st publ. in 1982).
—— 'Justice, Freedom, and Basic Income', in Horst Siebert (ed.), *The Ethical Foundations of the Market Economy: International Workshop* (Tubingen: J. C. B. Mohr (Paul Siebeck), 1994).
—— *Justice as Impartiality* (Oxford: Clarendon Press, 1995).
—— 'Spherical Justice and Global Injustice', in David Miller and Michael Walzer (eds.), *Pluralism, Justice, and Equality* (Oxford: Oxford University Press, 1995), 67–80.
Becker, Lawrence C., *Property Rights: Philosophic Foundations* (London: Routledge & Kegan Paul, 1977).
Beetham, David, 'What Future for Economic and Social Rights?', *Political Studies*, 43 (1995), 41–60.
Beitz, Charles, *Political Theory and International Relations* (Princeton: Princeton University Press, 1979).
—— 'Sovereignty and Morality in International Affairs', in David Held (ed.), *Political Theory Today* (Cambridge: Polity Press, 1991), 236–54.

Beitz, Charles, 'International Justice: Conflict', in Lawrence C. Becker and Charlotte Becker (eds.), *Encyclopedia of Ethics* (London: Garland, 1992), 621–4.
—— 'Cosmopolitan Liberalism and the States System', in Chris Brown (ed.), *Political Restructuring in Europe: Ethical Perspectives* (London: Routledge, 1994), 123–36.

Bell, Daniel, *Communitarianism and its Critics* (Oxford: Clarendon Press, 1993).

Belsey, Andrew, 'World Poverty, Justice, and Equality', in Robin Attfield and Barry Wilkins (eds.), *International Justice and the Third World: Studies in the Philosophy of Development* (London: Routledge, 1992), 35–49.

Bentham, Jeremy, 'Principles of the Civil Code', in John Bowring (ed.), *Works of Jeremy Bentham*, i (Edinburgh: William Tait, 1843).
—— 'Anarchical Fallacies' (1843 [1796]) and 'Supply Without Burthen or Escheat Vice Taxation' (1794), in Jeremy Waldron (ed.), *Nonsense upon Stilts: Bentham, Burke and Marx on the Rights of Man* (London: Methuen, 1987).

Binswanger, Hans, and Pierre Landell-Mills, *The World Bank's Strategy for Reducing Poverty and Hunger* (New York: World Bank, 1995).

Brown, Chris, *International Relations Theory: New Normative Approaches* (Hemel Hempstead: Harvester-Wheatsheaf, 1992).
—— (ed.), *Political Restructuring in Europe* (London: Routledge, 1994).
—— 'International Political Theory and the Idea of World Community', in Ken Booth and Steve Smith (eds.), *International Political Theory Today* (Oxford: Polity Press, 1995), 90–109.

Buchanan, Allen, 'Justice as Reciprocity versus Subject-Centered Justice', *Philosophy and Public Affairs*, 19/3 (1990), 227–53.
—— 'The Morality of Inclusion', in Ellen Frankel Paul, Fred D. Miller, Jr., and Jeffrey Paul (eds.), *Liberalism and the Economic Order* (Cambridge: Cambridge University Press, 1993), 233–57.
—— 'Secession and Nationalism', in Robert E. Goodin and Philip Pettit (eds.), *A Companion to Contemporary Political Philosophy* (London: Blackwell, 1993), 586–96.

Burke, Edmund, *Reflections on the Revolution in France*, ed. Conor Cruise O'Brien (Harmondsworth: Penguin, 1968).

Caney, Simon, 'Liberalism and Communitarianism: A Misconceived Debate', *Political Studies*, 40 (1992), 273–89.
—— 'Individuals, Nations and Obligations', in Simon Caney, David George, and Peter Jones (eds.), *National Rights, International Obligations* (Oxford: Westview, 1996), 119–38.

Carens, Joseph H., 'Aliens and Citizens: The Case for Open Borders', in Will Kymlicka (ed.), *The Rights of Minority Cultures* (Oxford: Oxford University Press, 1995), 331–49.
—— 'Complex Justice, Cultural Difference, and Political Community', in David Miller and Michael Walzer (eds.), *Pluralism, Justice, and Equality* (Oxford: Oxford University Press, 1995), 45–66.

Cassese, Antonio, *Human Rights in a Changing World* (Oxford: Polity Press, 1990).

Chomsky, Noam, 'The US and Human Rights', *Lies of Our Times* (1993).

—— *Year 501: The Conquest Continues* (London: Verso, 1993).

—— *World Orders, Old and New* (London: Pluto Press, 1994).

Cohen, G. A., 'Freedom, Justice, and Capitalism', in *History, Labour, and Freedom* (Oxford: Clarendon, 1988), 286–304.

—— *Self-Ownership, Freedom and Equality* (Cambridge: Cambridge University Press, 1996).

Cohen, Joshua, 'Review of Michael Walzer, *Spheres of Justice*', *Journal of Philosophy*, 83 (1986), 457–68.

Crocker, David A., 'Hunger, Capability, and Development', in William Aiken and Hugh LaFollette (eds.), *World Hunger and Morality*, 2nd edn. (Upper Saddle River, NJ: Prentice-Hall, 1996), 211–30.

Dasgupta, Partha, *An Inquiry into Well-Being and Destitution* (Oxford: Clarendon Press, 1993).

Dinwiddy, John, *Bentham* (Oxford: Oxford University Press, 1989).

Donaldson, Thomas, 'Kant's Global Rationalism', in Terry Nardin and David R. Mapel (eds.), *Traditions of International Ethics* (Cambridge: Cambridge University Press, 1992), 136–57.

Dreze, Jean, and Amartya Sen, *Hunger and Public Action* (Oxford: Clarendon Press, 1989).

Dworkin, Ronald, *Taking Rights Seriously* (London: Duckworth, 1977).

—— 'Rights as Trumps', in Jeremy Waldron (ed.), *Theories of Rights* (Oxford: Oxford University Press, 1984).

—— *A Matter of Principle* (Oxford: Clarendon Press, 1985).

—— *Law's Empire* (Cambridge, Mass.: Harvard University Press, 1986).

Elfstrom, Gerard, *Ethics for a Shrinking World* (London: Macmillan, 1990).

Ellis, Anthony, 'Utilitarianism and International Ethics', in Terry Nardin and David R. Mapel (eds.), *Traditions of International Ethics* (Cambridge: Cambridge University Press, 1992), 158–79.

Elster, Jon, 'The Empirical Study of Justice', in David Miller and Michael Walzer (eds.), *Pluralism, Justice, and Equality* (Oxford: Oxford University Press, 1995).

Falk, Richard, *On Humane Governance: Toward a New Global Politics* (Cambridge: Polity Press, 1995).

Feinberg, Joel, *Social Philosophy* (Englewood Cliffs, NJ: Prentice-Hall, 1973).

—— 'The Nature and Value of Rights', in Philip Pettit, *Contemporary Political Theory* (New York: Macmillan, 1991), 19–39.

Fishkin, James S., 'Theories of Justice and International Relations: The Limits of Liberal Theory', in Anthony Ellis (ed.), *Ethics and International Relations* (Manchester: Manchester University Press, 1986).

—— *The Dialogue of Justice: Toward a Self-Reflective Society* (London: Yale University Press, 1992).

Fletcher, George P., *Loyalty: An Essay on the Morality of Relationships* (Oxford: Oxford University Press, 1993).

Freeman, Michael, 'Nation-State and Cosmopolis: A Response to David Miller', *Journal of Applied Philosophy*, 11 (1994), 79–87.

Friedman, Marilyn, *What are Friends For? Feminist Perspectives on Personal Relationships and Moral Theory* (Ithaca, NY: Cornell University Press, 1993).

Frost, Mervyn, *Towards a Normative Theory of International Relations* (Cambridge: Cambridge University Press, 1986).

—— 'Constituting a New World Order', *Paradigms*, 8/1 (Summer 1994), 13–22.

—— *Ethics in International Relations: A Constitutive Theory* (Cambridge: Cambridge University Press, 1996).

Galbraith, John Kenneth, *The Good Society: The Humane Agenda* (London: Sinclair-Stevenson, 1996).

Gewirth, Alan, *Human Rights: Essays in Justification and Applications* (Chicago: University of Chicago Press, 1982).

—— 'Economic Justice: Concepts and Criteria', in Kenneth Kipnis and Diana T. Meyers (eds.), *Economic Justice: Private Rights and Public Responsibilities* (Totowa, NJ: Rowman and Allenheld, 1985).

—— 'Rights', in Lawrence C. Becker and Charlotte Becker (eds.), *Encyclopedia of Ethics* (London: Garland, 1992), 1103–9.

Godwin, William, *An Enquiry Concerning Political Justice and its Influence on Morals and Happiness*, 3rd edn., 1798, in *Political and Philosophical Writings of William Godwin*, ed. Mark Philp (London: William Pickering, 1993), iv.

Goodin, Robert E., *Protecting the Vulnerable: A Reanalysis of Our Social Responsibilities* (Chicago: University of Chicago Press, 1985).

—— *Reasons For Welfare: The Political Theory of the Welfare State* (Princeton: Princeton University Press, 1988).

—— 'What is So Special about Our Fellow Countrymen?', *Ethics*, 98 (1988), 663–86.

—— 'The State as a Moral Agent', in Alan Hamlin and Philip Pettit (eds.), *The Good Polity: Normative Analysis of the State* (Oxford: Blackwell, 1989), 123–39.

—— 'Government House Utilitarianism', in Lincoln Allison (ed.), *The Utilitarian Response* (London: Sage, 1990), 140–60.

—— 'Utility and the Good', in Peter Singer (ed.), *A Companion to Ethics* (Oxford: Blackwell, 1991), 241–8.

—— *Utilitarianism as a Public Philosophy* (Cambridge: Cambridge University Press, 1995).

Gorovitz, Samuel, 'Bigotry, Loyalty, and Malnutrition', in Peter G. Brown and Henry Shue, *Food Policy* (New York: The Free Press, 1977), 129–42.

Grahame, Kenneth, *The Wind in the Willows* (London: Methuen, 1926).

Gray, John, *Liberalism* (Milton Keynes: Open University Press, 1986).

Hampshire, Stuart, *Morality and Conflict* (Oxford: Blackwell, 1983).

—— 'Justice is Strife', Presidential Address to the American Philosophical Association, Western Division, 1991.

Hardimon, Michael O., *Hegel's Social Philosophy: The Project of Reconciliation* (Cambridge: Cambridge University Press, 1994).

Hardin, Garrett, 'Lifeboat Ethics: The Case Against Helping the Poor', *Psychology Today*, 8 (1974), 38–43.

—— *Living within Limits* (Oxford: Oxford University Press, 1993).

Hardin, Russell, *Morality within the Limits of Reason* (Chicago: The University of Chicago Press, 1988).

Harman, Gilbert, *The Nature of Morality* (New York: Oxford University Press, 1977).

Hart, H. L. A., 'Between Utility and Rights', in Alan Ryan (ed.), *The Idea of Freedom* (Oxford: Oxford University Press, 1979).

Hegel, G. W. F., *Phenomenology of Spirit*, tr. A. V. Miller (Oxford: Oxford University Press, 1977).

—— *Elements of the Philosophy of Right*, tr. H. B. Nisbet, ed. Allen W. Wood (Cambridge: Cambridge University Press, 1991).

Held, David (ed.), 'Democracy, the Nation-State and the Global System', in his *Political Theory Today* (Cambridge: Polity Press, 1991), 197–235.

—— *Democracy and the Global Order* (Cambridge: Polity Press, 1995).

Herman, Edward S., and Noam Chomsky, *Manufacturing Consent: The Political Economy of the Mass Media* (New York: Pantheon Books, 1988).

Hill, Jr., Thomas E., 'The Importance of Autonomy', in Eva Feder Kittay and Diana T. Meyers (eds.), *Women and Moral Theory* (Lanham, Md.: Rowman and Littlefield, 1987), 129–38.

Hinsley, F. H., *Sovereignty*, 2nd edn. (Cambridge: Cambridge University Press, 1986).

Hobbes, Thomas, *Leviathan*, ed. C. B. Macpherson (Harmondsworth: Penguin, 1968; 1st publ. in 1651).

Hoffman, Stanley, *Duties Beyond Borders: On the Limits and Possibilities of Ethical International Politics* (Syracuse: Syracuse University Press, 1981).

Hohfeld, Wesley N., *Fundamental Legal Conceptions as Applied in Judicial Reasoning* (New Haven, Conn.: Yale University Press, 1919).

Howard, Rhoda E., 'Cultural Absolutism and the Nostalgia for Community', *Human Rights Quarterly*, 15 (1993), 315–38.

—— *Human Rights and the Search for Community* (Oxford: Westview Press, 1995).

Hurka, Thomas, *Perfectionism* (Oxford: Oxford University Press, 1993).

—— 'The Justification of National Partiality', in Jeff McMahan and Robert McKim (eds.), *The Morality of Nationalism* (Oxford: Oxford University Press, 1997).

Hurrell, Andrew, 'International Political Theory and the Global Environment', in Ken Booth and Steve Smith (eds.), *International Political Theory Today* (Oxford: Polity Press, 1995), 129–53.

Johnston, David, *The Idea of a Liberal Theory: A Critique and Reconstruction* (Princeton: Princeton University Press, 1994).

Jones, Peter, *Rights* (London: Macmillan, 1994).

Kagan, Shelly, 'Does Consequentialism Demand Too Much?', *Philosophy and Public Affairs*, 13 (1984), 239–54.

Kant, Immanuel, 'On a Supposed Right to Lie from Altruistic Motives', in *Immanuel Kant: Critique of Practical Reason and Other Writings in Moral Philosophy*, ed. and tr. Lewis White Beck (New York: Garland, 1976), 346–50 (1st publ. in 1797).

—— *Foundations of the Metaphysics of Morals*, 2nd edn., tr. Lewis White Beck (London: Collier Macmillan, 1990).

—— *Perpetual Peace*, in *Kant: Political Writings*, ed. Hans Reiss (Cambridge: Cambridge University Press, 1991).

—— *Metaphysics of Morals* (Cambridge: Cambridge University Press, 1992; 1st publ. in 1797).

Kelly, P. J., *Utilitarianism and Distributive Justice: Jeremy Bentham and the Civil Law* (Oxford: Clarendon Press, 1990).

Kukathas, Chandran, and Philip Pettit, *Rawls: A Theory of Justice and its Critics* (Cambridge: Polity Press, 1990).

Kymlicka, Will, *Liberalism, Community, and Culture* (Oxford: Clarendon Press, 1989).

—— *Contemporary Political Philosophy: An Introduction* (Oxford: Clarendon Press, 1990).

—— 'Some Questions about Justice and Community', Appendix I, in Daniel Bell, *Communitarianism and its Critics* (Oxford: Clarendon Press, 1993), 208–21.

Landesman, Bruce, 'Justice: Cosmic or Communal?', in Keith Kipnis and Diana T. Meyers (eds.), *Economic Justice: Private Rights and Public Responsibilities* (Totowa, NJ: Rowman and Allenheld, 1985).

Locke, John, *Two Treatises of Government*, ed. Peter Laslett (Cambridge: Cambridge University Press, 1988; 1st publ. in 1689).

Lloyd Thomas, D. A., *Locke on Government* (London: Routledge, 1995).

MacCormick, Neil, 'Rights in Legislation', in P. M. S. Hacker and Joseph Raz (eds.), *Law, Morality, and Society: Essays in Honour of H. L. A. Hart* (Oxford: Clarendon Press, 1982).

MacIntyre, Alasdair, 'Is Patriotism a Virtue?', The Lindley Lecture (Lawrence, Kan.: University of Kansas, 1984).

—— *After Virtue: A Study in Moral Theory*, 2nd edn. (London: Duckworth, 1985).

Malthus, Thomas, *An Essay on the Principle of Population* (New York: Dutton, 1914).

Miller, David, 'The Ethical Significance of Nationality', *Ethics*, 98 (1988), 647–62.

—— 'In What Sense Must Socialism be Communitarian?', *Social Philosophy and Policy*, 6 (1988–9), 51–73.

—— *Market, State, and Community* (Oxford: Oxford University Press, 1989).

—— 'The Resurgence of Political Theory', *Political Studies*, 38 (1990), 421–37.

—— 'In Defence of Nationality', *Journal of Applied Philosophy*, 10 (1993), 3–16.

—— 'The Nation-State: A Modest Defence', in Chris Brown (ed.), *Political Restructuring in Europe* (London: Routledge, 1994), 137–62.

—— *On Nationality* (Oxford: Clarendon Press, 1995).

—— 'Nationality: Some Replies', *Journal of Applied Philosophy*, 14 (1997), 69–82.

—— and Michael Walzer (eds.), *Pluralism, Justice, and Equality* (Oxford: Oxford University Press, 1995).

Moon, J. Donald, *Constructing Community: Moral Pluralism and Tragic Conflicts* (Princeton: Princeton University Press, 1993).

Morgenthau, Hans, *In Defense of the National Interest: A Critical Examination of American Foreign Policy* (New York: Alfred Knopf, 1951).

Nagel, Thomas, *Equality and Partiality* (Oxford: Oxford University Press, 1991).

Nardin, Terry, *Law, Morality, and the Relations of States* (Princeton, NJ: Princeton University Press, 1983).

Nathanson, Stephen, 'In Defense of "Moderate Patriotism"', *Ethics*, 99 (1989), 535–52.

—— *Patriotism, Morality, and Peace* (Lanham, Md.: Rowman and Littlefield, 1993).

Nickel, James W., *Making Sense of Human Rights: Philosophical Reflections on the Universal Declaration of Human Rights* (London: University of California Press, 1987).

—— 'How Human Rights Generate Duties to Protect and Provide', *Human Rights Quarterly*, 15 (1993), 77–86.

Nozick, Robert, *Anarchy, State, and Utopia* (Oxford: Blackwell, 1974).

Okin, Susan Moller, *Justice, Gender, and the Family* (New York: Basic Books, 1989).

O'Neill, Onora, *Faces of Hunger: An Essay on Poverty, Justice and Development* (London: Allen & Unwin, 1986).

—— 'Hunger, Needs and Rights', in Steven Luper-Foy (ed.), *Problems of International Justice* (London: Westview, 1988).

—— 'Transnational Justice', in David Held (ed.), *Political Theory Today* (Oxford: Polity Press, 1991), 276–304.

—— 'International Justice: Distribution', in Lawrence C. Becker and Charlotte Becker (eds.), *Encyclopedia of Ethics* (London: Garland, 1992), 624–7.

—— 'Ending World Hunger', in Tom Regan (ed.), *Matters of Life and Death*, 3rd edn. (London: McGraw-Hill, 1993), 235–79.

—— 'Justice and Boundaries', in Chris Brown (ed.), *Political Restructuring in Europe: Ethical Perspectives* (London: Routledge, 1994), 69–88.

—— *Towards Justice and Virtue: A Constructive Account of Practical Reasoning* (Cambridge: Cambridge University Press, 1996).

Parfit, Derek, *Reasons and Persons* (Oxford: Clarendon Press, 1984).

Phillips, Derek L., *Looking Backward: A Critical Appraisal of Communitarian Thought* (Princeton, NJ: Princeton University Press, 1993).

Plant, Raymond, *Modern Political Thought* (Oxford: Blackwell, 1991).

Pogge, Thomas W., *Realizing Rawls* (Ithaca, NY, and London: Cornell University Press, 1989).

Rachels, James, *The Elements of Moral Philosophy*, 2nd edn. (New York: McGraw-Hill, 1993).

Rawls, John, 'Two Concepts of Rules', *Philosophical Review*, 64 (1955), 3–32.

—— *A Theory of Justice* (Cambridge, Mass.: Harvard University Press, 1971).

—— 'The Law of Peoples', in Stephen Shute and Susan Hurley (eds.), *On Human Rights: The Oxford Amnesty Lectures 1993* (New York: Basic Books, 1993), 41–82.

—— *Political Liberalism* (New York: Columbia University Press, 1993).

Raz, Joseph, *The Morality of Feedom* (Oxford: Clarendon Press, 1986).

Rorty, Richard, *Contingency, Irony, and Solidarity* (Cambridge: Cambridge University Press, 1989).

—— 'Human Rights, Rationality, and Sentimentality', in Stephen Shute and Susan Hurley (eds.), *On Human Rights: The Oxford Amnesty Lectures 1993* (New York: Basic Books, 1993), 111–34.

Sandel, Michael, *Liberalism and the Limits of Justice* (Cambridge: Cambridge University Press, 1982).

Scanlon, T. M., 'Rights, Goals, and Fairness', in Samuel Scheffler (ed.), *Consequentialism and its Critics* (Oxford: Oxford University Press, 1988).

Scarre, Geoffrey, *Utilitarianism* (London: Routledge, 1996).

Scheffler, Samuel, 'Families, Nations and Strangers', Lindley Lecture 1994 (Lawrence, Kan.: University of Kansas, 1995).

—— Review of Martha Nussbaum *et al.*, *For Love of Country*, *The Times Literary Supplement*, 27 Dec. 1996.

Schneewind, Jerome B., 'Autonomy, Obligation, and Virtue: An Overview of Kant's Moral Philosophy', in Paul Guyer (ed.), *Cambridge Companion to Kant* (Cambridge: Cambridge University Press, 1992).

Shue, Henry, 'Rights in the Light of Duties', in Peter G. Brown and Douglas MacLean (eds.), *Human Rights and U.S. Foreign Policy* (Lexington, Mass.: Lexington Books, 1979), 65–81.

—— 'Exporting Hazards', in Peter G. Brown and Henry Shue (eds.), *Boundaries: National Autonomy and its Limits* (Totowa, NJ: Rowman and Littlefield, 1981), 107–45.

—— 'Mediating Duties', *Ethics*, 98 (1988), 687–704.

—— 'Morality, Politics, and Humanitarian Assistance', in Bruce Nichols and Gil Loescher (eds.), *The Moral Nation: Humanitarianism and U.S. Foreign Policy Today* (Notre Dame: University of Notre Dame Press, 1989).

—— *Basic Rights: Subsistence, Affluence, and U.S. Foreign Policy* (Princeton, NJ: Princeton University Press, 1996), 2nd edn. (1st edn., 1980).

—— 'Solidarity among Strangers and the Right to Food', in William Aiken and Hugh LaFollette (eds.), *World Hunger and Morality* (Upper Saddle River, NJ: Prentice-Hall, 1996), 113–32.

Simmons, A. John, *The Lockean Theory of Rights* (Princeton: Princeton University Press, 1992).

—— 'Associative Political Obligations', *Ethics*, 106 (1996), 247–73.

Singer, Peter, 'Famine, Affluence and Morality', *Philosophy and Public Affairs*, 1 (1972), 229–44. Repr. in Charles Beitz *et al.* (eds.), *International Ethics* (Princeton: Princeton University Press, 1985), 247–61.

Sivard, Ruth Leger, *World Military and Social Expenditures 1989* (Washington, DC: World Priorities, 1989).

Sullivan, Roger J., *Immanuel Kant's Moral Theory* (Cambridge: Cambridge University Press, 1989).

—— *An Introduction to Kant's Ethics* (Cambridge: Cambridge University Press, 1994).

Sumner, L. W., *The Moral Foundation of Rights* (Oxford: Clarendon Press, 1987).

Tamir, Yael, *Liberal Nationalism* (Princeton: Princeton University Press, 1993).

Taylor, Charles, *Reconciling the Solitudes* (Kingston and Montreal: McGill-Queens, 1993).

Thompson, Janna, *Justice and World Order: A Philosophical Inquiry* (London: Routledge, 1992).

Unger, Peter, *Living High and Letting Die: Our Illusion of Innocence* (Oxford: Oxford University Press, 1996).

United Nations Development Programme, *Human Development Report, 1995* (New York: Oxford University Press, 1995).

Van Parijs, Philippe, 'Competing Justifications of Basic Income', in Philippe van Parijs (ed.), *Arguing for Basic Income* (London: Verso, 1992), 3–43.

Vincent, R. J., *Human Rights and International Relations* (Cambridge: RIIA/ Cambridge University Press, 1986).

Waldron, Jeremy (ed.), *Nonsense upon Stilts: Bentham, Burke and Marx on the Rights of Man* (London: Methuen, 1987).

—— *The Right to Private Property* (Oxford: Clarendon Press, 1988).

—— *Liberal Rights: Collected Papers 1981–1991* (Cambridge: Cambridge University Press, 1993).

—— 'Rights', in Robert E. Goodin and Philip Pettit (eds.), *A Companion to Contemporary Political Philosophy* (Oxford: Blackwell, 1993), 575–85.

Walzer, Michael, *Just and Unjust Wars* (New York: Basic Books, 1977).

—— 'Philosophy and Democracy', *Political Theory*, 9 (1981), 379–99.

—— *Spheres of Justice: A Defence of Pluralism and Equality* (Oxford: Basil Blackwell, 1983).

—— *Interpretation and Social Criticism* (London: Harvard University Press, 1987).

—— 'Nation and Universe' (including 'Two Kinds of Universalism' and 'The National Question Revisited'), Tanner Lectures 1989, in G. B. Petersen (ed.),

The Tanner Lectures on Human Values, xi (Salt Lake City: University of Utah Press, 1990), 509–56.

Walzer, Michael, *Thick and Thin: Moral Argument at Home and Abroad* (Notre Dame and London: University of Notre Dame Press, 1994).

—— 'Response', in David Miller and Michael Walzer (eds.), *Pluralism, Justice, and Equality* (Oxford: Oxford University Press, 1995), 281–97.

Wellman, Carl, Review of Henry Shue, *Basic Rights*, in *Human Rights Quarterly*, 3 (1981).

Wertheimer, Alan, 'Coercion', in Lawrence C. Becker and Charlotte Becker (eds.), *Encyclopedia of Ethics* (London: Garland, 1992), 172–5.

Williams, Bernard, 'Persons, Character, and Morality', in *Moral Luck: Philosophical Papers 1973–80* (Cambridge: Cambridge University Press, 1981), 1–19.

Wood, Allen W., *Hegel's Ethical Thought* (New York: Cambridge University Press, 1990).

Zinn, Howard, *A People's History of the United States* (London: Longman, 1980).

—— *Declarations of Independence: Cross-Examining American Ideology* (New York: HarperCollins, 1990).

INDEX

Karen Morley
Oxford, 1999.